Wildflowers among the Cotton Seeds

Wildflowers among the Cotton Seeds

*Childhood Memories of Growing Up on
Farms and in Cotton Mill Villages in
Greenville and Pickens Counties, South Carolina,
1941–1959*

DOYLE R. PORTER

CHAPEL HILL
PRESS, INC.

ISBN-10: 1-59715-034-7
ISBN-13: 978-1-59715-034-7
Library of Congress Catalog Number 2006931655

First Printing

This book is dedicated to the memory of my father,
Curtis Dewitt Porter,
and to my mother,
Eleanor Thomas Porter,
and my four siblings,
Grace Satterfield, William H. Porter,
James D. Porter, and David B. Porter

———

The contents of this book are gifts of knowledge to my children,
Brian Keith Porter, Dawn Michelle Porter, and Tracy Lynn Porter Payne,
and my stepchildren,
Robert Jason Cooper and Caroline Ashley Cooper,
and to my grandchildren,
Emily Caroline Porter, Joshua Ryan Porter, Lori Elizabeth Porter,
and Mason Alexander Payne

———

In appreciation to my wife,
Pamela A. Porter,
For her love, understanding, and patience while this book was written

Contents

Prologue

This book is about children. The primary purpose of this book is to provide insight into the lives my siblings and I lived as we were growing up. I have written about circumstances of hardship we found ourselves in and the difficulties we faced. I have also written, almost incessantly, with pride and excitement, about numerous games and adventures my siblings and I experienced as children, collectively or individually. It was not my intention to write a book about the lives of adults. However, the lives of adults and children in my family were inherently intertwined, and the adults' lives, including previous to the births of us children, heavily influenced the lives of my siblings and me. Therefore, the end result is that this book also contains a story of my parents' lives that runs parallel to the story of my siblings and me.

This book is not a history book, so it does not contain an abundance of information about local, state, or national history. However, there are some tidbits of historical information sprinkled within its pages that coincide with the lives of my family. Also, our lives are, in reality, history.

I remember where we were living when each event of our lives occurred, but I have difficulty remembering the order in which the events occurred. Therefore, I have chosen to write my memories in chronological order relative to different places where I lived when I was growing up, rather than in chronological order of events as they occurred. I have relied largely on my own memory of events that I experienced or witnessed, and I am very pleased that

I remember so many adventures, misadventures, and games from that period of my life. I kept no diary or notes during my years of growing up, so some of the details of incidents I have written about may be slightly distorted or exaggerated. Some of my memories may be a mixture of events that I actually recall and stories I just happened to hear over and over in family conversations as I was growing up, but remembering a story is also a memory. Also, some of my memories come from listening to the radio and reading numerous books and articles over many years that provided me with some valuable historical information that applied to the early years of the lives of my parents and to my own younger years on farms and in cotton mill villages.

I have read numerous stories about cotton mill villages and cotton farms that were once a way of life in upstate South Carolina. My perception is that most of the authors have never actually lived in a cotton mill village, never worked in a cotton mill, and never experienced life on a cotton farm. The authors were probably mostly historians, or people who, for some strange reason, became interested in writing about a way of life that has now all but disappeared from South Carolina. Of course, a few authors may have actually experienced glorious lives while working on a farm or while living in a cotton mill village, but I have doubts about that. In their stories and books, some writers have portrayed the cotton mills and cotton farms as wonderful places for local inhabitants to work and live. They actually seem to believe that the days of cotton farms and mills were a glorious time in history and that the farmers and mill workers are sad to see them gone. Although cotton mills definitely provided a means of avoiding starvation in difficult times for many southerners, based on my experiences most of the writings that portray cotton mill villages and cotton farms as glorious places to live and work are pure fiction.

Although the families of most cotton mill workers and cotton farmers I knew when I was growing up were kind, caring, loving, and friendly people, their lives were a paradox. On one hand, most of them were happy to be with their families, among friends, and just to have jobs so they could survive through difficult times. On the other hand, many of them were disheartened and depressed to the point of near hopelessness because they were trapped in a way of life they could not escape from. I know about the way of life in a cotton mill village and working on cotton farms because I lived it. Although my family, friends, and I had many wonderful times on farms and in cotton mill villages, from my perspective, there was absolutely nothing glorious about that way of life.

I grew up in cotton mill villages and on farms in the northwestern area of the state of South Carolina at a time when the United States was still struggling to overcome World War I, the Great Depression, World War II, and the Korean conflict. South Carolina was a rural state that had little diversity of industry; therefore, job opportunities were limited. If a person in the area where I grew up wasn't wealthy enough to own a business or fortunate enough to work in a business, he either worked on a farm or in a cotton mill. Very few business opportunities were available, so my family farmed and worked in cotton mills. All of my family members and I have picked cotton, and my parents were also involved in the processing of cotton into cloth in cotton mills.

I perceived myself and the other children of the farmers and cotton mill workers to be much like the wildflowers that grew on area cotton farms, yet were so different from the cotton plants. We were born and were growing up among the cotton mills and farms, but most of us were different because we believed we would survive to become something other than cotton mill workers or farmers. Many of us were involved in a desperate struggle for survival and eventual freedom to choose our own direction in life. We were especially seeking freedom to work in our own way and freedom from the bondage of poverty that had a stranglehold on many area families. Our struggle was often painful and sometimes perilous, but it was also full of adventure and fun.

My siblings and I were not attention-starved, malnourished, or unhappy children. In fact, the opposite was true. Perhaps our parents did not express their love for me or my siblings with words and shows of tender affection, but they did express their love, care, and concern through enabling us to survive, regardless of circumstances, and through great personal sacrifice and hard work. As we were growing up, none of us children ever heard the words "I love you" spoken to us by either of our parents; however, all of us always knew that we were loved by them. Believe it or not, the lack of words and shows of affection by almost the entire generation of my parents was not uncommon throughout the United States at that time, especially in our community. I have spoken to many people of my generation about this issue, and most of them stated they had the same experience in their homes we had in ours. My guess is the generation that included our parents, now known as "The Greatest Generation," was born into difficult circumstances, forced to work adult jobs that denied them the enjoyment of childhood, and compelled to make other great sacrifices. Their lives were heavily influenced by World War I, the crash of the stock market, the Great Depression, and World War II. I believe that many of them, including my parents, were hardened for life by the circumstances of their youth. It was not our parents' idea for us to experience or inherit the same problems that confronted them. However, there was no way they could shield us from the life they were living. Their life was our life, and anything they had to contend with, so did we.

My family pulled together in our efforts to survive and succeed, and we did succeed. Sometimes the inability to earn enough money to provide for the individual needs of each family member caused dissent and exasperating disappointment in our already severe life crisis, and at times it seemed that our family would not survive as a whole unit, but at other times the cohesiveness of the family unit was quite obvious.

My siblings and I were very close in age, so we were able to develop close relationships with each other. Our closeness enabled the older siblings to teach the younger ones and for all of us to share effortlessly and play harmoniously. We spent much time together, as we did with our parents. I have many fond memories that originated from observations of and activities with my parents; however, the games and adventures of us children are my most prominent memories.

A few years ago, I read an e-mail that was passed on to me by a friend named Dr. James E. Kelley of Atlanta, Georgia. The author of the original message was listed as "unknown." I copied the message and then I deleted parts of it and rearranged the remainder into what I thought was a more appropriate communication about how things were when I was born and as I was growing up. The following is my version:

Our lives were governed by the Ten Commandments, good judgment, and common sense, and we were taught to know the difference between right and wrong and to stand up and take responsibility for our actions. Sundays were set aside for going to church as a family, helping those in need, and visiting with family or neighbors. My parents and grandparents got married first, and then lived together. We were the last generation to believe that a lady needed to have a husband to have a baby. Every family that I knew had a mother and a father. Until I was twenty-five, I called every man and woman older than I "Sir" and "Ma'am," and after I was twenty-five, I still called policemen, firemen, and every man with a title "Sir." All women, even most who were younger than I, were called "Ma'am." Serving your country was a privilege, and just living here was a bigger privilege. A person could buy a brand-new automobile for just over six hundred dollars, but who could afford one? It was too bad that we didn't own an automobile because gasoline was only thirteen cents a gallon. Mailing a letter cost three cents, and a postcard was only one cent. Ice cream cones, phone calls, streetcar rides, Pepsi Cola, and Coke all cost just a nickel each. Admission to a movie, soft drink, and popcorn cost a total of sixteen cents. We had five-and-ten-cent stores where a person could actually buy something for five and ten cents. Almost every boy over twelve had a rifle or shotgun that his father bought for him and taught him how to use and respect. They even went hunting and fishing together. We thought fast food was when Mother hurried in the kitchen, and having a meaningful relationship meant getting along with other family members, especially cousins. I was born before television was invented. Man had not yet invented air conditioners, dishwashers, or clothes dryers. Clothes were hung out to dry in the fresh air and sunshine. We never heard of FM radios, tape decks, CDs, electric typewriters, word processors, or computers. Software wasn't even a word. Draft dodgers were people who closed their front doors when a breeze began to blow, and time-sharing meant time the family spent together, not purchasing condominiums. If you saw anything with "Made in Japan" written on it, it was junk. Polio shots, frozen foods, Xerox machines, contact lenses, Frisbees, and birth-control pills were not invented. There were no ballpoint pens, police radar, credit cards, or laser beams. Man had not yet walked on the moon. There had never been a gay-rights issue, males wearing earrings, or pantyhose. The term "making out" meant how well you did on a school exam. There was no such thing as computer-dating, dual careers, group therapy, or daycare centers. "Grass" was a lawn to be mowed, "Coke" was a cold drink, "pot" was something to cook in, and "rock music" was a lullaby. McDonald's, Pizza Hut, Hardee's, instant coffee, and yogurt were unheard of. "Aides" were helpers in the school principal's office, "chip" was a piece of wood, and "hardware" was found in a hardware store. We listened to the Grand Old Opry, the Lone Ranger, Jack Benny, the Great Gildersleeve, and Amos and Andy on our radios, and I never heard of anyone blowing their brains out listening to Tommy Dorsey.

When I was growing up, we lacked many things that would have made our lives much easier in comparison to today's standards; however, nothing can take the place of curiosity, imagination, and ingenuity. Those were the primary tools of inventors who have enhanced our way of life through the years, and those were the tools we used when working, attending school, making toys, inventing games, and enjoying our daily adventures. Our way of life may not have been easy, but we discovered that happiness or sadness is just a state of mind. At one time or another, each of us experienced pleasure, joy, and even exhilaration, but all of that was countered by hardship, depression, and heartbreak. Overall, my perception is that our lives were normal and well balanced.

A Touch of History

$\mathcal{T}$he United States was economically sound at the beginning of the twentieth century, and most citizens were quite happy. The citizens were feeling more confident about the national economy and were more eager to invest their capital for future benefits at the turn of the century than at any other time in history. With national prosperity and new prominence in world affairs, the people of the United States had good reason to feel proud of their accomplishments, and they had great expectations for a prosperous future. Factories were busy, and incomes were on the rise. New inventions such as the telephone, the electric lightbulb, and the automobile were rapidly changing the way people lived. The United States was the world's largest industrial power, and its annual output of goods and services was close to nineteen billion dollars. The United States had almost half of all of the world's railroad mileage. Half the world's freight was shipped by the United States. Approximately half the world's oil was pumped in the United States, and approximately a third of all the steel in the world was made in the United States. In addition, the United States mined a third of the world's gold. The population was more than seventy-six million people, and by 1912 (the year of my father's birth) there were forty-eight states. The entire country was getting bigger, stronger, and seemingly more wonderful.

Although changes relative to industry and the economy were taking place at a rapid pace, some features of the nineteenth century were still in existence. More than 60 percent of all Americans lived in rural communities of fewer than twenty-five hundred people. The largest occupation was farming, and most families still used a horse and buggy for transportation. Many families still made their own clothing. Sugar cost four cents a pound, and a pair of men's shoes cost approximately two dollars and fifty cents.

The magnitude of immigration was so great that just a few years after the turn of the century the country was rapidly expanding and becoming more urbanized. There were more than eighty-five million Americans by 1910. Although urbanization was rapid, the nation's farms still produced more than half the world's cotton, half its corn, and most of its tobacco.

The United States had become a major industrial and economic power, and it was inevitable that the nation would be involved with at least some foreign nations when it came to developing and controlling world trade. As a result of attaining great industrial and economic power, it became necessary for the United States to have a very powerful navy to protect the interests of the nation at home and around the world. The development and control of world trade and the building of a powerful navy were carried out vigorously and with much enthusiasm. However, the citizens, industrial developers, military personnel, and political leaders of the United States did not anticipate that the economic battles going on in Europe and other parts of the world would draw the United States into a world war.

Tensions had been mounting in Europe for years, and on July 28, 1914, an armed conflict broke out between Austria-Hungary and Serbia. That conflict was transformed into a general European war on August 1, 1914, when Germany declared war against Russia. Eventually, the war involved thirty-two nations. The United States became officially involved when it declared war on Germany on April 6, 1917, and later declared war against Austria-Hungary on December 7, 1917. However, the United States had been indirectly involved in the war, behind the scenes, for several years prior to those dates. Supporting other countries at war was costing the United States a major loss in economic power around the world, and as a result the country began to experience decreased business activity, falling prices, and unemployment. The economy grew even worse after the United States became directly involved in the war.

My parents were both born near the beginning of the twentieth century, so I became interested in learning about life in America during the turn-of-the-century era and beyond. I now have at least a partial understanding of the economic conditions in the United States at the turn of the century, and I am also somewhat familiar with the causes of difficult circumstances that both of my parents' families experienced during the early years of my parents' lives. In addition, I have some degree of understanding of the circumstances of my parents' lives at the time of their marriage and after the births of their children. Most importantly, I learned that my parents and their families were proud, ambitious, and hard-working individuals who fell on hard times because of a failing economy and war. The harsh and sometimes tragic circumstances of their lives were also prevalent in the lives of almost every other family in the communities in which they lived and worked. I am happy to have learned that my parents and grandparents were honorable people who, because of circumstances beyond their control, became struggling survivors. I am also happy to know that, through it all, my family and their numerous friends and acquaintances in the communities in which they lived managed to maintain some degree of a healthy sense of humor while struggling to survive and attempting to create a desirable future. The events that controlled their lives, some good and some terrible, have now become an integral part of American history.

I have researched my mother's side of my family as far back as my great-great-grandfather Henry Pierson Thomas and his wife Hannah Turner Thomas. I am continuing to research in an attempt to find the roots of that side of my family that possibly began in Europe. I have been informed by some family members that the Thomas family ancestors were originally from Wales. So far, I have not been able to confirm that. However, I have located a crest that is published as the Arms of the Thomases of Wales. It is reportedly the most widely used of all Thomas Coats of Arms.

The following is information I have attained relative to my Thomas ancestry: I have not been able to find the names of the father and mother of Henry Pierson Thomas; however, Henry Pierson Thomas was my great-great-grandfather, and Hannah Turner Thomas was my great-great-grandmother.

Henry Pierson Thomas had three brothers and one sister. Their names were John, Huey, Pete, and Lucy. I have no information about the children of John, Huey, Pete, and Lucy.

Henry Pierson Thomas was born on June 23, 1806, and died on September 6, 1884. His wife Hannah Turner Thomas was born on June 20, 1816, and died on March 31, 1865. The children of Henry Pierson Thomas and Hannah Turner Thomas were Joseph Berry (possibly Joseph Barry but family members have always called him Joe Berry), Mansel, Lovell, Harriett, Jane, Angeline, Levica, and Lavada. I have no information relative to the children of his siblings; however, Joseph Berry Thomas was my great-grandfather.

Joseph Berry Thomas was born on October 10, 1844, and died on December 31, 1913. He was married to Charlotte Elmina Aiken. She was born on January 4, 1848, and died on February 14, 1903. Joseph Berry Thomas had a second marriage to Theresa Mauldin. The children of Joseph Berry Thomas and

Joseph Berry Thomas

Charlotte Elmina Aiken Thomas

Henry Palmer Thomas *Vesta Odella Sanders Thomas* *Nancy Ellender Harris Sanders*

Thomas Siblings: Back Row – L to R: Lewis, Cliff, Clyde, Willie, Joe.
Front Row – L-R: Nellie, Eleanor, Ollie Mae, Iola. Photo taken approximately 1970

Hannah Turner Thomas were Matilda, Lizzie, Pinkney, George, and Henry Palmer. Etta was the child of Theresa and Joseph Berry Thomas. Henry Palmer Thomas was my grandfather.

Henry Palmer Thomas was born on October 2, 1881, and died on March 3, 1934. His wife Vesta Odella Sanders was born on January 30, 1883, and died on April 6, 1951. The father of Vesta Odella Sanders was William Henry Sanders, and he was Cherokee Indian. His wife was Nancy Ellender Harris Sanders. The children of Henry Palmer Thomas and Vesta Odella Sanders Thomas were Joseph, Willie, Iola, Ollie Mae, Clyde, Eleanor, Cliff, Nellie, and Lewis. My mother is Eleanor Thomas Porter.

I have attempted to research my father's family, but I have not been as fortunate as I was with my mother's family. I know my grandfather was William Brunner Porter, and his wife was Annie Mae Brock Porter.

Annie Mae Brock Porter

My grandmother's father was William B. Brock. My father was Curtis Dewitt Porter, and he had eight siblings. Their names are Bill, Hoyt, Annie Lou, Flora, Adele, Ethel, Irene, and Eulelia (Lay).

My parents were born during prosperous and exciting times, only to see the prosperity and excitement in their community all but disappear before they were old enough to realize what they had just lost.

My father, whom I called "Daddy," but herein will be called "Dad," was born in July 1912, at a time when Europe was heavily armed and torn by national rivalries and jealousies. William Howard Taft was president of the United States.

Dad and his family were living a life near poverty and were experiencing hardships within a couple of years after he was born. By the time Dad was two years old, war had broken out in Europe as a result of the Austrian archduke's assassination on June 28, 1914. The economic impact of war on the United States, even though the United States was not yet directly involved, was taking its toll. Dad's family was hit hard by the economic losses that trickled down to their small farm in the hills of northwestern South Carolina.

My mother, whom I call "Mother," was born in December 1915, at a time when the war in Europe was spreading very rapidly from country to country. Woodrow Wilson was the president of the United States. Mother's family, also in northwestern South Carolina, had already been hit hard by economic losses, and the family was still taking a pounding. Their prosperity was diminishing rapidly. However, the worst was yet to come.

When the United States officially entered World War I, Dad was four years and nine months old and Mother was seventeen months old. Survival became the top priority for both families. Their parents struggled mightily just to provide a little food and shelter for their families as the war wore on. When the war finally ended, it had lasted four years, three months, and fourteen days. It ended with the signing of the Armistice on November 11, 1918. President Woodrow Wilson was in office during all of the United States' direct participation in World War I.

The end of World War I was a welcomed and memorable time; however, it did not end the economic problems of my parents' families. Their way of life continued in a downward spiral for many years. Both families had continued to survive during the war by farming their small plots of land, but neither family could survive by farming alone after the war ended. They sold, or lost, their small farms and moved closer to the small town of Liberty in Pickens County, South Carolina. A cotton mill had been built in Liberty by Woodside Mills, and it was the primary source of income for most inhabitants of Liberty and the surrounding area. The mill was operated as a fully integrated print cloth manufacturer. The two families of my parents became cotton mill workers, no longer owning anything but their clothing and a few home furnishings. In reality, the cotton mills had become a major industry throughout the southern United States, and although employee earnings were meager, the jobs saved many families from losing everything they owned and from starvation.

The families of my parents grew until eventually each of my parents had eight siblings. Neither of my parents was the oldest or youngest of the children in their families.

I have been told two separate theories relative to why families were so large back then. One theory is that farmers wanted to have large families because the more children in a family, the more farm work they could do. The other theory is that conditions of financial insufficiency create a system of alliance between men and women, with one result being the creation of children. In the second theory, the man alone usually cannot, or will not, support the family. As a result, the father will abandon the family and leave the raising of the children to the mother. The second theory sounds more like a modern explanation of single mothers being enrolled into the welfare system because the father of her children has not taken parental responsibilities. I guess the first explanation must have applied to my parents' families because neither father abandoned his wife and children, but both families still did some farming. Neither of my parents' families applied for, or received, financial assistance from the government. They did not depend on only one vocation to earn a living. They worked very hard on farms and in cotton mills.

President Woodrow Wilson left office in 1921, and William G. Harding was elected. President Harding died of a massive heart attack on August 2, 1923, and Vice President Calvin Coolidge finished out the term as president. He was subsequently elected to a full term from 1925 to 1929.

Although America's economy in the 1920s had improved considerably after World War I, my parent's families were still having extreme difficulties. In fact, the Roaring Twenties were a contradiction of sorts. The decade is often characterized as a period of optimism and prosperity in America: social clubs and speakeasies with live bands, floor shows, and lively music for patrons using dance floors, illegal homemade bathtub gin, the Model T Ford automobile that provided a newfound freedom because it was actually affordable for many middle-income workers, a five-dollar workday, the first trans-Atlantic nonstop flight by Charles A. Lindbergh, and motion pictures being shown in theatres. On the other hand, there was World War I, child labor in factories and mines, the rise of the Ku Klux Klan, restrictive immigration laws, Prohibition, moral decline, city slums with poor sanitation, and great social conflict. Overall, the twenties are often viewed as a period of rising optimism and severe cynicism, of increasing and decreasing faith, and of great hope and great despair. Unfortunately, both of my parents were subjected to child labor in a cotton mill.

As soon as Dad completed the sixth grade, he had to stop attending school to go to work on a farm. It was, according to his father, absolutely necessary that the family income be increased for the family to survive. When Dad was fourteen years old, he was forced to become a cotton mill worker so that he could even better assist the family financially. He became an employee of Woodside Mill in Liberty, South Carolina. Although his earnings were meager, his contribution to the family income was much needed. Dad never attended school again, and whatever dreams and ambitions he might have had were swept away because he lost sufficient confidence in himself due his lack of an adequate education. Even though his removal from school was beyond his control, I think Dad regretted for the rest of his life not getting an education.

When Mother entered the sixth grade, one of her classmates was Dad's sister. Mother and her classmate became close friends. Mother told me that she was visiting her friend one day when Dad walked into the room. Prior to that day, Mother had never seen Dad, nor did she know that her friend had a brother. Dad and Mother became friends soon after that day.

At age fourteen, after completing the sixth grade in school, Mother was also forced to quit school and go to work in Woodside Mill because her family needed additional income. I was told that it was not unusual during that period of time for children in families suffering from financial difficulties to be forced from school and into the cotton mills after they had completed the sixth grade. However, Mother told me she attempted to resist being removed from school. She said she loved school and was hoping that a good education would enhance her chances for a prosperous and comfortable future, but her fate was much the same as Dad's. She never returned to school and still regrets that her educational opportunity was snatched away by the immediate financial needs of her family.

In the cotton mill, both my parents worked in the spinning room. They talked to each other regularly and eventually began dating; however, Mother told me that she was never allowed to go *out* on a date. Dad had to come to her house, and they just sat around talking and listening to music. Mother loved dancing, but she was not allowed to dance, especially with boys. During the twenties and early thirties, the Charleston was popular with everyone, so it was only natural that Mother wanted to dance the Charleston with Dad. Instead, she could only dance in secrecy with her sisters and girlfriends. Obviously, my parents did about as much together at work as they did on dates.

Mother told me that she and Dad worked fifty-five hours each week for a paycheck of seven dollars and seventy cents each. That came to fourteen cents an hour for each of them. As the economy worsened, they were expected to do more work for the same pay. They had to comply with the expectations of their supervisors and the cotton mill owners or lose their jobs, so they worked harder and faster to produce more goods.

President Calvin Coolidge left office in 1929, and Herbert Hoover began serving as president of the United States. The economy of the United States had been fluctuating up and down for years and was seemingly on the rise; however, in October 1929, the stock market crashed during President Hoover's first year in office. The faltering economy, resulting from the stock market crash, put many millions of people out of work. My mother's father lost his job, as did some of her siblings, leaving Mother and one of her sisters to support their entire family of eleven. Dad was in almost the same predicament. He and two siblings were able to keep their jobs to support their family of eleven. I have heard Dad and Mother speak about "Hoover Days" many times. The entire nation suffered for several years.

Franklin D. Roosevelt became president of the United States in 1933. After taking office, he immediately began creating program after program to give relief, create jobs, and stimulate the U.S. economy. He was responsible for getting Congress to pass the Emergency Banking Act and the creation of the Federal Deposit Insurance Corporation to insure deposits up to five thousand dollars. This action helped restore citizens' faith in banks by eliminating the fear of losing all of their savings in a bank failure. President Roosevelt was also responsible for the establishment of many government-sponsored work programs, among which were the Civilian Conservation Corps that taught men and women of America how to live independently. The Civil Works Administration instituted a public work program that gave jobs to the unemployed. Those workers were responsible for building or repairing roads, bridges, airports, parks, and so on. The Public Works Administration was responsible for projects that included the building of the Grand Coulee Dam on the Columbia River. The Homeowners Loan Corporation had the responsibility of helping people keep their houses by providing refinanced mortgages for middle-income homeowners. The Agriculture Adjustment Administration tried to raise farm prices by using proceeds from a new tax to pay farmers not to raise specific crops and animals. They believed lower farm production would decrease supply and increase demand, which would result in higher prices. The program was designed to assist farmers, but it was instituted while many Americans were starving, and it was very unpopular. That program was later declared unconstitutional.

Although most of these programs did not directly affect my parents, the significance of the programs was that my parents began to have a little better life. Some of their family members were able to get back into the workforce, and wages of many workers were increased. Dad began earning thirteen dollars for fifty-five hours work, and Mother earned twelve dollars for the same number of hours. That worked out to twenty-three and a half cents per hour for Dad and about twenty-two cents per hour for Mother. They weren't getting wealthy, but they were doing a lot better than some people.

When Dad was twenty-one years old and Mother was almost eighteen, they were married on November 18, 1933. Mother turned eighteen in December 1933. Between the two of them, they earned twenty-five

Curtis Dewitt Porter and
Eleanor Thomas Porter in 1933

17

dollars per week. They could not afford to buy or even rent a house, so they lived with Mother's parents and siblings for the first three months of their marriage. The residence was 12 Fourth Street in Woodside Mill village in Liberty, South Carolina. Mother told me that those three months were extremely difficult because the entire house had only four rooms. No one had any privacy, and everything was shared.

After three months, when Dad and Mother could afford to move, they moved into a small house in what was known as Old Town, which was part of the same mill village community. The house was approximately one-half mile from Fourth Street. They lived in only two rooms of a five-room house, but they were happy to have some privacy.

After they lived in Old Town for three months, the mill company offered Dad and Mother a house directly across the street from Mother's parents at 14 Fourth Street (current name of Fourth Street is Iselin Street). They immediately moved into the four-room house. The living conditions in the house were not fantastic, but they were much better than my parents had been used to. The house had a sink with running water in the kitchen, but there were no built-in kitchen cabinets. The bathroom had a commode and a sink, but no bathtub.

They went into debt to buy a limited amount of furniture. Mother had to cook on a cooking stove that was heated by burning wood in one side of it. That type of cooking stove was commonly called a "woodstove" by people of that era. The only other source of heat in the house was a heater that was heated by burning coal and/ or wood inside it, commonly called a "coal heater." Dad and Mother were happy to be working in the cotton mill, and everything seemed to be going well for them.

William – 1 year 4 months,
Grace – 2 years 7 months

When Dad and Mother moved into their house, Mother was already pregnant.

My sister Grace was born on November 22, 1934, one year and four days after Mother and Dad were married. They were proud parents, but they apparently were not satisfied to have only one child. I find it difficult to believe, but in the three years Dad and Mother lived in that house, they had three children. My brother William was born on February 25, 1936, and my brother James was born on April 25, 1937. All three births occurred within a period of two years and five months.

Because of growing financial difficulties that come with raising children, Dad and Mother were having a difficult time feeding and clothing their family. Unfortunately, Mother was out of work a lot. Dad was trying hard, but he was not earning enough money to enable him to provide adequately for his rapidly growing family. Mother's father died before William was born, so Mother and Dad could no longer seek financial assistance from him. According to some of my relatives, the death of Mother's father was also affecting Mother emotionally. They told me that Mother was very close to her father, and she was never again the same happy person that she had been previous to his death.

In 1937, Dad quit his job at Woodside Mill. He decided that he wanted to be a farmer. He and Mother could no longer live in the mill-owned house after Dad quit his job. Mother had no other choice but to move with Dad to a farm in Pickens County, and they moved into a five-room house on the farm. The primary source of heat in the farmhouse was a fireplace in which they burned wood. Mother told me that the floors were wood, with cracks so wide between the flooring that she could stick her fingers through them. She had her wood-burning cookstove that helped supply a little heat, but even with a fire going in both the stove and the fireplace, there was not enough heat to warm the house. They had a well outside the house that was equipped with a rope and bucket on a crank that had to be turned by hand to get water. There was a sink on the back porch rather than in the kitchen, and instead of a bathroom there was an outhouse. Without electricity, they had to use candles and kerosene lamps. Although the small farm on which they were living was government subsidized, they received none of the money because they were renting the house and sharecropping. Mother said moving to that farm was the stupidest idea Dad ever had. The whole family almost starved to death, and it was all Mother could do to keep her babies alive during the winter months. They lived in that house for about one year before moving to a house on another farm in the same county.

The second farmhouse was not much better than the first. It had five rooms with a fireplace as its primary heat source. One difference between the two farmhouses was that the floors in the second one did not have wide cracks. Mother still had her wood-burning cookstove to supply a little heat, but the total output of heat was still inadequate. The well at the second farmhouse was on the back porch. Although they again had to crank water up in a bucket, they didn't have to carry it quite as far as they did at the first farmhouse. The only sink at the second farmhouse was also on the back porch rather than in the kitchen. They had another outhouse instead of a bathroom. They had no electricity, so they used candles and kerosene lanterns. They didn't fare much better there than they had at the prior location. They were still renting someone else's house and sharecropping. The lack of conveniences was bad enough, but Mother was even more miserable than she otherwise might have been because she was pregnant again. She was already having difficulty trying to feed and clothe three small children, so having a fourth child was more than likely to bring on more hardship. However, on June 7, 1939, my brother David was born. Shortly thereafter, the family moved back to Liberty.

The family had electricity and running water again at the house on Front Street in Liberty. However, Mother and Dad were still having a great deal of difficulty feeding and clothing the family because Mother was frequently out of work to take care of her four small children. Eventually, their situation improved, and both of them again worked regularly in Woodside Mill. I don't know any details of the arrangement, but I do know that the mill company allowed them to live in the house only because Dad worked in the mill.

Apparently the cotton mills had some kind of unwritten rule that a family could live in a mill house only so long as the male head of the household worked in the mill. Mother learned that the hard way. When Dad went to

Greenville, South Carolina, and got a job on the third shift at Monaghan Mill, she was told that she would have to move out of the house in Liberty. It didn't matter that she was still working regularly at Woodside Mill.

Mother went to Greenville and also got a job on the third shift at Monaghan Mill, which meant that Mother and Dad were both working from twelve o'clock at night until eight o'clock in the morning. Soon after Mother landed her job, the family moved into a house on Cedar Lane Road in Greenville County. Mother was unable to work in the mill and take care of four small children twenty-four hours a day so she had to hire a babysitter. Marie Whitaker, a family cousin, was hired to stay with the children while Dad and Mother were working the midnight shift at the cotton mill. In addition to babysitting services, she assisted Mother with washing clothes and house cleaning.

Although a cotton mill did not own the house on Cedar Lane Road, it was no better than a mill house, maybe worse. The house was old and weatherworn. Although it had five rooms, the rooms were so tiny that the whole house was no larger than a normal three-room house. The interior of the house was very dark, and during inclement weather it was necessary to burn lanterns or candles in the middle of the day. The house had no electricity, but there was running water. However, although there was a commode, the house had no bathtub.

To make matters worse, a family of bootleggers lived in a house next door, and another family of bootleggers lived in a small log cabin directly behind them. According to Mother, she and Dad were afraid all the time because the bootleggers and their visitors were occasionally involved in fights, cuttings, stabbings, and shootings. Many violent incidents took place within their sight and hearing. Mother said that she wanted to find another house somewhere else because she was afraid that some family member would be hurt or killed. As a matter of fact, I was told by family members that someone actually entered a bedroom of my family's house through a window late one night while the family was sleeping. Grace was awakened, and she began screaming. The burglar quickly exited through the same window. A large, muddy footprint was left inside the house, and footprints were in the mud outside. Although law enforcement personnel and others attempted to track the burglar the next morning, the culprit escaped.

The house, however, proved interesting for reasons other than its lack of comfort, the constant fear of neighbors and their visitors, and the burglary. I recall a story about a ghost of a woman that visited the house on two occasions. I have heard Mother tell a story about the ghost many times. To this day, Mother swears the story is true and that the house was haunted.

Mother told us that she was alone in bed one night and all of the children were fast asleep. She said she was awakened by something, and when she opened her eyes, there was a figure of a woman dressed in white standing at the foot of her bed. She said she was so terrified she just stared at the woman but said nothing. After awhile she got herself under control enough to light a candle. The figure disappeared instantly when she lit the candle.

Mother said she began to hear footsteps in the children's bedroom so she got up to check on the children. When she opened the door to the children's bedroom, the footsteps stopped. Mother did not see anything unusual in the children's bedroom, and the children were still asleep. She closed the children's bedroom door as she went back to her bedroom. She blew out the candle and lay down to go to sleep. She opened her eyes, and the figure was standing at the foot of her bed again. She lit the candle, and just as before, the figure disappeared and she heard footsteps in the children's bedroom. When she opened the children's bedroom door again, the footsteps stopped. Mother said she left the children's bedroom door open and kept a candle burning the rest of the night while she sat up in a chair. As soon as Dad walked through the doorway the next morning, Mother told him of her experience.

On numerous occasions, Dad has confirmed that Mother told him about her nightmarish experience and that she exhibited a great deal of fear while telling the story to him. There was no doubt in Mother's mind that she had seen a ghost.

Mother was not the only person to have a frightening experience with what was believed to be a ghost in my parents' bedroom. Marie Whitaker had what she described as the exact type of experience as Mother's one night while Dad and Mother were working the midnight shift at the cotton mill. The ghostly figure appeared at the foot of my parents' bed but, after a lantern was lit, it disappeared and footsteps were heard in the children's bedroom. Marie also sat up all night with a lantern burning. Shortly after that incident, my family moved away from Cedar Lane Road.

Amazingly, the old house on Cedar Lane Road was still there in the year 2002 when I visited that location. The old log cabin behind it that was once used by bootleggers was also still there. I have driven by there many times, and each time I wondered whether or not the "lady in white" still occupied the residence. I also wonder who she might have been and why she occupied the residence in the first place. Is she a person who was killed there? Was she attempting to reveal something to my mother and Marie?

My family moved from Cedar Lane Road to Haynesworth Street in the Monaghan Mill village in Greenville County, South Carolina.

Monaghan Mill was incorporated in February of 1900 by two cousins named Lewis and Thomas Parker. The mill began operations in 1902. The mill and the mill-owned village of approximately 210 houses were built on

Monagham Mill. Photo Courtesy of Greenville County Historical Society. Greenville, South Carolina.

325 acres of land adjacent to a road that is now called Smythe Street. I think the mill owned a gymnasium and a baseball field. In addition, the mill owned and operated a health clinic and a company store. Monaghan Elementary School and a couple of churches were also in the Monaghan community.

Even though some historians have written stories about Monaghan and other mill villages that portray them as having been comfortable and desirable places to live and work, living conditions for my family were not as good as they were for some other families. The mill company provided inexpensive housing for mill employees, but my parents and siblings had to live in only three rooms of a five-room house. Mother was pregnant again, so she was unable to work regularly. The family was sometimes suffering from hunger, and my parents were having a difficult time providing ample food. The services at the medical clinic at the mill were not adequate for my mother's condition. Grace would soon be ready to enter the first grade at Monaghan Elementary School, and there was not enough money to buy her necessities. Credit at the mill-owned store was both good and bad. It allowed my parents to purchase items on credit, and the mill company collected the debt from their pay before they received their paychecks at the end of each week. The end result was that they rarely received a paycheck. It was as though the mill enslaved them because all of their earnings went back to the mill company via the company store. I was the baby Mother was pregnant with, and my parents didn't want to bring me into the world while living in such circumstances.

Dad decided to quit his job at the mill to run a small café on Cedar Lane Road. He thought he could earn a better living running a café than he could as a cotton mill worker. He had no way of knowing at the time he made that decision, but it almost cost him his life. One day when Dad was working in the café a fire erupted, and he was trapped in the rear of the building. Everyone else escaped. In order to save Dad, the rescuers had to chop their way through the back wall of the café. When they reached him, he was badly burned. They got him out, and his wounds eventually healed. However, his skin was discolored for the rest of his life. Amazingly, he had no permanent visible scars, just some discolored skin. After his recovery, he went back to work in the cotton mill. However, he wasn't too happy about going back to the mill.

Mother described one other incident that occurred near Haynesworth Street prior to my birth. An electrical power plant that was located less than a quarter of a mile from my family's house suddenly exploded. Windows were shattered, and the whole area vibrated. Mother said the explosion sounded like a bomb, and a ball of fire larger than a house just floated right over the top of my parents' home. Mother said the whole neighborhood was terrified. The blast and the fireball were over in less than three minutes, but the memories are just as vivid to her as if the incident had happened yesterday. I was born within a couple of months of that explosion.

Life at Monaghan, Taylors, Poe Mill, and Cateechee

*F*ranklin D. Roosevelt was serving as president of the United States when I was born on April 6, 1941. I already had a sister and three brothers at the time of my birth. Based on the story I have heard my parents repeat many times, I know that I was neither expected nor wanted. Although I am very happy I was born and very grateful that my parents chose to do their best to raise me, there have been a couple of times in my life that I regretted I was not the additional girl they had dreamed of and named in anticipation of her birth. However, I have found this event to be quite humorous much more than regretful. Instead of Betty Jean, they got me. After getting over the initial shock and disappointment of having another boy, my parents frantically searched for a name, and I was named Doyle.

I was born in Saint Francis Hospital in Greenville County, South Carolina, the only child of my parents to have been born

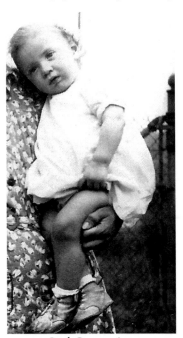

Doyle Porter – Age 1

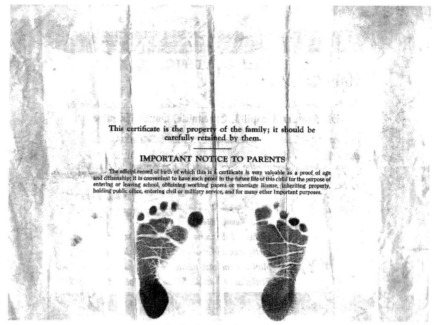

Backside of my birth certificate.

in a hospital. I still have the hospital-issued birth certificate with my footprints on the back of it. When I was six to eight years old, I loved looking at my birth certificate. I could not believe my feet had ever been so tiny. It was really special to me because I was the only one in the family with a hospital-issued birth certificate. Of course, all of my siblings were issued birth certificates at some point in their lives. The differences were that theirs were issued by the state, and I had the only one with footprints on it.

All of my siblings were born in the houses where our parents lived at the time of each birth. I don't know why they chose to go to a hospital for my birth unless it was because the hospital was just a short distance from where they lived, less than ten miles. When my siblings were born, the hospital was either too far away, there was no available transportation, or a hospital was just not an option my parents could afford. Numerous times in our years of growing up, our parents had no automobile, a situation that made traveling difficult. I don't know whether or not Mother ever had difficulty giving birth to a child, but giving birth in a location other than a hospital always sounded very frightening to me.

Unfortunately, when I was born, the United States was entering another war era. The whole world was in turmoil again, and on December 7, 1941, Japan bombed Pearl Harbor in Hawaii. That act drew the United States into World War II. Within a short time after the war started, the U.S. government was rationing food, coffee, sugar, shoes, automobiles, gasoline, automobile tires, and many other items. Although our parents were able to continue working, we were experiencing hard times. My parents and siblings had never known anything else but hard times, so I was just being introduced to a normal way of life. The minimum wage in 1941 was $0.43 per hour, and my parents were earning just $0.48 per hour. Their combined income per week for forty hours each was approximately $38.40. They were earning approximately $2,000 annually on which to provide for a family of seven. I just don't see anything glorious about working as hard as they did in a cotton mill for that small amount of pay.

We moved away from Monaghan when I was little more than one year old, so I asked Mother to inform me about events that occurred at Monaghan and to describe our living conditions there. Even so, I have often wondered about what kind of place the total Monaghan village was like at that time. I visited Monaghan to see the first house I ever lived in, only to discover it is no longer there, perhaps the result of a fire. Mother said that Monaghan was not much different from all the other cotton mill villages in upstate South Carolina. I could only imagine how it must have been for my parents to live there. Our entire living area at Monaghan was not much larger than the den in my current home. Our family of seven was very cramped due to living in only three small rooms of a house that was probably built to house only one family. I was a baby, so I slept in our parents' bedroom, at least some of the time, and all of my siblings slept in the one other bedroom. The third room was a kitchen. There was also a very small room the size of a small closet at the rear of the house that housed a commode, but there was no sink or bathtub. Fortunately, we had a sewer connection.

We had electricity, but it consisted of only one drop cord with a light at the end of it hanging in the center of each room. We had running water, but it consisted of only one faucet that furnished only cold water on the back porch. We had to heat water in a large pot, pour it into a large tin tub, and mix in just the right amount of cold water to get it to a decent temperature for taking a bath. It was difficult, even for us children, to take a bath in our tub because it was small and round. To make matters worse, many times all of us children had to take a bath using the same water. Our parents had no choice but to also take baths in the tin tub. I think their baths were probably short, with absolutely no time for relaxing or soaking.

We heated the house with a heater in which we could burn wood or coal. Our parents used mostly coal because wood was not as readily available in town as it was in the country where people could just cut down a tree. A truck came through the neighborhood delivering coal to anyone who could afford to buy it. Coal was not really expensive but our parents bought only one or two fifty-pound bags at a time because they had little money.

We had no automobile, so my parents had to take a taxi or depend on relatives or friends for transportation to the grocery store or to travel to downtown Greenville to shop.

Mother used a woodstove for cooking, so it was necessary to have at least some wood available daily. The woodstove helped heat the house when it was in use, and we enjoyed the heat it produced. However, we rarely used the woodstove other than when preparing meals because we couldn't afford to waste wood.

Wood was also a necessity for washing clothes because Mother had to wash clothes over a fire in the yard. She had a very large, probably thirty-gallon, black cast-iron pot. She placed the legs of the pot on bricks and built a fire under it. While the fire was burning, she filled the pot with cold water and then waited for the water to get hot enough to boil. Once the water was boiling, she placed the clothes she wanted to wash into the boiling water and added soap. As the water boiled, she used a long stick to keep the clothes punched down, and the boiling water and soap cleaned the clothes.

Mother had two very large tin tubs that she filled with clean, cold water to rinse the clothes she had just washed. When the clothes had boiled enough to be clean, she used the punching stick to move them from the washing pot to the first rinsing tub. She moved the clothes up and down in the cold water with the stick until they were cooled off enough for her to use her hands. Then she continued to clean them, using a rub-board or a batting board to ensure that she removed most of the dirt and soap. She moved the clothes to the second tub of cold, clean water, where she continued to rinse soap from them. If it was necessary at that point, she would start the process over again. If the clothes appeared to be thoroughly cleaned, they were ready to be wrung and dried. As heavy as the wet clothes were, Mother would wring as much water as she had the strength to from each piece of clothing. Then she carried the clothes to a clothesline where she hung each piece to dry. Needless to say, washing clothes for a family of seven was an all-day job, sometimes more. However, clothes that have been freshly washed and dried must also be ironed.

Mother began preparing to iron clothes by placing her two flatirons on the coal-burning heater or in front of an open fire. When the irons were hot enough to use, she picked up one and began ironing with it until it got too cool to take the wrinkles from the clothes. Then she placed it back in front of the fire and picked up the other one. She ironed like that for hours on end, switching irons as she worked. I don't remember how many days a week Mother washed and ironed clothes, but we always had clean clothes. We were all proud to be clean. The thing I wonder about the most is how Mother worked in the cotton mill so many hours each week and still had the energy to do all the work she did at home. On one occasion, when all five of us children had the chicken pox simultaneously, Mother was so exhausted that she almost didn't make it through the week. Life for Mother was a living hell, and it wasn't much better for the rest of us.

Other family members have agreed that Mother's description of our living conditions at Monaghan is fair. Life was just simply not easy back then.

When we moved away from Monaghan, we moved into a house on Pendleton Street in Greenville County. We lived on Pendleton Street for only a month, and then we moved into a house on Reid School Road in Taylors, which was a rural community that was also in Greenville County.

The house on Reid School Road was a small, four-room, run-down house that our parents rented from a person who lived nearby. It was not such a shack that it resembled an old weatherworn and damaged barn more than it did a house, but I have seen barns recently that were in better condition. Its condition was worse than most mill village houses. Our family probably should not have inhabited it, but my parents were doing the best they could at the time. We had a living room, kitchen, and two bedrooms, and all five of us children shared one bedroom. The only source of heat was a fireplace in which we burned only wood because coal was not delivered to our area. Of course, Mother still had her woodstove for cooking, which provided some heat. We had electricity, but no running water. We had a well for household water on the back porch, but we had to go to a spring, about fifty yards from the house, to get water for washing clothes. We had only a small bucket for transporting water from the spring to the house, so sometimes when we washed our clothes someone had to make many trips to the spring and back. William learned quickly that carrying water from the spring to the house was probably the most difficult chore on the farm. However, most of the time, Mother washed our clothes at the spring rather than carrying water or having someone else carry water such a long distance. Mother's process for washing, drying, and ironing clothes at Reid School Road was pretty much the same as it had been at Monaghan.

We had an outhouse instead of a bathroom. There was a sink next to the well on the back porch, but none inside the house. There were no built-in cabinets. The floors were hardwood with no floor coverings. There were large cracks between the boards of the floor that I could stick my whole hand through. Admittedly, my hands were small, but needless to say, the house was not easily heated or cooled. We had great difficulty getting the house warm enough so that we could remove a jacket during the winter.

Outside, we had chickens running loose in the yard, and sometimes the chickens would walk under our house. I remember dropping breadcrumbs and corn through the cracks in the floor to feed the chickens.

Mother told me that we had gotten into that mess because Dad had quit his job at Monaghan and the mill forced us to move out of the mill's house. When Dad quit, the mill fired Mother. We were just as bad off, in every way, as our family had ever been. It was as if we were traveling backward instead of forward.

Although we were living on a farm, both of our parents had jobs in another cotton mill. The name of the mill was Southern Worsted, and it was located in the small community of Paris, in Greenville County. I don't know whether or not Southern Worsted had mill houses, but we never moved to Paris.

Our parents were not considered farmers, but we had a large garden in which both of our parents toiled many hours preparing for growing season. I don't know whether Dad had bought a mule or was just using one that he had borrowed from a neighbor, but I can just barely remember seeing him plowing our garden with a mule. I was about two years old, maybe three.

After Dad plowed the garden, it was raked clean of grass and weeds, and then Dad and Mother planted their seeds and plants. Occasionally, during growing season, they had to hoe the new grass and weeds from the garden. No matter how tired they might have been from working in the mill, they could not let the garden be taken over by weeds and grass. The garden supplied food that we could not afford to buy. Besides, the war was still going on and food was being rationed, so we were lucky to have a garden.

When our garden began to produce vegetables, we had some really delicious meals. However, Mother also had to prepare vegetables for canning. She stood in the kitchen for hours canning food for later use. Because of war rationing, Mother could not get enough sugar, salt, and preservatives to can enough food for an entire winter, so we were very hungry sometimes. Even though we had a garden and there were times when we had animals to slaughter, sometimes we didn't know where our next meal was coming from. When we had food, leftovers were common. Dad and Mother didn't believe in wasting food, and we couldn't afford to waste food anyway. Some of the meals Mother had prepared were even better the second day.

In the mill village, we had survived by eating pinto beans, fat meat from hogs (fatback), turnips, turnip greens, cornbread, biscuits, gravy, and molasses. At times, we survived the same way in the country. I loved those foods, so it wasn't as if I knew we were eating less desirable food than some other people. However, I was aware that when we didn't have enough food to feed the whole family, Mother skipped meals to make sure her children were fed. When I grew a little older, I was ashamed and embarrassed to admit that we had to live like that. I overcame those feelings, and now I have great respect for the sacrifices my mother made in the course of raising her children.

We had chickens, hogs, and at least one cow on the farm, but I don't really remember actually seeing the hogs. I know the hogs were there because I remember that Mother killed a rooster with the stick she was using to stir the hog's feed when she was on her way to feed the hogs one evening.

We had a very large rooster running loose in our yard. For years, I did not know how to spell the name of the type of rooster it was, but Dad and Mother pronounced it "Dominecker." I learned at some point that the true name for that particular breed of fowl is "Dominique." Dad aggravated that rooster all the time. In fact, he had aggravated it so much that it became aggressive toward all of us.

On one particular day, some of us children chased and threw rocks at the rooster almost the entire day. That evening, William and David were going to the barn when the rooster came from under our house and attacked David. The rooster pecked and spurred him so hard David was bleeding. William and David fought the rooster off and ran back to the house.

Just a few days later, the rooster came after me while I was outside playing. I was wearing a bright red cap and playing near the house when I was suddenly knocked to the ground. Our rooster was all over me, pecking at my red cap. I was screaming and crying as the rooster pecked, spurred, and flogged me. The rooster managed to get the cap off my head, and I was terrified. Fortunately, Mother heard my screaming and crying and came running out of the house and chased the rooster away. I was not injured, just frightened. The incident of the rooster attacking me is one of my most vivid memories from the farm.

The same day the rooster attacked me, Mother carried a bucket of food (we called it "slop") to our hogs. As she was walking toward the hog pen, she was stirring the slop with a large stick, and suddenly the rooster flew onto her back and began to flog her with its wings. Mother was so startled that she didn't even realize what was happening, but she swung the stick over her shoulder and struck the rooster very powerfully right on top of its head. The rooster was killed instantly, and Mother continued on to feed the hogs. On the way back to the house, Mother picked up the rooster and brought it along. She cleaned the rooster and cooked it, and we all enjoyed that meal immensely.

While we were living on Reid School Road, our great-grandfather Brock, Dad's grandfather, came to live with us. It was difficult for me to understand that he was the father of the mother of my father. I also did not understand why he came to stay with us, but he lived with us for a long period of time. I guess he came because his health was getting bad, or he came to help our mother with us children because both Dad and Mother had to work in the mill in their quest to earn enough for living expenses. Our great-grandfather provided a much-needed childcare service for us. Even so, we were even more cramped in that small four-room house.

Our great-grandfather was an amusing and funny character who loved children very much. He came into the yard every day, weather permitting, to play with us. He walked with a cane, so he had to sit most of the time. He would always have something funny to say to us, but we were always a little wary of him because he seemed to instigate competitive games among us, then watch us hurt each other. However, sometimes he would also participate in our games.

Great-grandfather Brock would get us to play some kind of game of tag, a game in which he would participate. Because he couldn't run like us, it was easy for one of us to tag him, and he was "it" most of the time when we played tag. When he was "it," he would just sit in his chair and say funny things to us, and he acted as if he wasn't even interested in tagging any of us. We would inch closer and closer to him, not realizing that he was actually luring us in. His voice would get softer and softer, until we could hardly hear him, and suddenly he would grab one of us with the crook of his cane; then the person he grabbed would be "it." It was absolutely amazing how many times he was able to lure us close enough to grab one of us with that cane. When I had to be "it," he would get me up in his lap, because I was so young and small, and help me capture someone else. Playing tag with him was really a lot of fun for all of us.

We had a large oak tree in our front yard that had limbs growing very close to the ground. My siblings could climb the tree easily, and they climbed it often. We also had a cherry tree that my siblings climbed. Our great-grandfather would pull them from the trees with the crook of his cane, but he never let them fall so hard that they would get hurt. They just had a lot of fun.

There was another game called "battle" that our great-grandfather had us playing a lot in the summertime when the maypops were ripe. Maypops are edible, yellow fruit that grow on a vine in the southeastern United States. Prior to the appearance of the maypop fruit, the vines are covered with purple and white flowers. Before the fruit ripens and turns yellow, it is a dark green color, similar to the color of cucumbers. While the fruit is still green, it is much harder than after it turns yellow. I don't know how the maypops got their name, but we called them "maypops" because of the popping sound they made when they struck us on the head and burst. *Pop!* Another reason for calling them "maypops" might have been because they were usually found on the vines during the month of May, but it seems to me that maypops didn't ripen until later in the summer. When the maypops were ripe, we gathered them by the dozens.

Great-grandfather Brock would send us to gather the maypops, and then he would choose the teams to battle each other. Sometimes he would participate, and I always wanted to be on his team because I knew he would protect me. Our battles would last until the last maypop had popped on someone's head. Once in awhile someone would get hurt—not seriously, but some maypops were harder than others, and the sting of a hard maypop would make us cry. Our great-grandfather would console us, but he always sent us right back into the battle. I think he taught us to be tough, but sometimes he seemed to enjoy just a little too much seeing us in pain. However, he also seemed to enjoy watching us just having fun. After a good battle with maypops, we were usually hot and sweaty, and our great-grandfather always seemed to think that just after a battle was a good time to enjoy the creek.

We went down to the creek and splashed around in the water until we had cooled off, and then we played games in and around the water. We had a large barrel that all five of us children could get into at one time, and we rolled the barrel to the top of the hill above the creek. Then we all got inside the barrel and rolled down the hill, all the time picking up speed, until we splashed into the creek. What a refreshing feeling! We repeated that ride over and over, sometimes all day. I was so young and small that I was always placed in the center of the barrel so I couldn't fall out. I can't remember ever having so much fun at any other time in my life, and I will always cherish the memories of our barrel rides to the creek.

Although I have some very pleasant memories from the farm, I also have some that are not so pleasant, like the time our dog had to be killed.

We had a small black and white dog named Trixie that Mother said was a feist, which just means a cur or mutt. William said the dog was a screw-tailed bulldog, but I believe the breed of the dog was Boston Terrier, which may or may not be a type of bulldog, but it resembles a small bulldog. No matter what else it was, it was a yard dog. Anyway, I have called it a terrier for many years, so I won't change the breed name. Our father took the terrier rabbit hunting with him and discovered that it was an excellent jump dog. The terrier could find and pursue a rabbit as well as a beagle, so Dad took him on many of his rabbit hunting trips. In fact, I believe that some of my siblings took the terrier hunting, and it actually caught a rabbit. I don't remember whether or not I was with them. Dad hunted frequently, and to Dad the terrier was a hunting dog, but to us children it was a lovable pet. All of us loved and played with Trixie.

Dad was at work in the cotton mill one day when the terrier began to act very strangely. It was running all over the yard and barking, and it approached Mother numerous times and barked and whimpered. After awhile, Mother began to pay a lot of attention to the dog, and she sensed that the dog was trying to tell her something. She noticed the dog was beginning to produce a lot of white, foamy-looking saliva. Mother told all of us children to get into the house. We watched the dog through the windows as it was running wildly around the yard and acting as if something was terribly wrong with it. Mother was afraid to let any of us go back outside. When Dad arrived, Mother shouted for him to be careful of Trixie, that something was wrong. Dad took one look and knew exactly what the problem was: Trixie had rabies. Dad came into the house, got his shotgun, and went back outside. The next noise we heard was the gun going off. Trixie was dead, instantly. We were all very sad that we had lost Trixie, but we were also very grateful to Trixie for making Mother aware that something was wrong. Trixie had apparently been bitten or scratched by some wild animal, and Trixie died making sure we didn't suffer from rabies.

Although we escaped injury from Trixie, we did not escape injury altogether. Numerous times we received injuries, some worse than others. I remember two incidents when David got his head split open with an axe. In one incident, David raised the axe above his head and couldn't hold it because it was too heavy for him and it landed on his head. In the other incident, James accidentally hit David on the head with the axe. I recall the incident when David cut himself a little clearer than the other because it was the one that produced the most damage and blood. The axe put a gash about five inches long into David's head, and the resulting scar is still visible. When James hit David, the cut was much smaller and with far less blood. I don't know which, but I think David must have been a little too brave or slightly accident prone back then.

David narrowly missed being seriously injured when a cow attacked him as he walked across the pasture. Apparently the cow thought David was posing a threat to her, so she butted him with her head. The cow didn't injure David, but as he flew over the fence, he learned the hard way that cow horns will hook!

A puzzling thing about my memories of the farm is that I cannot remember us children ever having any kind of interaction there with either of our parents. I can't even remember them talking very much to us. I guess they were so busy trying to provide *for* us that they didn't have time to spend *with* us.

Our parents just seemed to be working themselves to death, but they were not accomplishing anything more than mere survival. On the other hand, all of us children were totally oblivious to the fact that we were living in conditions bordering on, if not in, poverty. We knew we sometimes ran out of food, but overall we were still happy. We romped and played as if nothing were wrong.

We lived on the farm at Reid School Road for approximately two years. World War II was raging as badly as ever, and survival on the farm had gone from bad to worse and had eventually become almost impossible. Our parents needed work where they could earn more money working fewer hours, and because of us children they wanted to be located closer to a school, grocery store, and medical facilities. Automobiles were rationed during wartime; we could not afford one anyway, so we did not own one. It was necessary for us to be within walking distance of any place we had to attend or visit. Regardless of how much we children wanted to continue living in the country, it became necessary to move closer to a town. Dad quit his job at Southern Worsted and took a job at Poe Mill.

Poe Mill. Photo Courtesy of Greenville County Historical Society. Greenville, South Carolina.

Poe Mill and the mill-owned village of 238 houses were built in 1895 to the west of the city of Greenville, adjacent to Old Buncombe Road. The mill was designed and laid out by a young man named J. E. Sirrine, who worked for a company named Lockwood-Greene. The 432,000-square-foot mill was built by a contractor named Jacob O. Cagle. The first production of the mill began in March 1896. The mill started production with ten thousand spindles and had increased the number of spindles to sixty thousand by the end of 1903. Poe owned and operated a large company store, and two churches and Poe Elementary School were also inside the village's boundaries. A baseball field was located just across Buncombe Road. I think there was a health clinic at the mill, but there was no gymnasium in the village.

At the time the Poe Mill village was built, the houses had no indoor plumbing. However, some minor improvements, including indoor plumbing and sewer service to all the homes, had been made before we arrived.

We moved into a house at the corner of Fourth Street and C Street. Within days, Mother also took a job at Poe Mill. Our family of seven was living, unbelievably, in three rooms of a six-room house. Fortunately, we had to live there only one month, and then we moved into a four-room house at 33 Third Street, where all five children still had to share one bedroom. Our great-grandfather went to live with other relatives in Georgia instead of moving to Poe Mill with us. Compared to the farm, except for food shortages, our living conditions had improved dramatically. We had running water again, but no hot water. We also had an indoor commode, but no bathtub or sink in that room. However, we did have a sink in the kitchen. We had electricity again, which consisted of one drop cord in the center of each room. We had an icebox rather than a refrigerator, and Mother still cooked on and in a woodstove. Our main source of heat was a small heater in which we could burn wood or coal, and Mother's woodstove provided additional heat when she was cooking. Mother's process for washing, drying, and ironing clothes continued as it was at previous locations, absent a spring or well.

Our biggest problem was that we no longer had a garden or animals to slaughter. Because of the war, food was still being rationed, and we had very

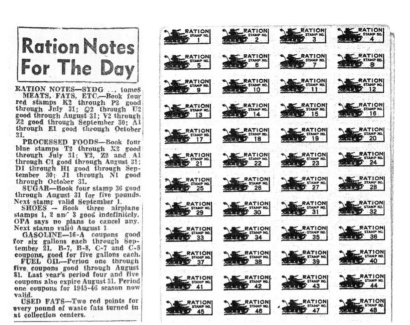

Ration Notes For The Day

RATION NOTES—STDG ... tomeS
MEATS, FATS, ETC.—Book four
red stamps K2 through P2 good
through July 31; Q2 through U2
good through August 31; V2 through
Z2 good through September 30; A1
through E1 good through October
31.

PROCESSED FOODS—Book four
blue stamps T2 through X2 good
through July 31; Y2, Z2 and A1
through C1 good through August 31;
D1 through H1 good through September 30; J1 through N1 good
through October 31.

SUGAR—Book four stamp 36 good
through August 31 for five pounds.
Next stamp valid September 1.

SHOES — Book three airplane
stamps 1, 2 and 3 good indefinitely.
OPA says no plans to cancel any.
Next stamp valid August 1

GASOLINE—16-A coupons good
for six gallons each through September 31. B-7, B-8, C-7 and C-8
coupons, good for five gallons each.

FUEL OIL—Period one through
five coupons good through August
31. Last year's period four and five
coupons also expire August 31. Period
one coupons for 1945-46 season now
valid.

USED FATS—Two red points for
every pound of waste fats turned in
at collection centers.

Ration Stamp Books with ration notes for the day – July 9, 1945.

little money. Even when we did have money, some items were impossible to purchase. Sometimes we had no food at all, and we were often hungry so we ate whatever we were able to scrounge. Sometimes, when we had flour, we had no milk, so Mother made bread with water instead. She also used water and coffee as substitutes for milk to make gravy. For meat, she fried slices of fatback. I even remember once eating some kind of roots that we dug from the ground. Mother was continuing to skip meals to ensure that the rest of us would have something to eat. Mother told me that she believed Dad was using some money from his pay to buy whiskey and food for himself instead of using it to feed the family.

Many people in our community didn't know where their next meal was coming from, and if a family didn't have a ration stamp for a certain item, they didn't get it from a store. We were very careful not to waste our ration stamps. As a matter of fact, I still have partials of War Ration Books one, two, three, and four. I also have some stamps called spares.

A very stern and powerful message was printed on the front cover of each War Ration Book. It stated that the book was the property of the U.S. government and that it was unlawful to sell or give it to any other person, or to use it, or permit anyone else to use it, except to obtain rationed goods for the person to whom it was issued. The book had to be returned to the War Price and Rationing Board, which issued it, if the person to whom it was issued was inducted into the armed forces of the United States, or left the country for more than thirty days, or died. The address of the board was printed on the cover. Anyone who found a lost War Ration Book had to return it to the War Price and Rationing Board. Anyone who violated the rationing regulations was subject to a ten-thousand-dollar fine or imprisonment, or both.

Obviously, one citizen could not give ration stamps to another. What they could do, in absolute secrecy, was trade goods they didn't use or need for goods they did need. If our parents needed sugar but had only coffee stamps and someone else needed coffee but had only sugar stamps, they got the items, using the appropriate stamps, and traded.

Although living conditions were terrible for our family, we were better off than some other families. At least we had shelter and some decent clothing, and both of our parents were with us. Some children's fathers were still at war, or had been injured, captured, or killed in the war. We just had to be grateful for all that we did have and not be too concerned about what we did not have. We just waited for some vendor to drive in from his farm and down our street, and we hoped that he would have something we could afford to buy that would feed all of us. Occasionally a farm vendor showed up, and we did eat at least something. Sometimes we purchased some really delicious food.

Farm vendors were not the only vendors who drove down our street. Two other delivery trucks traveled on Third Street each day; one was the ice truck, and the other was the coal truck. I didn't pay a lot of attention to the coal truck, even though we bought coal from him, but I was always waiting for the ice truck. I don't recall whether or not refrigerators had been invented at that time, but I do remember that we had an icebox for food storage. I believe the name on the icebox was Ice-way, but I'm not positive. We usually bought ice in twenty-five- or fifty-pound blocks, and all of our neighbors also bought large blocks of ice. The ice deliveryman had a set of ice tongs he used to carry the ice into the neighborhood houses. He also had an ice pick that usually stayed in the back of the truck with the ice.

All of us children loved to eat chunks of freshly chipped ice, and we knew the easiest way to get it was to steal it from the iceman. We waited until the deliveryman left his truck to deliver a block of ice to someone, and then we jumped into the rear of the truck and chipped off small pieces of ice for each of us to eat. I was only four or five years old, but I knew how to chip ice with an ice pick. I could also climb into the ice truck. I got my own ice many times. I think the ice deliveryman knew we were stealing from him because he always seemed to be in a hurry to get back to his truck. We had to work fast and run away before he returned.

I remember one day that I went to get ice and the truck was already rolling slowly away, but I ran and caught it. I climbed into the rear of the truck and chipped off a small piece of ice to eat. When I started to jump off the truck, it was moving faster than I realized. I jumped, but I fell onto the asphalt and skinned my elbows and arms, so I never tried that trick again. I always made sure the truck was parked after that.

Another type of ice we all loved was snow, and I will never forget the first time I can recall ever seeing snow. It snowed so much on December 24, 1945, that I experienced my first white Christmas the next day. The snow was beautiful, and there was so much that we had snow on the ground for several days. However, the snow also did a lot of damage to trees and knocked down power lines. Many people were without power, but we were not even affected by that. We burned coal in our heater for warmth, and Mother cooked our meals in her woodstove. We used candles and kerosene lanterns to provide ample indoor lighting. We were allowed to play in the snow, and we built snowmen and threw snowballs over a period of two or three days. We had a lot of fun, and I don't recall any injuries sustained by any of us. I guess we were just lucky. All of us were tough, but not so tough that we couldn't get hurt. In fact, we were injured many times while playing. The incidents had nothing to do with snow, but I recall several incidents when one of us was injured, or one of us injured someone else.

When David, who was two years older than I, was in the second grade, a group of boys were always picking on him. They chased him home or jumped on him after school almost every day. One day one of the bullies started a fight with David, and a much older boy who happened to be aware of what had been happening to David saw what was going on. He picked up a hard, cardboard tube and handed it to David and told him to hit the bully across the head with it. David hit the bully right in the corner of his eye. The bully's eyeball popped out of its socket and was hanging down on his face. Everyone was shocked, and the bully was terrified. David was scared half to death also. Someone had to take the bully to the hospital, and David ran home. I never heard of those bullies bothering David again. In fact, I don't recall that they ever bothered any members of our family after that incident.

In another incident, David was playing cowboys and outlaws with a group of boys one summer afternoon when a boy who was several years older than David captured him. The boy decided to hang David the way he had seen the cowboys do in the movies. He made a noose with a long piece of rope and placed it around David's neck, and he was about to hang David, for real, when an adult neighbor just happened to see what was going on. The neighbor screamed at the older boy just in time to save David from being hanged. There was no doubt that the neighbor saved David's life. Having a brother almost lose his life made us appreciate each other a little more, but nothing seemed to stop us from participating in dangerous activities. In fact, we all received our share of injuries, and the only thing that slowed us down besides injuries was sickness, and we all seemed to get sick at the same time.

On one occasion, all five of us children had the mumps simultaneously. On another occasion, we all had the whooping cough simultaneously. Doctors actually made house calls back then, and I remember that we had a doctor to visit us in both instances. I don't recall specifically which doctor came each time but Dr. Joe Converse, Dr. David Reese, and Dr. Asa Scarborough all visited our house on separate occasions over a period of several years.

It was as if Mother were living in a nightmare when all of us children were sick and confined to the inside of the house. Mother was working herself to death taking care of us, which she did with much care and concern. However, we were all confined to our house, and that must have driven her almost out of her mind. I have never enjoyed being confined to the inside of a house, so the confinement also bothered me considerably. I loved my brothers and my sister, but spending time with them under those conditions was not something to dream about. I much preferred spending time with them outdoors and on my own terms. We loved playing games together, and we played some type of game outside, weather permitting, almost every day when we were not sick.

The first game I can recall playing after we moved to Third Street was hopscotch. We drew eight squares that connected with each other and formed the shape of a twice-crossed *T*. From somewhere, we managed to get several pieces of flat, broken glass. We took turns throwing our individual pieces of glass into each square we hoped to advance to, starting with the first square at the bottom of the *T*. If we succeeded at landing our pieces of glass in the first square, we were allowed to hop on one foot over the block with the piece of glass in it to the next square and the next, then hop with one foot landing in each of the first side squares of the first cross of the *T*. Then we had to hop into the next square on one foot, and then hop with a foot landing in each of the squares of the last cross of the *T*. Then we had to jump into the air and turn around, while still in the air, and land facing the direction from which we had started, with one foot in each of the squares we had just jumped from. Then we hopped into the next square on one foot, then into the two side squares with one foot in each. Then we hopped on one foot into the next two squares, stopping before we hopped into or over the last square, which held our piece of glass. We had to bend over, while standing on one foot, and pick up our piece of glass, and then hop into the square and out of it to our starting point. If we succeeded at completing that entire process without making a mistake, we got to try advancing to the next square. However, we had rules. One of the rules was that we were not allowed to step on a line or step out of a square we were hopping into. That was a miss and would cost a loss of turn. Another rule was that if we failed to land our piece of glass in the correct square, we lost our turn. The glass could not be partially in a square; it had to be totally inside, not touching a line. Also, if someone else had already advanced to another square, the person whose turn it was could not hop into any square where someone else's glass was located. The game sounded simple and looked simple, but for a chubby little three- and four-year-old, it was a nightmare.

Not only did I have a problem playing hopscotch, I had a problem pronouncing some words. For example, when I missed a throw or a jump, I inevitably said, "Ut oh, I messed." Well, my brothers and sister thought my mispronunciation of the word "missed" was the cutest thing they had ever heard. Therefore, they allowed me to have every other turn, regardless of who was really supposed to be up. To make matters worse, I was a fat little boy, so my brothers and sister called me "Fat Belly." To give my brothers and sister a little something extra to adore, I could not pronounce the word "belly." My pronunciation was "bolly."

I didn't realize it at the time, but I was being given extra turns just so my brothers and sister could have a little fun. I was excited to be playing with them, and I thought I was big! I would throw my piece of glass and miss a square. Then, I would say, "Ut oh, I messed." One of my brothers or my sister would say, "Fat Belly missed." Then, I would say, "Mother, make them quit calling me 'fat bolly.'" No matter what position I was in, I always missed and went through that same dialogue, and so did my brothers and sister. I stayed more frustrated and angry with them than I did at the game. I also got upset with Mother because she never seemed to stop the name calling. I didn't realize that she was also getting a kick out of listening to me mispronounce words. I don't know how old I was when we discontinued playing hopscotch, but I don't recall ever playing that game after we moved away from Third Street.

Another game that brought all of us children together was old maid. In fact, Mother even participated sometimes. I don't have any idea where the cards came from, but I loved to play the game. I thought I was the slickest old maid player in the county. When I was dealt the old maid card, I always stuck it right in the middle of my hand, with at least half the card protruding above the rest of my cards. I thought that was really being smart. To me, that would entice the person drawing from me to choose the old maid card. I should have realized that I was making the old maid card so obvious that no one would ever choose it. Sure enough, I was always stuck with the old maid card at the end of each game.

After watching me lose so much, my brothers and sister must have started feeling sorry for me because I started to win occasionally. I had no idea they were letting me win; I just felt good about being able to finally laugh at those losers!

The period of time we lived on Third Street gave me my first memories of spending time alone with Grace. Although I remember all of us children playing together when we lived on Reid School Road, I don't recall ever being alone with Grace until Third Street. I remember that we had a swing on our front porch. Grace would get me in the swing with her, and we would spend hours just swinging. I don't know about her, but I still enjoy a swing. However, I vaguely recall that Grace enjoyed a rocking chair even more than a swing, and so did I. Even now, when we are together, if there is only one rocking chair in the room, we each try to get to it before the other. Grace taught me a lot, and she was a positive influence in my young life. I still cherish those times we spent together in the swing.

At some point our parents bought a used piano, and Grace began taking music lessons. Because she was attending school, studying for school, or practicing her piano lessons, I didn't get to spend as much time with her as I wanted to. That didn't make me too happy but it was good for her.

I also vaguely remember spending some time with Dad when we lived on Third Street. I recall that I wanted to go with him everywhere he went, and occasionally he would let me go with him to the company store. I always tried to take steps as long as his, and the neighbors laughed and commented about my stride. Although I remember walking with Dad and wanting to go with him, I have few recollections of him playing with me but I knew he loved me. Otherwise, I would not have wanted so badly to spend time with him. I credited the lack of play activity with my parents to their hard work during hard times.

Another fond memory I have involved a schoolteacher who stopped at our house almost every day on her way home from work. Her name was Hattie Barnes, and she spent a lot of time with me. She taught me things that many children learn in kindergarten today. I learned how to spell simple words, to add and subtract, and how to write my name. A few years later, Mrs. Barnes was my fourth-grade teacher, and I loved her very much. Of all the schoolteachers I had over the years, Mrs. Barnes was the first of three who left a positive, lifetime impression on me.

We had a next-door neighbor, Mr. Andrews, who also impressed me, not because of anything he taught me, but because he just seemed to love me so much. When he was outside, he would play with me or, in a kind and funny way, pick at me to get me to say things that made him laugh. I had difficulty pronouncing a lot of words, and he seemed to enjoy my mispronunciations. He never attempted to correct me. He just laughed and gave me cookies and candy. We rarely had the kinds of treats that he gave to me, so I was always happy to see him. His birthday was on the same day of the year as mine, so

Poe Mill Store. Photo Courtesy of Greenville County Historical Society. Greenville, South Carolina.

maybe that's what made me special to him. I don't recall whether or not he treated my siblings and the other neighborhood children the way he did me. On my fifth birthday, I put soot from our chimney on my hands and went over to his house to wish him a happy birthday. I asked him to bend down, and when he did, I put soot on his face. In return, he put shaving cream on my face, and then he gave a birthday cake to me. He also gave me a small bucket and shovel for my birthday. I played with them for the next two years, until I broke both. Shortly before my sixth birthday, we moved away, and I don't remember ever spending any time with Mr. Andrews again, even though we did return to live in that mill village.

Another person I enjoyed visiting was Mr. J. M. Trammel, the manager of the Poe Mill Store, which was located across the street from the mill. I never knew the store by any other name. The company that owned the mill also owned the store, so everyone called it the "company store." Mr. Trammel would start playing with me the second I entered the store. I never had more than a nickel to spend, and most times less. When I was only four years old, he began sitting me up on the counter and having me spell words, such as "dog," "cat," " rat," and other simple words. I guess he was intrigued that I

49

could spell words at that age. I always left the store with my stomach full of candy that Mr. Trammel paid for, and I wanted to go in and spell for him every day. Mr. Trammel must have felt the same way. I don't recall the circumstances that would provide me with adequate insight relating to why, but I remember very clearly that Mr. Trammel wanted to adopt me. He spoke with my parents about adopting me on numerous occasions. Although he never attempted to purchase me, he did offer to provide financial assistance to my family if he could adopt me. Who knows what the remainder of my life would have been like if the adoption had taken place? Mr. Trammel was a very good person and I liked him very much, but I am happy that I was able to remain with my own family.

One other place I enjoyed visiting was the ice cream parlor at a place that I remember as the Ape Yard. The area I recall being described as the Ape Yard was an area about two square blocks that was located across the street from the mill village at Buncombe Street and D Street. I have heard other people say they believed the Ape Yard was at a different location. Anyway, I have heard two stories about how the Ape Yard got the name. The first story was that a man was drunk at a beer joint in the area and got himself all worked up in an argument with someone else about all the hair on his body. Suddenly, he ripped off all of his clothing and began running all over the area screaming, "I'm an ape, I'm an ape." From that day forth, the area was called Ape Yard. The other story was that a circus was passing through the area when a real ape escaped. The circus animal handlers, along with law enforcement personnel, were scouring the area looking for the ape. There was a lot of commotion that attracted the attention of many people, including the news media. Finally, the ape was captured and taken away, and the name "Ape Yard" has remained ever since. I have never been able to verify either story, so either story could true or both stories could be false.

The ice cream parlor in the Ape Yard served many different flavors of ice cream, but my favorite was called Florida fruit. My pronunciation was "flada flute." In the summertime, every time I could get my hands on a nickel, I went straight to the ice cream parlor. I think the people who managed the parlor enjoyed my coming because they always acted happy to see me. In retrospect, I think they enjoyed listening to me talk more than anything else.

One day, when I was five years old, Mother gave me fifty cents to buy ice cream for three of us children. Why she sent me instead of one of my older brothers is something I will never understand, because I had to cross a major roadway to get to the parlor. As I was running across the road, the half-dollar flew out of my hand and I didn't see where it went or hear it land or roll. I had lost the money, and I knew that fifty cents was a lot of money to us. I was frightened and afraid to go home, and although I searched the road, I couldn't find the money. I began to cry.

After searching for a long time, I gave up. I expected to get a whipping when I arrived home with no ice cream and no money, so I tried to prepare myself mentally for it. When I got home, instead of a whipping, Mother sent David and me to search for the money with instructions to buy ice cream if we found it. Within ten minutes David found the half-dollar, and we bought ice cream and walked home. Our evening ended happily for all of us, and we visited the ice cream parlor many times after that day, but I always held tightly onto my money.

Crowd waits for Roosevelt Funeral train at Greenville Railroad Depot.
Photo Courtesy of Greenville County Historical Society. Greenville, South Carolina.

It was while we lived on Third Street that President Franklin D. Roosevelt died in Warm Springs, Georgia, on April 12, 1945. That occurred six days after my fourth birthday, but I vaguely remember that some people in our community were saddened by the death of President Roosevelt. The train that carried President Roosevelt's body to Washington, D.C., traveled through Greenville. The route the train traveled took it just behind Poe Mill, and many people stood and watched as it passed.

World War II ended on September 2, 1945. Although I was only four years and five months old, I remember that day well. I heard Dad in the distance, long before he arrived at our house, yelling, "Yippee, the war's over!" Within just a few minutes, the whole community was outside their homes and yelling as well. We heard the mill whistle blowing and church bells ringing. We carried pots and pans outside and began beating them. I believe some people were firing guns into the air. The whole neighborhood was jubilant. Dad must have yelled the same exclamation forty times before he finally reached our house. It was obvious that he had been drinking alcoholic beverages of some type. After listening to and being involved in all of the commotion, going to bed that night was the last thing on my mind. When I think about that incident now, I can see some humor in it. In fact, in retrospect, I can see a lot of humor in a lot of things we said and did back then.

With the war over, a feeling of relief came over all of America. We had won the war, our military personnel were returning to their families, and everyone in our community seemed to be happier. The war rationing program ended, making food and household supplies available again. Shoes, gasoline, automobiles, and automobile supplies and equipment were also available. In fact, whatever a citizen wanted, if it was manufactured and one could afford it, there was nothing to stop him from purchasing it. America was on the rise. Our community was more social than before, and it was a fun place to live. Our parents and our neighbors sat on their porches, and the neighborhood children laughed and played together. We weren't any better off financially, but we were relieved that the war was over.

It was shortly after the war had ended that I heard and repeated the first joke that I can recall ever hearing or telling. It still makes me laugh, not because the joke was so funny, but because of the way I told it and the audience who heard it. I was only four years old, so I must have heard some older person tell that joke; otherwise, I would never have known to say the words I did. I was playing with Roy Bagwell, a neighborhood friend who was about thirty yards away from me, so I had to talk loud, or yell. I said, "Hey, Roy, can you run fast?" Roy said he could, so I said, "Can you paint good?" He said he could, so I said, "Well, I just let a fart. If you can run fast and paint good, why don't you catch it and paint it green?" About that time, I heard a roar of laughter coming from the front porch of the Garlands, who lived directly across the street from us and from two other neighbors' houses. I had no idea anyone was around, especially adults. I ran as fast as I could to the rear of our house and hid. Later, some of the neighbors told our parents what they had heard, and I was ready to take a whipping. Instead, our parents laughed just as loud as the neighbors had. I was relieved, but I always looked around first before I told another joke. As much as we enjoyed laughing and playing, everything that happened in our lives was not humorous.

During the summer of 1946, we could not play as often as we wished. It was then that I discovered life on Third Street was not all play for me, because I suddenly was expected to assist with work. All of us were expected to work, which we did in a variety of ways. Picking cotton was one type of work I was introduced to at the age of five.

I can just barely remember climbing into the back of some type of pickup truck and traveling away from the mill village to the country, where we picked cotton. The cotton fields were so large that I could not even see from one end to the other of any of them. I felt as I imagined an ant would feel as it crawled through a cornfield. I knew I was going to have to walk to the opposite end of the cotton field; I just couldn't see that far because I wasn't tall enough.

Mother had sewn shoulder straps onto a large flour sack that was draped around my shoulders for me to fill with cotton. Each of us had to start at the beginning of a cotton row, and we were expected to pick every piece of cotton from every cotton boll on every plant all the way to the other end of the row.

Cotton grows on small, shrublike plants, which looked like small trees to me. The flower bud, known by us as a square, would blossom and develop into an oval boll. I always thought we were talking about a cotton "bowl"; and I still believe that the Cotton Bowl, where football games are played, got its name because someone else thought the same thing. Anyway, when the cotton boll matured, it would split open, revealing the cotton inside.

Picking cotton might have been a much easier task if there had been no impediments. The first problem I recognized was that picking cotton took place in the summertime and required dry weather. Dry weather meant that we had to work under a blazing summer sun. Drinking water was an absolute necessity. Pouring water over our heads to cool off was pure pleasure, but we knew we had better not let our parents catch us doing such a thing. Water had to be carried into the fields, and it was not to be wasted. We found out the hard way that some form of punishment came soon after we wasted some of our precious water. The one thing that helped us get through a hot day was that our bodies would sweat profusely. The sweat helped cool us down, especially if just the slightest breeze was blowing.

To us children, the most dangerous and worrisome problem was the little prickly, briarlike stickers on the cotton bolls. If we weren't careful, we would receive some painful injuries to our hands. Picking cotton with gloves on was not an option. In the first place, we didn't have any gloves, but our parents wouldn't have allowed us to wear them if we did, so we did what we had to do. We picked cotton and licked our wounds later.

A major problem for me was that I was too young and small to be picking cotton in the first place, or so I thought. I could barely reach into a cotton plant to pull the cotton from the boll. I was scared to death of the stickers on the bolls, so I picked cotton very carefully, which also meant very slowly. The slowness was an added hazard for me because our parents didn't have a lot of patience, and they thought slowness meant laziness. They also didn't understand that small children were sometimes fearful. My fear of the stickers was quickly dismissed with a demanding order to get to work. I would pick as fast as I could, but it was never fast enough to fill up my flour sack before lunch. It was amazing to me how much cotton one could stuff into a flour sack, but it still didn't weigh much. I guess I was not cut out to be a cotton picker because the most cotton I could pick in a day was probably no more than thirty to forty pounds. Mother could pick over three hundred pounds of cotton a day. I was young, and I didn't measure up to the other family members when it came to work.

When we finished picking cotton at the end of the day, it was time to weigh our pickings and receive our earnings. Since I had to dump whatever cotton I had picked into one of our parent's large bags, I don't recall ever receiving any earnings. The money earned went to take care of the whole family, not for any individual to buy toys or candy or to otherwise enjoy. We worked hard but went home empty-handed. At least, that's the way I saw it. I always felt somewhat unappreciated for the work I did in the cotton fields. However little it was, I wanted to receive a hug or a thank-you, or just have someone tell me that I had done a good job, but that never happened. However, my siblings performed very well, and they didn't receive praise for their work either.

I didn't get any praise for my cotton-picking ability, but I do remember one day when I got some very special attention in the cotton field, more attention than I wanted. I was picking cotton rather slowly, as usual, when I looked up and noticed that all the others were way ahead of me on their rows. I wanted to get some praise for all the cotton I picked that day, and the best place to get praise for picking cotton was at the scales. Every day, the person who picked the most cotton was at least identified. To me, that was a form of praise, so I decided that if I put a few rocks in with my cotton, I would get the praise I wanted so badly. I picked up some rather large rocks and put them into my flour sack. Well, when I carried my sack to the end of the row, instead of dumping it into Mother's large sack, I asked to have my sack weighed separately.

Mother must have become suspicious because she picked up my sack and shook it. She heard a noise coming from the sack, a noise that sounded like rocks banging together, and she took the cotton from the sack and discovered the rocks. I was really frightened because I knew I was caught. By the time she finished with me, I regretted ever trying to get attention, and I wished I had not even seen a rock that day. I had received more attention than I had ever imagined, and I had a difficult time getting through the rest of the day. I preferred not to be noticed much after that episode.

When cotton-picking time came to an end, apple-picking time wasn't far off. I was involved with apple picking for the first time at age five. I remember climbing into that old pickup truck we traveled in on our cotton-picking trips again and traveling away from the mill village and into the countryside. I believe the apple orchard was in Oconee County, but I'm not positive about that. It could have been in Greenville or Pickens. Regardless, we were given buckets and sent into the apple orchard to pick apples. I didn't mind picking apples so much because I got to climb trees and the weather was much cooler than when we picked cotton.

We picked all the apples we could reach from the ground, and then we climbed trees to pick other apples. I had a small bucket, maybe two or three gallons, to fill with apples. Everyone else had larger buckets. When our buckets were full, we dumped them into bushel baskets near the trees. We repeated that activity all day. I wasn't allowed to climb very high in a tree, but because I was quite small, I could reach some apples others could not. I could go out onto small limbs and drop apples I picked to someone else. To me, that was fun.

One of the benefits of picking apples was that we got to eat some. Of course, it was not that we were allowed to eat the apples; we just had a lot of opportunities to eat one quickly while no one was looking. At least I don't think we were ever observed eating apples, because I never got the same attention I did for placing rocks in the cotton sack. Perhaps our parents just didn't mind if we ate some apples, because if we ate apples, they had to feed us less. Anything to save the little amount of money we earned.

At the end of the day, the apples we picked were counted by the bushels, and we were paid according to the number of bushels we picked. Just as with the cotton, I had to dump my apples into someone else's container; therefore, I never saw any of the money for picking apples.

I recall that our parents always were allowed to take two or three bushels of apples home; however, I never knew if that was a portion of our pay or the orchard owner was just a very kind and generous person. I know we certainly enjoyed some delicious apple cobblers; Mother would make apple jelly, apple butter, and preserves, enough she hoped to last until the next apple season. In the middle of winter, it was good to find fresh-cooked biscuits and apple jelly on the table for breakfast.

Sometimes, we would wrap apples individually in newspaper and pack them away for use at Christmas. When Christmas arrived, we would have some of the best apples ever tasted. I tried to eat all of them, but I had three older brothers and a sister with the same idea. I was limited by the number they ate.

When apple season was over, we began to look forward to Christmas. We looked through a Sears Roebuck catalog for hours in attempts to find a toy we hoped to receive. We also looked at various newspaper ads from stores in downtown Greenville. I counted the number of pictures of Santa Claus that were in the *Greenville News* every day, and I kept up with the number of shopping days left until Christmas. Although it arrived a month before Christmas, I don't even remember Thanksgiving 1946.

Before Thanksgiving arrived, a tragic accident occurred that attracted the attention of our entire community. As a matter of fact, it probably received national attention. We thought we were being bombed! The Ideal Laundry, located at Buncombe Street and Echols Street, just inside the boundaries of the city of Greenville, had a propane gas explosion on November 19, 1946. The result was tragedy. The laundry was within one mile of our house, and our house shook violently. We later learned that the laundry, ten houses, and the fire department next door to the laundry were destroyed. We also learned that ten people were killed and more than one hundred others were injured. Plate glass and other windows were shattered in many buildings and homes as far away as one mile from the laundry. I don't recall whether or not windows were broken at our house, but I know that the explosion frightened the whole community. That incident happened within a few hours after the Christmas parade in downtown Greenville. Thanksgiving was only six days away. Aside

Ideal Laundry. Photo Courtesy of Greenville County Historical Society. Greenville, South Carolina.

Aftermath of Ideal Laundry Explosion. Photo Courtesy of Greenville County Historical Society. Greenville, South Carolina.

from thoughts of Christmas, I guess the tragedy is a major reason that I have no memory of Thanksgiving in 1946. December 25 was just a little more than a month away, so there was ample time for a five-year-old to forget the tragedy and think about Christmas again before it actually arrived.

Christmas 1946 was my most memorable Christmas ever. I remember it so well because my brothers allowed me to assist them in finding any Christmas presents that might be hidden in the house. A couple of days before Christmas, our parents had left all of us boys at home without any supervision. I don't recall whether or not Grace was also there, but it seems to me that she was never around when we boys got into our greatest mischief.

With our parents gone, and no one to stop us, we decided it was time to search the house. We went into every room in the house and looked into every conceivable hiding place. We had just about given up on finding any Christmas presents when we decided to look in the most forbidden place in the entire house: our parents' bedroom closet. That was the one place we knew we were never to go into, no matter what season of the year it was.

Then it happened! William uncovered the most beautiful red wagon I have ever seen in my life. It was huge, with side rails that made it look even larger than it was. I think it was called a Radio Flyer or Western Flyer, but I'm not positive about the name.

We pulled the wagon out of the closet at just the wrong time—when our parents returned home! We were scared out of our wits! We were just going to look at the wagon and put it back. We certainly didn't want anyone to know we were sneaking a peek at something we might be receiving for Christmas. We were frantically attempting to put the wagon back into the closet when our parents walked into their bedroom. We were caught!

The good thing about that day was we didn't get the whipping we all expected. Instead, we were allowed to play with the wagon. We were surprised beyond expression when Mother told us that we could take the wagon outside to play with it. I got into the wagon with David and James, and William pulled it all over the neighborhood. We were having the time of our lives.

We traveled what seemed like forty miles on the sidewalks of the mill village, when it was actually probably no more than one mile.

A few hours after we had begun playing with our wagon, we heard some adult neighbors talking to our parents. They were telling them how terrible it was for us to be playing with our Christmas gift two days before Christmas. Our parents told them to mind their own business. Although I didn't understand why our neighbors were complaining, that was one time when I was happy to see our parents angry.

Because World War II had not been over long, we did not receive any other toys for Christmas that year. The wagon was for all five of us children to share. Financially, that was the best our parents could do, but to us children, our parents couldn't have done better.

We played with our wagon as often as we could. In fact, we spent a lot time playing, either with the wagon or some game that we already knew or created. We were a little on the wild side from time to time, probably because we thought having fun was what life was all about. However, in our zeal to have a good time, we sometimes made mistakes that either caused us to receive bodily injuries or to receive unwanted attention from our parents. All of us children experienced the liberty to enjoy activities of play so long as we obeyed our parents and stayed out of trouble. Most of the time, we were treated with a degree of kindness. However, when we disobeyed or got into some type of trouble, we knew we would be disciplined. Some of the harshest instances of discipline I can recall during my years of growing up occurred while we were living on Third Street at Poe Mill. Although I may have contributed to the cause for discipline in two separate incidents, the harshness was beyond what I believe should have been necessary.

Dad and Mother were very strong, short-tempered, quick to react, and totally unforgiving when one of us children did something they perceived to be wrong. The standard method of disciplining us was whipping. I learned, as I got older, that the harshness of discipline and the methods of my parents were almost universal within mill villages and on farms during that era. I emphasize that fact because it should be understood that my siblings and

I were no different from most other children whom we grew up with. Our parents were just as normal and loving as our neighbors were, and whippings were the standard punishment throughout our community.

We did not receive whippings every day, not even every week. Sometimes we went months without punishment. However, when we got a whipping, the memory of it lasted for several weeks, and a few have lasted a lifetime. At times, we probably deserved a spanking or some form of tough discipline, and at other times we were totally innocent and got a whipping anyway. There is no way to know how many whippings we got overall, but I recall just a few very clearly.

Most of the time, Mother whipped us with what she called a "hickory." However, I called them "tree limbs." Sometimes she just slapped us, anywhere her hands happened to strike, including across the face. Mother had hands as hard as nails, and the sting of a slap from her lasted for quite some time. When she used a hickory, she always picked out what she called a "keen hickory." To me, that meant a hickory that would cut right through my clothing and make bright red stripes everywhere it hit. If I had a choice, I preferred to be slapped, because the mark from a slap faded away faster than the stripe of a hickory. I wanted to play with my friends without obvious signs that I had just been whipped.

Dad had the strength of a weight lifter. He had worked on farms and in cotton mills most of his life, but I don't think he ever realized how strong he was. He whipped us with either a belt or a hickory, whichever he thought would be the most effective at the time. As a young child, I don't remember ever walking away from one of his whippings without screaming and crying. The pain was absolutely excruciating and sometimes lasted ten minutes or more. The whipping was remembered for days.

The first incident of discipline that I remember clearly occurred shortly after we moved to Third Street. At the time, I was only three years old. I guess I recall the incident so well because all three of my brothers took a whipping that I should have received, if any one of us deserved a whipping at all. I lied, convincingly, to save my own skin, and I am still sorry today that my brothers took a whipping; however, at the time, I was so scared that I would have done anything to avoid being hurt by Dad.

Because World War II was still going on and food rationing was still in existence, fresh fruits and vegetables were extremely hard to come by. However, Dad and one of his brothers, Hoyt Porter, had discovered that a shipment of bananas had arrived at a location near our mill village. Dad, Mother, Uncle Hoyt, and his wife Viola left all of us boys at home while they traveled to the location to attempt to purchase some bananas. A short time later, they came back with twenty-four bananas, all ripe, with a beautiful yellow color. I had never seen so many bananas before. In fact, that might have been the first time I had ever seen a banana at all. They looked so good I wanted to eat them immediately, but Mother wanted to make a pudding. All of the adults left the house again to attempt to locate some vanilla wafers for a banana pudding.

The adults had been gone no longer than three minutes when one of my brothers decided he wanted to eat a banana, so he broke one off and took it outside. Then, each of my other brothers did the same thing. I guess that gave me the idea it was okay to eat the bananas, so I broke one off, peeled it, and took a bite of it. It was so good that I just had to have another one, then another one, and another one, until I had eaten twenty-one bananas! I don't recall the size of the bananas, just the color and taste; however, they must have been small for a three-year-old to eat so many. When I finished eating all of the bananas, I went outside to play with my brothers.

About fifteen minutes later, the adults returned, having found and purchased some vanilla wafers. When Mother walked into the kitchen, the first things she noticed were that the bananas were gone and the trash can was full of banana peelings. Of course, Mother was immediately angry; however, she was also concerned for our health. That was kind of odd because on one hand she wanted to kill all of us, and on the other hand she wanted to prevent us from becoming sick. There's a little bit of humor in that. I guess mothers are just that way. Mother immediately yelled for Dad to come into the kitchen.

When Dad realized what we had done, he was very upset. He called all of us boys into the house. It was obvious what was about to happen, because Dad's face was red and he had his belt in his hand. He asked who ate the bananas, and my brothers admitted that each of them had eaten one banana. They were telling the absolute truth. I admitted that I had eaten only three bananas. I was telling an absolute lie. Dad did not believe, for one second, that my brothers had eaten only one banana each, so he took them, one by one, into a bedroom, where he whipped each of them for what seemed like five minutes. I could hear them screaming and crying and begging Dad to stop whipping them, and I was petrified. Then Dad came for me.

My uncle was my savior that day. By the time Dad had finished whipping my brothers, my uncle had me up in his lap. He had asked me several times how many bananas I had eaten, and I just kept repeating the number "3." Dad told me to come with him, and I started to climb out of my uncle's lap, but my uncle held onto me. He told Dad that he believed I was telling the truth. He said there was no way a small boy like me could have eaten more than three bananas, and he said that, because I had told the truth, I should not get a whipping. Eventually, he convinced Dad not to whip me, and I have been grateful for the intervention of my uncle ever since. He quickly became a favorite uncle of mine.

I credited Mother and Dad for the discipline my brothers received that day; however, one other person deserved some credit. As I said, Mother was angry but worried about our health at the same time. She had contacted a doctor to find out what effect eating all of those bananas would have on us. The doctor told her the bananas would not harm us; however, he added that Mother and Dad should just "beat the hell" out of us. I guess Mother thought the doctor was prescribing a beating. I often wonder what the doctor would have said if he had known all of the adults left four small children, ranging in ages from three to eight, at home alone with absolutely no supervision. Maybe he would have believed that the lack of proper supervision had something to do with our behavior. I'm glad prescription discipline is no longer on the market. However, I was lucky to have an uncle protect me against it at least one time. Later in life, I wasn't so lucky.

When I was four years old, I committed an act that was so dangerous my life could have been lost at any second. I didn't realize I was in danger; however, the reaction I got from Dad was almost equally dangerous.

Mother was working in the cotton mill, all of my siblings were in school, and Dad was supposed to be taking care of me until some of my siblings got home. Then he was supposed to go to work on the second shift, and Mother would come home.

Dad left me at our house alone while he supposedly ran some errands. I still don't know where he went, but he was gone a long time. I went into our bathroom to do whatever act of nature I had to do, and while I was in the bathroom, I noticed two large glass jugs, one full of a clear liquid and the other almost empty of what looked like the same type of clear liquid. As I sat on the commode, I began playing with the two jugs. I opened both jugs and smelled the contents, and both of them had the same, strong, distinct odor. I realized that both jugs contained the same type of liquid so I decided that each jug should contain an equal amount. I picked up the full jug and began pouring some of the liquid into the other jug. The jug was a gallon-size jug, and it was very heavy for a four-year-old. As I was pouring, I was spilling about as much as I was getting into the other jug. When I thought I had the two containers equally filled, I stopped to measure them visually. I had poured too much, so I needed to pour some back into the first jug. This activity continued for several minutes, with me spilling the liquid all over the floor.

Even though I was busy playing, I heard Dad when he came into the house. I heard him call out my name as he walked through the house; the tone of his voice indicated to me that he had already smelled the liquid I was playing with. I jumped from the commode and commenced to pull up my pants. I had all intentions of running some place to hide because I knew I must have been doing something wrong. I also knew it would mean terrible consequences if I were.

Before I could get my pants up and fastened, Dad entered the bathroom. He grabbed me with a viselike grip and jerked me off the floor like a rag doll. He carried me into a bedroom and whipped me until I was screaming and crying and begging him to stop. His face was red, his eyes had an angry look, and his knuckles on the hand that held the belt were white. He left stripes all over my legs, arms, and back that took a couple of hours to fade away.

When Dad stopped whipping me, he started lecturing me. I was never to touch that liquid again, not to even go near it. He would beat me half to death if he caught me near it again. I guess he didn't realize I thought he had just done that. Anyway, I learned the liquid I had been playing with was kerosene, and I had been playing with it within only about twelve feet of a lit kerosene heater. I was lucky he came home when he did but unlucky to receive such a whipping. I guess the whipping was not only discipline but was also his way of showing that he loved me.

I now realize I got into that situation because Dad shared some of the blame through his negligence. If I had not been left at home alone at the tender age of four, the incident never would have happened. Even so, Dad's reaction, in my opinion, was totally wrong. Instead of jerking me up and beating me, he should have picked me up and hugged me and explained to me what the liquid was and the danger it posed. I could have understood that even at the age of four. Unfortunately, showing compassion and understanding were not things Dad did best. Mother was not so great at showing them either. However, the whippings were meant to be parental guidance.

I remember one act of discipline that occurred when I was still just four years old that involved Mother. She and I began playing, and it is the only time in my life that I can recall when Mother actually played with me individually, but this is not to say that she never did. She was swinging me around and around, holding me by my arms, and she would occasionally let me fall gently to the floor. I was having a great time, laughing and playing. Suddenly, without any warning whatsoever, Mother violently slapped me right across the left side of my face, and I immediately screamed and began to cry. I was so shocked by the slap that I didn't know what to do. As I was crying, I asked Mother why she had slapped me, and she replied that I was trying to look up her dress. At that age, looking up my mother's dress would have been the last thing I would have thought about doing, and if I did, I was a totally innocent child. I remember that I had only been looking into her face and enjoying the fact that she was actually laughing and playing with me. The slap caused both of my ears to ring for several minutes. I don't recall that Mother ever played with me individually again. Maybe I should be happy for that.

I don't recall ever seeing Grace get a whipping with a hickory or a belt, but I do remember one incident when Mother slapped her across the face. When I received my first slap, I understood how Grace must have felt.

Not long after Mother slapped me, William received a terrible whipping from Dad. Dad had been drinking whiskey, which clouded his ability to think rationally, and William was totally innocent of any wrongdoing.

A neighbor asked William and one of his friends to climb a pear tree and get some pears for her, and William and his friend gladly helped the lady. Later that day, a male neighbor reported to Dad that he had seen William and his friend stealing some pears from the lady's tree.

Dad didn't even bother to determine what the truth of the incident was; he just came in and began to whip William with a belt. The belt was one that I had chewed on when I was an infant, and the end of it was twisted and hard. Every time he struck William, the belt was leaving a welt, and William was screaming and crying. Then Dad struck a blow that caused the belt to wrap around William's neck. When Dad jerked the belt back, a large piece of William's skin was jerked from his neck. William began bleeding profusely, and Dad stopped whipping him. The injury was not intentional, but it was bad enough to visually upset and anger Mother.

Mother had Chief Davis, the mill village police chief, come to the house to look at William. Chief Davis stated that there was nothing he could do about a father whipping his own child, regardless of the severity. However, I believe that two positive outcomes occurred. The first outcome was that Dad was so frightened by his own actions that he discontinued drinking alcoholic beverages immediately. I never saw him again when he appeared to have been drinking. The second outcome was that William never again received a severe whipping from Dad. In fact, I don't recall that William ever received any

Norris Cotton Mill in Twelve Mile River at Cateechee, S.C. Photo Courtesy of Jerry Alexander—Pickens, South Carolina.

whippings at all after that incident, and I can only remember two or three whippings that any of us received after that day.

We lived on Third Street for about three years before Dad quit his job again. I thoroughly enjoyed living on Third Street, and the fact that I have so many memories from there is very special to me.

We moved away from Third Street in March 1947. We did so because Dad and Mother got jobs in a mill village called Cateechee in Pickens County, South Carolina. Cateechee was the name of a legendary Cherokee Indian maiden who rode a horse from the Cherokee village of Keowee to Fort Ninety Six to warn her white lover of an impending Indian attack on Fort Ninety Six. Ninety Six got its name because early settlers believed that the distance between their community and the Keowee village was ninety-six miles. When Colonel D. K. Norris founded Cateechee, he named it in honor of the Indian maiden.

The Norris Cotton Mill and mill-owned village of ninety houses, company store, barber shop, hotel, post office, jail, company offices, church, and school had been built in 1896. I don't recall seeing a jail, barber shop, post office, or hotel when we lived in Cateechee, but that doesn't mean they no longer existed. I just don't recall seeing them. I remember that I was intrigued when I saw that Norris Mill sat right in the middle of Twelve Mile River. The first cotton mill I ever actually visited was Norris Mill in Cateechee. The mill was many miles from any town or city. I guess one could call it a country mill. I don't recall anything that would have been considered to be a commercial business within five miles of the mill, other than the company store, where they sold groceries and just about anything else a family in Cateechee needed, and a grocery store on a nearby highway. The mill had its own village for its workers, including a school. The only other buildings I remember are the mill office complex and two churches that were located on the highway nearby. We attended one of those churches.

It was like going backwards again when we moved to Cateechee. We moved into a small, four-room house with no bathroom, and the outhouse was a good thirty yards from the house. I will never forget the stench of the

Four-room house in Cateechee, similar to the Porter residence in 1947. This house was next door to our house when we lived in Cateechee and it looks almost identical to ours. Our house was destroyed by fire sometime after we moved away from Cateechee.

chamber pots (we called them "slop jars") we used at night and then emptied into the outhouse every morning. We had running water and a sink on the back porch, but no hot water, and we had no sinks anywhere inside the house. We also had no floor coverings.

We had no built-in cabinets, but we did have electric lights, one bulb hanging in the center of each room. Mother had her wood-burning cookstove, and the only other heat source was a small heater in which we could burn wood or coal. All five of us children had to share one bedroom, and we were still taking baths in our round tin tubs and washing clothes over a fire.

Even though World War II had been over for more than a year, food was not readily available to us because we had very little money. I think Dad believed that we could have another garden and raise some hogs, and that we could produce enough food to provide for the family. Dad's desire to have a garden might have been a primary motivator for our move to Cateechee.

We had a hog pen in the woods, about a hundred yards from our house, but I don't recall how many hogs we had. However, I do recall hog-killing time. Someone shot a hog between the eyes to kill it, and then the hog was raised, and then lowered by chain fall, into a large vat of boiling water. The boiling water caused the hair on the hog's body to loosen, so it could be scraped off. Once the hair was scraped off, the hog was gutted and washed clean. The next step was to saw the hog in half, lengthwise, and place the two halves on a large table for cutting up. The meat was processed into cured hams, pork chops, sausage, roasts, and so on. Mother usually took a large piece of fresh pork and cooked it while others were processing the rest of the meat. Once finished, we went inside to enjoy a tasty meal.

We planted a garden soon after we moved in, but the garden was a long distance from our house and across a river. The garden produced a lot of food, but it was difficult to get to and difficult to work. We had only hand tools such as rakes and hoes, and we needed a tractor to work the garden. We also needed a tractor so we could be high off the ground for protection from the snakes that were in or near our garden. When our family went to work in the garden, I had to go along. I was not going for the purpose of working because

I was not strong enough to work very well with garden tools. I was there because there was no one else to watch me. We had no money for babysitters, but I preferred to be with the family anyway.

While the rest of the family worked in the garden, I walked around in the garden between the rows of vegetables. One day, when they were all hoeing weeds and grass from the garden, I became bored and decided I would walk over to the river, which was only about twenty yards away. I wanted to see what I could see in the water. I also wanted to play in the water, but I knew Mother would not permit me to do that.

I walked to the water's edge and began to look for minnows. Twelve Mile River originated in the nearby mountains, and the water was crystal clear. I could easily see the bottom of the river. I saw a few minnows swimming rapidly into an area near the riverbank and out of my view. I wanted a closer look, so I started down the embankment. As I reached the water, a large water snake swam by, no more than two feet from me. I was so frightened that I scrambled back up the embankment and ran over to Mother. When I told her what had happened, she scolded me for getting too near the river. Although I was tired of walking around in the rows of the garden, I stayed away from the river the rest of the day. I had just celebrated my sixth birthday on the sixth day of April, and because I was so young, I was frightened by snakes. However, that incident was not the only encounter I had with snakes at Cateechee.

A group of black racer snakes started chasing us when my brothers and I were walking near the river one day. We ran away from them, but they followed us. When we stopped running, the snakes stopped. We ran again and the snakes followed us again. That activity continued for several minutes before we started throwing rocks at the snakes, but they kept following us. Finally, after much rock throwing, we chased the snakes away. The time that passed while we were being chased by snakes was a very scary few minutes. Though we never experienced another scary incident involving snakes while we lived in Cateechee, we did experience a scary but humorous incident involving a mouse.

My brothers and I, a cousin named Randolph Stancil (whom we called Randy), and another friend were walking through the woods one afternoon.

Cateechee Elementary School.

We saw what we thought was a bird's nest in the branches of a small tree. My brother James decided to climb the tree and get the nest. I think he said he wanted to take it to school to exhibit it on a science table.

He started climbing the tree, but he suddenly jumped back to the ground and started screaming and crying. We had no idea what was wrong with him. He started screaming that something was in his pants leg, near his crotch area. Although we were trying to help him, he was jumping around so much that no one could check to see what was in his pants. Randy and someone else grabbed James and held him while William took off James's pants. When they got James's pants down to his knees, there was a small mouse in the pants. They killed the mouse and then checked to see whether or not the mouse had bitten James. There were no bite marks, just some tiny red marks where the mouse's claws had apparently been digging in as the mouse was climbing. After about five minutes, all the rest of us stopped laughing, except intermittently. Somehow, James never did think that incident was funny. The rest of us have laughed about it for over fifty years. Whenever I think about the mouse incident, I also think about the Cateechee village in which we lived, Twelve Mile River, and Norris Mill.

Almost every cotton mill I ever saw had a river, creek, or pond adjacent to it. Usually, there was a creek that fed into an area where the mill had placed a dam, thereby creating a large pond. Probably at the time the cotton mills were built, no major electrical power company could provide power to all the mills in the area, or the water sources enabled the power companies that did provide electrical power. Either that or the mills just chose to provide their own power. I don't really know; however, I think most mills had their own electrical power station right on the property. As the water flowed over a dam, electrical power was generated. With that arrangement, each mill could be self-sufficient, with no dependence on major electrical power companies and no electric bills to pay.

I was actually allowed to visit the inside of Norris Mill with Mother, We walked across a pedestrian-only bridge that was high above the river and entered into the upper level of what appeared to be an enclosed brick tower, and then we walked down the steps inside the tower to the lower level where the mill was located. When we exited the stairway, we were inside the mill. When we arrived at Mother's work area, the noise of the machinery was almost deafening. I recall wondering why Mother would want to work in such a noisy place. I began to look for the river, but from inside the mill no one would have known that the mill sat in the middle of a river. I could not see or hear the river, just the sound of mill machinery. I was ready to go back home. At least I could explore the area near our home, even when my siblings were in school. I loved exploring more than anything.

One of the places I explored near our house was our outhouse. I guess I was fascinated by things in and around the outhouse because I was only six. I always paid particular attention to the critters crawling and flying around inside and outside the outhouse. There were more flies than I had ever seen gathered in one place before, and most of them were quite large. Many of them were a very bright green in color, with black eyes and transparent wings. I spent a lot of time trying to catch them, but they were too fast for the hands of a small child. However, I learned that I could swat them with a folded newspaper, but then I had to throw the newspaper into the pit beneath the carved-out wooden seat. I didn't waste a lot of newspapers killing flies. I don't even know whether or not toilet paper had been invented at the time, but I do know that we certainly never seemed to have any. Instead, we used old catalogs or newspapers. The catalogs were much more difficult to use than newspapers because the pages were thick and slick, and that's why I never wasted the newspapers on flies.

Another group of insects I noticed in the outhouse were maggots. They were the larvae of the flies, and they were on the feces in the bottom of the outhouse pit. They were white in color, and they squirmed around like small, fat, short worms. Even though the stench of the pit was terrible, I watched the maggots crawl and squirm for long periods of time.

One other critter I saw in the outhouse was a large black widow spider. At age six, I already knew the danger of being bitten by a black widow, so I wasted no time killing it with a heavy catalog.

I looked to the top of the inside of the outhouse and saw very large, red wasps clinging to a nest they had apparently built there. The nest was grayish in color and appeared to be made of paper and about four inches in diameter. There must have been a minimum of thirty wasps clinging to the nest, and I was a little frightened of them. I was very careful not to disturb the wasps; however, I told Dad about them. I think Dad threw gasoline on them because they disappeared. I had heard Dad say that gasoline would kill wasps instantly. They just fall to the ground, dead by the time they land.

Although I saw many other wasps while we lived there, there was never a new nest inside the outhouse. There were, however, several nests under the overhang of the outside of the outhouse. Dad killed them when he could, and we always entered and exited the outhouse very carefully. Other dangerous creatures lived there also.

On the wall in the corner of the inside of the outhouse, I saw a dirt-dauber crawling into its nest. The dirt-dauber is a wasp-like insect, which can also sting like a wasp. However, it builds its nest with mud and water. I guess that's why it's called a dirt dauber. The nest I saw was a reddish clay color, with three separate sections. I think each section is a different chamber for the larvae to hatch in. I did not tamper with the nest for fear I would be stung. Someone else removed it.

I saw a number of granddaddy longlegs spiders just outside the outhouse and in other locations but I was never afraid of them. I just picked them up and played with them.

I observed small lizards scrambling up and down the outhouse walls and sometimes disappearing into the cracks between the wall boards. I was always afraid to grab one because I thought they had sharp teeth, which they didn't. I chased them until they found places to hide well enough to prevent my finding them.

I suppose I was the only family member that was intrigued by the outhouse and the immediate area surrounding it because I never noticed any of the rest of the family lingering there very long when they had to visit it. However, all of us boys were intrigued by the Twelve Mile River. In fact, we were fascinated by the river and the surrounding woods.

I remember that seven of us, including us brothers, a cousin, and two neighbors, went for an exploratory walk in the woods behind our house and discovered that the same river that was adjacent to our garden and ran around Norris Mill also ran through the woods behind our house. We also discovered we could walk through the woods to get to the river, to our garden, and to the mill. We were so excited to make that discovery we could hardly contain ourselves. We discovered many large rocks at the river, some as big as a house, scattered throughout the water. We could jump from shore to a rock and then jump from rock to rock all the way across the river. The water was not very deep at that location either. The depth was ideal for us to play in the water and not worry about drowning. We had visions of swimming holes and fishing. The river would be our paradise! However, we discovered that our paradise was somewhat limited by our inability to swim. Downstream the water was quite deep, and upstream the water was even deeper. Our cousin, Randy, was a very strong swimmer so he loved the deeper water, but my brothers and I stayed away from any areas where the water was more than chest deep. We just pretended we were swimming.

We went to the river as often as we could. Sometimes, if we had any, we took potatoes and other foods with us. Of course, we had to sneak food from the house; it wasn't just given to us. When we took potatoes, we found small limbs and brush to build a fire. We built a fire on the rocks in the middle of the river to avoid causing a forest fire. We let the fire burn down until there were only some bright red coals, and then we placed our potatoes on some coals and covered them with more coals. Of course, while the potatoes were cooking, we played in the water. When we thought the potatoes had cooked long enough to be ready to eat, we used a long stick to rake them away from the hot coals. We let them cool for a few minutes and then cut them open. The potatoes were almost like charcoal on the outside, but soft, white, and delicious on the inside. My very first lessons in outdoor cooking were at the river. Picnicking was never more fun.

Discovering Twelve Mile River was synonymous with discovering a fishing hole. Long before we moved to Cateechee, we knew that many fish were in the rivers in that area. Dad had fished the rivers in the area since his childhood, and we had heard many of his fishing stories. We were eager to try our luck.

I had never heard of a rod and reel at that time. We just found a canebrake near the river and cut canes to use as fishing poles. We tied fishing line to the end of a pole and attached a hook on the other end of the line. We placed a lead sinker on the line, near the hook, to hold the hook under the water. Finally, we attached a cork, or float, onto the line, about three feet from the sinker, and our equipment was ready.

We could not fish without some type of bait, and for us the easiest way to get bait was to dig for it. We used a mattock and a shovel to dig into the black, rich, moist soil near the river. We found a variety of worms, mostly grubs and reds. Worms are natural fish food, and just about any kind of fish will eat a worm. Once we had our bait, we were ready to fish. We walked along the riverbank to get to the deeper areas of the river where we believed our chances of catching fish were best, and then we tossed our worm-laden hooks into the water and waited. The corks bobbed on top of the water while we watched in anticipation of a nibble. Sometimes, the corks began to bob up and down in rapid succession. We knew a fish was probably bumping the hook, perhaps trying to get the worm into its mouth. Suddenly, the cork would disappear under the water, and we would jerk our pole up in an attempt to catch the fish. Many times, we missed the fish because we jerked too soon; however, the fish rarely missed stealing our bait. We needed to be a lot more patient, but very young fishermen are sometimes easily excited and too eager. On occasion, we jerked the pole at just the right time and the hook was firmly stuck into the fish's mouth. Then the battle to get the fish to shore began. To us, a fish was not caught until we had it on a stringer. Once we got a fish on a stringer, we repeated the process over and over again. We caught several types of fish, mostly perch, suckers, and small catfish.

After catching the fish, we went home as quickly as possible, cleaned the fish, and turned them over to Mother. She washed and drained them, then prepared them for cooking. When they were cooked, the entire family had a very delicious and filling meal. Having a good meal was a natural incentive for us to go fishing as often as possible, and every time we decided to go fishing, I was always jumping for joy.

Aside from picnicking, fishing, and attempting to learn to swim, there were other activities at the river. I sometimes wish I never had, but I learned to smoke cigarettes. An older boy, Jerry Harriston, who lived a couple of houses away from us, had a father who was a heavy smoker. He smoked brands that were very strong. Back then there was no such thing as a filtered or menthol cigarette, at least not that we knew about. Jerry snuck packs of cigarettes from his father's cartons and went to the river, where he went out on the big rocks to smoke them. I watched him steal and smoke cigarettes numerous times before he offered one to me. When he offered a cigarette to me, I readily took it and placed one end in my mouth, and he struck a match and held it to my cigarette. I took a draw and the fire lit the cigarette, but I choked on the smoke. I coughed until I was able to breathe fresh air again. Jerry just laughed at me, but he said he could teach me how to smoke without coughing and I was eager to learn. I took another draw and choked again, but that did not deter me. I wanted to learn how to smoke a cigarette, inhale the smoke, and blow the smoke out through my nose like Jerry could do. I listened and watched as Jerry showed me how to inhale the smoke without choking. He inhaled smoke and blew it out through his nostrils numerous times without so much as a small cough. When my turn came, I took a draw and did exactly as he had told me to do, but I choked again. I smoked two cigarettes the first day but could never inhale the smoke without choking. However, after a few more days of trying, I finally learned to inhale without choking and to blow the smoke through my nostrils. At the ripe old age of six, I thought I was a hero. I had no idea that I was playing with real danger. I would sneak and smoke from that day until I went into the military at age eighteen. While I was in the military and no longer sneaking, I smoked up to three packs of cigarettes per day. However, I quit smoking at the age of twenty-four and I have not smoked a cigarette since. I am happy today that I had enough sense, combined with enough self-discipline, to quit smoking at an early age. I strongly believe smoking is a health hazard that, if not discontinued, will slowly bring on death. In some cases death from smoking cigarettes comes at an early age, and it disturbs me greatly when I see young people smoking.

Another dangerous and nasty thing I learned about in Cateechee was the act of chewing tar that came from the surface of the roads. I never really participated a lot, except just to taste it, but my brothers and cousins walked on the roadways in the hot summer sun until they found a place where the sun had caused the road tar to soften and pool up. They pulled from the roadway some of the tar that had no gravel in it and placed it in their mouths. They chewed it like chewing tobacco, but they tried hard not to swallow any of the resulting dark-colored saliva. When they spit, the saliva looked like the tobacco juice that a person chewing tobacco would spit out. I think they chewed the tar to imitate adults who chewed tobacco.

I remember two other unpleasant events that involved all five of us children. The first time, all five of us children were jumping around screaming and crying for several days when we all broke out with a bright red rash all over our bodies. Our parents had no idea what was wrong with us, but we were scratching and clawing on ourselves and sometimes writhing around on the floor crying from pain. Our parents had us examined by a doctor and the doctor said that we were suffering from something called "the itch." He prescribed a salve that had to be rubbed all over our bodies. When our parents began to apply the salve, the process was far more painful and undesirable than the itch we had been experiencing. All of us were screaming at the top of our lungs and crying tears that were falling like rain. The salve had to be applied twice a day for several days, and each time we went through the same painful process. After a few days, the rash went away. However, that was not the only unpleasant incident that all of us experienced simultaneously while living in Cateechee.

The second event had all of us children scratching our heads at the same time. Mother got one of my brothers to sit next to her and began looking through his hair. After a few minutes, she said that he had head lice, and then she looked at all the rest of us. Within a few minutes, she had determined all of us had head lice. Most people we knew associated head lice with filth. We were dirt poor, but we knew we were not filthy people, so having head lice was very embarrassing to all of us. Of course, we immediately blamed the situation on some neighborhood children who lived close by. We figured we must have caught the head lice from them, because they didn't appear to be as concerned with cleanliness as we were. Mother treated us with some kind of medication and combed our hair diligently for several days until none of us had head lice anymore. She also told us not to play with the children we had blamed for our having the head lice. We obeyed, and we never played with those children again the whole time we lived in Cateechee. I later learned that head lice are usually airborne, and head lice are usually attracted to clean hair rather than dirty hair. We were innocent of being filthy, and the children that we chose not to play with were probably just as innocent.

We had many pleasant experiences and some unpleasant experiences in Cateechee, but I had one very good experience that stood out above the rest. For the first time in my memory, we attended church. If Cateechee did nothing else for me, it began the development of some degree of morality within me. I am thankful for that, because without a developed sense of morality, one could lose his way in life.

Other than the adventures and games of us children, I remember very little about our lives in Cateechee. After all, we lived in Cateechee only four months, and Cateechee was a very isolated country mill village. Fortunately or unfortunately, I learned a lot, both good and bad, in that short time span.

Mother became dissatisfied with life in Cateechee and wanted to return to Greenville. It wasn't long before we were on the move again. Our parents traveled back to Greenville and got jobs at Poe Mill again.

Return to Poe Mill

$\mathcal{W}$e returned to Poe Mill in the summer of 1947. There was only one house available in the entire village, and it was a small, four-room bungalow on Fifth Street. We had no choice but to move into it. However, the mill company did promise our parents a larger house as soon as one came available. We had to move such a great distance from Cateechee that we spent almost all of our money just to hire a moving van to get us into the house at Poe. The house we moved into was not much larger than the house our family was living in when I was born. All of us children were growing rapidly so, needless to say, we were somewhat cramped in such a small house. To make matters worse, we had only been living there one week when Grandmother Annie Mae Brock Porter moved into the house with us.

Grandmother moved in with us because Dad's father, William Brunner Porter Sr., was suffering from the effects of a couple of strokes. His health was severely damaged, and he was hospitalized in Columbia, South Carolina. Within a couple of years, Grandfather Porter died.

Grandmother could not care for herself because she was an invalid whose total body was ravaged by crippling arthritis, especially her hands and feet. She was in a wheelchair, so Mother's life became more complicated than ever. All of us children were too small to help with Grandmother's needs, and Dad helped her only after she was dressed and ready to move from her bed to the wheelchair. Sometimes, Dad helped her from her wheelchair back to the bed.

However, Mother did most of the lifting plus everything else for Grandmother. She bathed her, helped her get dressed, helped her use the bedpan, cooked for her, kept her room cleaned, brushed her hair, and anything else that had to be done for her. Mother was strong, but lifting Grandmother was extremely difficult because Grandmother couldn't assist the person lifting her. It was like lifting dead weight. We all loved Grandmother, but the burden of taking care of her and five growing children was almost more than Mother could bear.

We didn't have time to get settled in on Fifth Street before the mill company offered our parents a larger house on Fourth Street. We moved immediately, including Grandmother, and I will never forget how we moved from Fifth Street to Fourth Street.

We had no money to hire a moving van, we had no automobile, and we had no friends or relatives who were available to help us, but we had an abundance of furniture and other belongings to move. Just as I was beginning to think we were not going to get to move into the larger house, Mother came up with a brilliant idea. She suggested that the big wagon we had gotten for Christmas could be used as our moving van. The house we were moving into was only one block away. We could just roll Grandmother to the new house in her wheelchair. We believed we could move all of the furniture with the wagon, so we got started.

Dad was at work in the cotton mill, so Mother began packing everything we owned. As she was doing that, all of us children started moving pieces of furniture, one piece at a time. I was only six years old, but I was able to help push the wagon. I was also able to help carry clothing, quilts, and other household items. One would be surprised how much stuff five children could carry. My brothers loaded a dresser or some other piece of furniture onto the wagon, and while one pulled and guided the wagon, the rest of us pushed. When we reached the big house, my brothers unloaded whatever we had moved. That routine was repeated all day. After we got all the furniture to the larger house, we brought the remaining household items.

By the time Dad finished his shift in the cotton mill, we had completed the move, with the exception of one piece of furniture, the piano. The piano had a solid steel back, and it took four very strong men to move it. I don't recall who moved it, but we got it there within a couple of days.

Almost every time Dad quit his job at a cotton mill, we had to move from our house; however, there were a couple of exceptions when they allowed us to stay because Mother worked in the mill. The house on Fourth Street was our fourth residence in the village of Poe Mill. I was just six years old, but that was our eighth residence since I was born.

We moved into a six-room house at 15 Fourth Street. The most significant thing about moving into that house was that *Grace had a bedroom of her own for the first time in her life.* Grace was thirteen years old. I know Grace had wanted a bedroom of her own for years, and she deserved it. All of us boys shared one bedroom. We might have been dirt poor and still living in difficult circumstances, but we were the happiest we had ever been. We finally had enough space to move without bumping into someone or tripping over something, even with Grandmother living with us.

The house had hardwood floors in every room, and there were no cracks in them. We had linoleum floor coverings in the living room and kitchen. We had electricity, running water, and a sink in the kitchen. We had an inside bathroom, but we still had no bathtub. However, even taking baths in the round tin tub seemed to be more pleasant than ever before. There was a commode in the bathroom but no sink. Our main source of heat was a heater in which we could burn wood or coal. Mother still used her woodstove for cooking, so we received a little heat from it when it was in use. Mother's process for washing, drying, and ironing clothes remained the same as it was previously.

The house was high enough off the ground on one side for me to walk underneath it. On the other side, it was so low that I couldn't even crawl under it. There was no underpinning, so the wind blew under the house and caused it to be extremely difficult to heat in the winter. Also, the house was not insulated. It was also difficult to cool in the summer. It was a two-story house, and all of us children slept in the two bedrooms upstairs. We loved having our bedrooms upstairs away from our parents, but in the wintertime the floors were as cold as ice.

We seldom had firewood, but we were able to purchase sacks of coal from a vendor who drove his truck through the neighborhood yelling, "Coal man." Dad called our small heater a "laundry heater," and he would get up very early and build a roaring fire in it. Dad's fires got so hot sometimes that they caused the entire heater and the connecting pipe that the smoke escaped through to the chimney to turn a bright, glowing red.

After getting the room warm he called us, and we jumped onto the cold floor and ran downstairs as fast as we could, carrying our fresh clothing in our hands. We stood near the heater for a few seconds to get warm on one side and then turned around to get warm on the other side. The bad thing was that the side away from the heater was always cold. We spent a lot of time turning around while putting our fresh clothes on. We ran into the kitchen to have breakfast after we got dressed. The wood-burning cookstove provided heat for the kitchen, so we could eat in comfort. We either went to school or outside to play after breakfast, depending on whether or not school was in session. However, if the weather was too cold or it was raining outside, we played in the room where the heater was or on the front porch. The front porch stretched across the entire front of the house, so it made a really nice play area for all of us children.

The house was so large that Mother even had space to set up her quilting frames without disturbing anyone. Someone made the quilting frames for Mother, but I don't recall the person's name. They were made of slender pieces of wood and nails that looked like finishing nails. The frames appeared to be, and were, very dangerous. There were sharp points of nails protruding from the wood about every two inches. I don't recall whether or not Mother got her quilting frames before or after we moved into the house on Fourth Street, but I remember that she made a lot of the quilts we slept under while we lived there. Those quilts, of which I still have some, helped us survive some very harsh winters on Fourth Street and many years afterward.

When Mother made a quilt, she attached a quilt lining she had made from flour sacks or rags from the Rag House (which I describe shortly) to all of the nails on the frames. Next, she rolled cotton quilt batting onto the lining and

84

covered it with a quilt top that she also attached to all the nails. After she had the quilt lining, cotton, and quilt top attached firmly, she began to sew the three layers together by hand. After sewing for hours, she got enough sewn to roll the sewn portion under so she could reach another section to sew. It usually took several days to complete a quilt, but when winter came there was nothing more comforting than cuddling under a quilt Mother had made.

I watched Mother make quilts for many years and sometimes I assisted her with the turning under of the sewn portions. In fact, I believe that I could make a quilt, but I hope I never have to try.

Clothing was another necessity for warmth. We rarely had money, so we had to wear hand-me-down clothing. Sometimes people gave us clothing that their children had outgrown, and sometimes our parents were able to buy clothing for us. Prior to Grace going to work, it was necessary for her to receive a share of the money we had available for new clothing. Once she started earning wages, my older brothers received most of the clothing money. When William and James outgrew their clothing, it was passed down to David and me. No matter how hard our parents tried, they just simply did not always earn enough money to afford new clothing for all five children at one time. Even after Grace started purchasing her own clothing, our parents still could not always afford to buy new clothing for all four of us boys at the same time. If I got anything new, which was rare, I had to wait my turn.

Our parents rarely bought new clothing for themselves either. Even if they had a little money to buy an article of clothing, they couldn't buy it because there were shortages of clothing for adults in the Greenville area, especially in 1946–47. However, the lack of clothing was more of a financial problem for us. Dad wore overalls to work, to garden, for recreational purposes, and sometimes to church. When he was finally able to do so, he purchased a suit to wear to church, and he always looked good in his suit. It's too bad he couldn't afford a really nice, expensive one.

Sadly, Mother never seemed to have any money left over for her, so she had to make her own clothing. She had a sewing machine that was given to her by her mother. Although she never had money to purchase a lot of cloth, she managed to find a way to make her clothing. She bought flour in large sacks that contained twenty-five pounds of flour. Most of the sacks had floral print designs on them, and she saved them until she had enough of the same print to make an item of clothing. When she had collected enough cloth, she sat at her sewing machine and produced whatever she needed. However, making whatever she wanted was not the same as making whatever she needed, and making whatever she wanted was usually not an option for her. She was an excellent seamstress, and her clothing was always pretty. Most people would never have believed that some of her clothing were made from flour sacks.

Another way Mother got cloth for making clothing was by going to a place called the Rag House on Poinsett Highway. Mother raced other women up and down the aisles to bundles of cloth that were piled all around the floor. Much of the cloth was just junky rags that were cheaply priced. If Mother got to a nice bundle fast enough, she was able to purchase it. However, numerous other women were competing in the foot race for the same bundles. Sometimes, my siblings and I went with Mother to buy cloth, and we got involved in the races. We were small but fast, and we were successful in helping Mother find some of the better cloth. We knew that we would occasionally get something made from the rag bundles, so we tried to find cloth that we thought we would like to have a shirt or blouse made from. We were completely oblivious to the fact that we were buying cloth that our parents' supervisors would have considered trash. Such was the way of life for the cotton mill workers.

We were all happy to get an additional item of clothing even though it might be a hand-me-down or made from rags. However, I remember asking Mother for new store-bought clothing on occasion. Her reply was usually something to the effect that she would patch what I had and it would be as good as new. We wore patched overalls most all the time, and I learned that taking care of the clothing we had was very important. Mother was an artist at patching or otherwise mending clothing, and she taught me how to darn socks, patch the knees and elbows of pants and shirts, and sew buttons onto items of clothing. It has seldom been necessary for me to do those things, but when it was necessary, it was nice to know how.

In addition to making and mending clothing for our family, Mother made and mended clothing for other families in the neighborhood. It was a way to earn some extra money and help the neighbors at the same time. Very few, if any, of our neighbors could make clothes, and the clothing shortage in the area created a need for someone who could make clothes. Hiring Mother to make items for them was cheaper than buying something similar at a store even if they could find it. Everyone who saw the clothing Mother had made marveled at her ability to turn almost nothing into an item of clothing to be proud of.

Another thing Mother was especially good at was cooking. I always thought she was the best cook on earth, and judging from the way my friends hung around the house at meal times, they must have thought so too. Not one of them ever hesitated to sit at our table when Mother asked them if they would care to eat with us. When we had ample supplies to do so, Mother always cooked enough to feed our friends and us.

Getting ample food supplies involved more than just having enough money to buy them. We never owned an automobile prior to moving to Fourth Street, and we only owned one automobile for a short period of time during the whole period of time we lived on Fourth Street. We had to hire a taxi or depend on friends and relatives for transportation. Buying groceries was an ordeal. Mother sometimes walked four blocks to Buncombe Street to catch a trolley that would take her to Kash and Karry grocery store, and then she had to hire a taxi to bring her and the groceries home.

Kash and Karry Grocery Store. Photo Courtesy of Greenville County Historical Society. Greenville, South Carolina.

She occasionally sent some of my siblings. They sometimes hired a taxi to bring them home, and they sometimes rode a trolley to Buncombe and A streets and then walked home while carrying the groceries. There were several occasions when Mother, some of my brothers, and I pulled our large red wagon to the grocery store and back. The grocery store was approximately a mile from our house, so pulling a wagon full of groceries was a difficult task for us. However, we somehow made it home with supplies for many excellent meals.

Mother could cook anything she desired to, and if she could afford the ingredients my favorites were biscuits and peach or blackberry cobbler. I remember when she would cook either, or all, in her woodstove. All of us children would almost come to blows to see who got to eat the first biscuit or the first bite of cobbler. Then the same struggle took place for the last biscuit or bite of cobbler. Sometimes, we ate like little pigs.

Mother bought the ingredients for making peach cobblers and biscuits, but if we wanted a blackberry cobbler, we had to go blackberry picking. When we went blackberry picking, we knew from the beginning that we were in for a tortuous few days. The torture began while we were still picking the berries. There was always something lurking in a blackberry patch. Sometimes there would be a snake and sometimes there would be another animal, but chiggers were always present. I don't recall ever being harmed by any snake or animal, but I don't recall ever picking blackberries without feeling the stinging bite of the tiny red chiggers. We would try every method known to prevent chiggers from getting on us, including putting kerosene on our arms and legs, but nothing kept them off completely. I don't know why that critter was ever made, but I know that chiggers must have the most painful bite of all insects. I believe that if a chigger were the size of a dog, pit bulldogs would quickly become extinct as a result of being attacked by chiggers. I know that I would much rather have dog-sized chiggers to guard my house than to have any breed of dog for the same purpose.

When we returned from our blackberry-picking trips, we took a hot bath and put rubbing alcohol all over our bodies. Even so, we woke up the next day with bright red splotches all over us, and we knew the splotches were the result of chigger bites. Scratching a chigger bite is the worst thing a person can do, because it makes the splotch larger and the sting far more intense. Apparently, scratching just causes the chigger to dig in a little deeper. When a chigger bites a person, the chigger enters the skin and remains there. It digs in and is almost impossible to get out. The best thing I know of to use for treatment of a chigger bite is fingernail polish. The fingernail polish dabbed over the chigger causes the chigger to suffocate or it just dies from the effects of the fingernail polish. Regardless of how the chigger dies, it's a big relief to know it is dead. The splotch will begin to go away within a couple of hours and be completely gone within a couple of days. I have always loved blackberries, but I much prefer that someone else pick them and just give me the resulting cobbler.

Mother started teaching all of us children to cook when we were so small that we had to stand on a chair to reach the top of the table or stove. She placed ingredients into a bowl and allowed us to mix them. One of the first things I learned to make while living on Fourth Street was a banana pudding. She started me out by allowing me to use the hand-cranked mixer to beat the egg whites until they were thick and fluffy. Next, she added the correct amount of sugar, and I beat the egg whites until they were turned into thick, creamy icing. Then I cut the bananas into small, round slices and stacked them alternately with vanilla wafers in a deep glass dish. Mother always made the filling, which required cooking, and poured it over the bananas and wafers. I spread the icing on top and placed the pudding into the oven to lightly brown the icing, and I always licked the spoon and bowl. As I got older, I was allowed to do more, and eventually I learned to cook almost anything Mother could cook, plus some of my own concoctions.

Although Dad rarely did so, he could cook anything he wanted to. However, the one food item he made that I loved most was his hotdog chili. I don't know if he made up his recipe or he got it from someone else when he was operating a café, but he made the best hotdog chili I have ever tasted. He taught me to make it, and I can now make hotdogs almost as good as his. He was a good cook, but he was a cotton mill worker first and foremost.

When Dad talked about his job, which was often, he always bragged that he was one of the best workers in the area, and he proved his claim many times. That's why we lived in so many different mill villages over the years. If something, or someone, upset him or he thought that he could earn just one cent an hour more somewhere else, he would quit his job. Then he would go to another mill and get another job doing the same type of work. I was always amazed that he could quit a job in the morning and go to work at another mill in the afternoon of the same day, but he was just that good at his type of work.

I learned that Dad was a doffer, which is a person who removes bobbins full of thread from a drawing or spooling frame. Until I learned that, I had never understood why Dad had bragged about how many frames he could work by himself in an eight-hour shift. Apparently, he could doff more frames per shift than most other cotton mill doffers.

I learned that Mother was a spinner, which is a person who repairs breaks or snags in thread as it is being spun on a number of drawing frames. I don't remember hearing her brag about her ability a lot, but I have been told that Mother was at least as good a spinner as Dad was a doffer. Every time Dad got

Mother — Working in cotton mill.

a new job, if she chose to do so, she did too. The family would be uprooted and moved to a new location. I believe Grace began working in a grocery store because of the constant moving and the fact that we just never seemed to be able to get much above the poverty level. She needed more than was being provided for her.

Grace got her first job as soon as she turned fourteen. She worked in a huge grocery store named Kash and Karry, which I have already mentioned, located on Buncombe Street, a short distance inside the Greenville city limits. The store serviced all of Greenville County and then some. She didn't get the job because she had a great desire to work four evenings after school each week and on Saturdays; she got the job because if she wanted to wear new or stylish clothing, she knew she would have to buy it herself.

Sadly, once Grace started earning wages, I don't believe she received any money for anything from our parents again, maybe with the exception of the purchase of her high school ring. She had to buy her own clothing and whatever else she needed, plus pay her way through high school. She even had to furnish her own bus fare and lunch money. In fact, Grace told me that Mother attempted to force her to give a share of her money to our parents; however, Grace refused. She took control of her own life, but she continued to reside with us. She was always too busy to play with us boys after she started working, She was a serious student in school and a dedicated church attendee, so when she wasn't working, in school, or at church, she was studying. We all respected her for that. Of course, Grace had friends whom she visited as often as possible.

Grace had continued with her music lessons since she received the piano when we lived on Third Street, and we had her piano in our living room. The same year she started to work at Kash and Karry, she was asked to play the piano at worship services at Poe Baptist Church, which was on Second Street in the mill village. She accepted the position, so she had to practice often. She also attended choir practice regularly. One thing I remember well is how we used to gather around the piano and sing gospel music, especially when some of our cousins came to visit.

We sang together often until Grace started dating, and I didn't see much of her at home after that. She was either in school, working, at choir practice, in church, on a date, or studying with her friends at their homes. I missed her, but I knew she had ambition and was working toward becoming something other than a cotton mill worker or a farmer. She wanted to break the chains that bound us to our way of life. In retrospect, I can see that she had already achieved a little bit of the freedom she had been seeking. Because her first job was not in a cotton mill, she had loosened her shackles. She was on a path away from cotton mills and farms, and I admired her more than she has ever realized.

Even at my young age, I had already decided that I didn't want to be a cotton mill worker or a farmer. I couldn't articulate it then, but I had witnessed my parents experience too much pain, sorrow, disappointment, rejection,

Back Row – L to R: William, James.
Front Row – L to R: David, Doyle

Grace – 1947

92

and failure. The lives of all of us children had been adversely affected, and I blamed all of it on cotton mills and farms. Although we probably didn't realize it then, all of us children were, in our own ways, looking forward to and working toward future freedom. Somehow, we knew that when we grew up, we would eventually escape our way of life. We boys might not have been as pretty as a flower, as Grace was, but we would eventually bloom into healthy and happy young men just the same. We were already growing like wildflowers, each with a different appearance, but all of us still had a long, hard journey ahead. As dreadful as some aspects of life were, there were also some very exciting and fun-filled times, and we took advantage of every opportunity to have fun. I think my life was even more fun-filled and exciting after I started to school.

I began attending school in the first grade in the fall of 1947. My brothers were in the third, fifth, and sixth grades, and Grace was in the seventh grade. I loved going to school because, aside from learning, it made me feel as if I were as big as my brothers. We woke up every morning, dressed, ate breakfast, and ran across the street to school. It was nice to have the school so close to our house.

The only negative thing that had any real significance for me when I started school was learning that, in comparison to some my classmates, I was from a poor family. The public school we attended was the same school that the children of the superintendent and overseers of the cotton mill attended. While I was wearing patched overalls, brogan shoes, and hand-me-down coats, they were wearing new and stylish clothing. They never hesitated to let me know the difference. I was very humiliated and embarrassed by their disparaging remarks, and at a very young age I learned that it was US against THEM. Us included all the poor cotton mill workers and their children who were close to being poverty stricken, and them included all of the families of affluent cotton mill bosses who lived inside the mill villages and businesspeople who lived outside the mill villages. It was extremely difficult to prevent myself from developing an inferiority complex. However, I had at least a couple of things in my favor. I had older brothers to play with, and poor kids like me greatly outnumbered the affluent children at that school. I had plenty of friends.

One other thing that made me realize we were poor was that I never had any money for puppet shows, magic shows, and so on, and someone put on shows at the school regularly. When I was in the first grade, I remember crying sometimes because a show cost five or ten cents, and I never had money to attend.

I recall one incident when I cried, but I also lied to my teacher. I claimed I had turned in my money to attend a puppet show when, in fact, I didn't have any money. All of the more affluent children who had paid to attend the show were lined up at the classroom door, and I lined up with them. The teacher counted the money she had collected and then she counted the children. She had one child too many for the amount of money she had, so she started asking questions. Unfortunately, I was the person she was asking all the questions. I started crying and adamantly claiming that I had paid my money. Of course, she didn't believe me.

The teacher told me she was going to ask my brother David, who was just down the hall, whether or not I brought money to school for the puppet show. She left the classroom and was gone for about five minutes. When she came back, she allowed me to attend the show.

When we got to the school auditorium, David was also there. Apparently, he had brought money for himself, and he must have told my teacher that I had also brought money. I never asked David, or anyone else at home, because I was afraid I would get a whipping if our parents discovered what I had done. I never lied again to attend a show, but I have always believed that it was wrong for school officials to have provided entertainment in the school for the affluent children when the school officials knew that most cotton mill workers' children could not afford even five or ten cents for a show. After that episode, I spent a lot of time with my brothers and friends, before and after school, and tried not to get too upset about things the more affluent children were privileged to do during school hours. However, I did discover one thing I could do to get positive attention that even the most affluent child in the classroom never got, and it was one of the things I loved to do most: catch insects and bring them to school.

It didn't take long for me to discover we had insects living all around us on Fourth Street. One of the first insects I noticed was the doodlebug. David pointed out the little conical-shaped holes that housed the doodlebugs under our house. He told me the only way to catch a doodlebug was to sing a tune he recited and, simultaneously, to stir around in the doodlebug's lair with a sharp stick. The little tune was to inform the doodlebug that his house was on fire. I guess if someone told me my house was on fire and punched me with a sharp stick, I would come out too. Anyway, there I was, singing to a doodlebug and stirring with a stick: "Doodle-bug, doodle-bug, you better come out, your house is on fire." To my surprise, the dirt in the doodlebug's hole began to move ever so slightly, and then the doodlebug appeared. It was a weird-looking creature, but I caught it.

I learned at school that the correct name for a doodlebug is "ant lion." They build their conical-shaped lairs with very dry, loose dirt. When an ant attempts to cross an ant lion's lair, the dirt slides to the bottom of the cone-shaped hole, taking the ant with it. When the ant reaches the bottom of the ant lion's lair, the ant lion quickly captures and eats it. Once I learned that a doodlebug eats ants, I spent hours catching ants to feed to doodlebugs. I guess I became the primary food supplier for the doodlebugs under our house. David told me that he always killed the doodlebugs by smashing them into the ground when he finished playing with them. I called them my pets, and I carried them to school many times for show-and-tell.

We found hundreds of tiny holes in our yard that appeared to be the homes of some type of insect, and we tried many times to figure out what was causing the holes to appear. Finally, James broke off a very small wild onion and pushed the stem into one of the holes. He left it in the hole for a few seconds and then pulled it out. To our amazement, a small, white, grublike worm was clinging to the wild onion. We had invented a new game! The person who caught the most grub worms within a limited time would be the winner. There were no prizes, just fun. The great thing about that game was that we got rid of the wild onions and the worms at the same time. Although I took some of the worms to school, I'm still not sure what species of worm they were. However, the name of the species was never important to me. What was important was that I got recognition for catching them and taking them to school.

There was a field of very tall weeds behind the house next door to ours. My brothers and I often played in the weeds because the weeds provided a good hiding place when we played games that required hiding, which many of our games did. One thing we had to be the most careful about in the field was running into the webs of writing spiders. The web of a writing spider is huge. When we did run into a web, it took a considerable length of time to get the web out of our hair and off of our faces and bodies. That wasted a lot of valuable playtime, so we didn't care for it at all, not to mention the sickening feeling of the web on our skin. The writing spiders were very large, so I guess that was one reason for such a large web. The spiders were a brilliant yellow with contrasting black legs and body markings. Their bodies were somewhat fat and their legs were long, making them look rather scary to small children. I don't think writing spiders are poisonous, but I don't know for certain. The proper name for the writing spider species is *Argiope aurantia*, but we called it a "writing spider" because of the design it places across the center of its web. The design appears to be some type of unintelligible writing. I don't have any idea why the spider places the design on its web; however, I think it might be to strengthen the web and to attract its prey.

I remember hearing a story about the writing spider and the danger of a person looking at the writing on the spider's web. If a person ever read his or her name on a writing spider's web, that person would die in a very short period of time.

Of course, I never believed that story, and I have spent many hours attempting to read the writing of many writing spiders. I also spent many hours catching writing spiders. I walked slowly through the weeds with a jar until I found a writing spider on its web. I got on the same side of the web as the spider and then placed the open end of the jar over the spider. The spider had no place to go because a writing spider cannot penetrate its own web. I forced the spider into the jar and placed the lid on the jar, and then I ran home and punched some air holes in the jar lid. I always considered the captured writing spiders to be my pets. Although we had a dog when we lived on Reid School Road, we could no longer afford to have one. We didn't have meat scraps anymore and we couldn't afford to buy pet food, so I made a pet of whatever I could catch that I didn't have to buy food for. Sometimes my pets would live only one day, but having a pet for one day was better than not having a pet at all.

The writing spiders were excellent for show-and-tell when school was in session. I don't think my teacher especially liked them but she always allowed me to talk about where and how I captured them. The other boys always seemed to be interested in my spiders, but most of the girls would scream, especially if I acted as if I was going to open the jar. Since the girls were afraid of writing spiders, it was only natural that I would take one to school as often as possible. When the spiders were safely on the science exhibit shelf, the girls would talk to me about them. They seemed to think I was brave. Well, some of them thought I was an idiot, but either way I was getting their attention. I loved the attention I got from my teacher also. The affluent children in my class seemed to envy me, and that made up for my not being able to pay for puppet shows and magic shows.

Another species of insect I found in the high weeds was grasshoppers. Some of the largest grasshoppers I have ever seen lived in that small field. Most of them were green and some of them were brown, but all of them had large wings and flew, probably more than they hopped.

I spent a lot of time catching grasshoppers. I crept up on one and tried to get in a position to its rear, and then I slowly reached my hand toward it until I had my fingers on each side of its closed wings. I quickly grasped the grasshopper by its closed wings. The grasshopper could not stick me with the sharp spurs on its long legs when I used that method. I placed the grasshoppers into jars, as I had done with the writing spiders, and kept them as pets. I usually placed strands of grass into the jars with the grasshoppers so they would have something to eat. Sometimes, the grasshoppers also made it to school for show-and-tell. No one seemed to fear the grasshoppers, but they were still attention-getters. There was nothing like being the center of attention for five minutes.

Although I still enjoyed school very much, I much preferred being out of school and in the company of my brothers and friends in the neighborhood. In the early morning hours, before school began, and in the late afternoon hours, when school was over for the day, all of us boys went onto the school grounds to play. Most of the time, some of our friends were also there. We played on the hand walkers until our arms got so weak that we couldn't hold on any longer. We also draped our legs over the bars, at the knees, and hung upside down. Some of the older boys were actually strong enough to hang upside down using only their toes.

We played on the hand-walkers until we were tired of them, and then we played on the swings. Sometimes, one of my brothers would push me so high that I thought the swing was going to circle the top bar. That was a little scary because I was afraid I was going to fall out of the swing. I loved to swing, and I could swing for hours at a time.

One morning we were on the school grounds before school started, and we saw the school principal, Mr. Devore, coming onto the playground. I wasn't aware there was a rule against our being on the school grounds prior to school hours, but someone in the crowd must have been, because I heard someone say that we should run and we did.

James was closer to Mr. Devore than the rest of us, and there wasn't much distance between the two of them. Mr. Devore chased him across the school grounds, across the street, and into our house. When James ran into our house, Mr. Devore also ran into our house. Apparently, the school principal was determined to catch James; however, Mother just happened to be inside our house also. She told Mr. Devore to get out of our house, and after a few words he left. When Dad came home from work, Mother told him about the incident with the school principal.

I was standing in front of the school the next morning, waiting for the doors to be opened so I could attend class, when I saw Dad approaching the school. Dad had a terrible one-sided argument with the school principal. It was

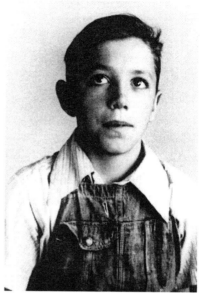

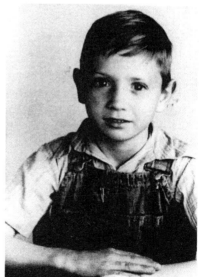

Porter Brothers in 1948. Top L to R: William, James. Bottom L to R: David, Doyle.

more like Dad was raising hell than just arguing. He threatened to beat up the principal and told him that he had better not ever set foot in our house again. I don't know whether or not the principal apologized for coming into our house, but I do know that he was very careful not to come near our house again.

William was also involved in an incident with the same principal. One day, for some reason, William was told to go from one area of the school to another area, and he refused to go. When Mr. Devore attempted to forcibly remove William by picking him up, William kicked him right in the mouth. Mr. Devore was injured and bleeding, but he left William alone. The principal reported the incident to our parents but took no further action against William. Our parents just felt that the principal got what he deserved, so no action was taken against William at home either.

Either the rule preventing us from playing on the school grounds when school was not in session was invalidated, or the school principal decided to allow our family and friends the privilege of playing there anytime we wanted to. We began playing on the school grounds in the mornings, evenings, and on the weekends.

One day we were playing baseball on the school grounds when I severely injured my right foot. I was on third base when someone hit a ball to shallow left field. I tagged up so I could run to home plate after the outfielder caught the ball, and as soon as the outfielder caught the ball, I headed for home plate. Just before I got there it looked as if I might be thrown out, so I slid to the plate. I was safe but I had slid across a sharp cinder. I was barefoot, so the cinder sliced the top of my foot wide open. Blood was pouring from the wound like water from a hose, and I guess I was about to go into shock. Someone picked me up and carried me to our house, where Mother attempted to get the bleeding stopped by pouring kerosene over the wound and wrapping the foot with a towel. Meanwhile, a neighbor came over and suggested that he should take Mother and me to a hospital.

I was immediately taken into the emergency room at the hospital where, after a few minutes, medical personnel had the bleeding slowed to just a little seeping. A doctor came in to sew the wound closed. I knew the doctor looked strange to me, but I didn't learn until later that he was a Filipino. I think his name was Dr. Geronimo, but my recollection of his name might be incorrect. The doctor picked up a curved needle that looked to me as if it were as large as a ten-penny nail and started sewing on my foot. I was screaming as loud as I could scream, and tears were streaming down my face. I was also attempting to fight anyone close enough to kick or hit. They were having a terrible time with me. Mother asked the doctor whether or not he had put anything on the wound to deaden it so I wouldn't feel so much pain. He gasped and admitted that he had not, and he had already sewn two stitches. He put a local anesthetic on the wound and waited a few minutes before he started sewing again. When he resumed sewing, the pain was not nearly as bad as it had been earlier, but I screamed and cried just the same; however, I didn't fight anyone that time. After I was sewn up, I was dismissed from the hospital to go home to heal.

It wasn't long before I was injured again, but that injury was a nose injury. My brothers and I were eating a watermelon on the school grounds when we decided to have a battle with watermelon rinds—similar to the maypop battles we had when we lived in the country. We broke the watermelon rind into small pieces, and each of us took several pieces. The battle began, but we weren't throwing the rinds very hard initially. However, someone must have gotten stung pretty badly because the rinds were suddenly being thrown hard. I was running, turning to throw, and running again. I turned to throw a piece of rind just in time to get hit full force with a large piece of rind right on the bridge of my nose. My nose began bleeding from both nostrils immediately. I ran home holding my nose and trying to stop the blood. When I got home, I had blood all over me. Mother came rushing out with a cold towel, but it didn't seem to help. A neighbor told Mother that she knew how to stop the blood flow, and she took me and started applying pressure to both sides of my face, right against my ears. To my astonishment, and I think to Mother's, the blood flow immediately began to slow. The neighbor had the flow of blood completely stopped within just a couple of minutes. However, my problem was not over.

A couple of days after I was injured by the rind, my nose had swollen until I could no longer breathe through my nostrils. Mother took me to the hospital, where the hospital personnel determined that my nose was infected. I was given a shot at the hospital, and I was given some medication to take at home. My nose was okay again after about ten days, but I never battled with watermelon rinds again.

One thing happened on the school grounds that I have wondered about for many years. A young man who lived in the mill village came to the school grounds regularly, and he always seemed to have his pockets full of loose change. He called all the children over to him, and then he pulled a hand full of change from his pocket and tossed it into the coal bin. The money fell between large pieces of coal and disappeared, and then he shouted that whoever found the money could have it. We jumped into the coal bin and threw coal everywhere in our search for money. Sometimes we emptied the coal bin before we found the last piece of change. We might find a nickel, or if we were lucky, we might find a half dollar. We didn't care what the last piece was; we just wanted some money. The man occasionally threw as much as five to ten dollars into the coal bin at one time. Poor children searching for that amount of money were searching for real treasure. By the time we found all the money and put the coal back into the bin, we were as black as soot from head to toe. The young man just laughed. However, before he left, I always saw him talking to a group of older boys, ranging in age from fourteen to eighteen.

That young man never bothered any members of our family, and I don't know that he ever bothered anyone. I have just always had a strange feeling about someone who would literally throw money away as he did. It was as if he was always attempting to attract the older boys' attention, and I never saw him talk to a girl. He was possibly a homosexual or a pedophile, but maybe not. I don't know. I'm just glad that my brothers were always there, because I always felt safe when they were around.

In the summertime, we had much more time to play in the neighborhood. Of course, some of my favorite memories have to do with catching and playing with insects. About mid-summer, we noticed some very large insects flying all over the neighborhood. They were everywhere, flying close to the ground. In fact they were flying so close to the ground that we were actually looking down on most of them. We could see that their backs were a dark green color. We asked our parents what they were, and they replied that they were June bugs. We decided to catch some of them, because it looked as if it would be easy to do. They were not difficult to catch at all; however, their legs had little spurs on them, which hurt when they stuck into our fingers. We had to be careful, but we continued catching them anyway.

Mother told us that when she was a child, she would tie a string to the rear leg of a June bug and let it fly while she held the string. That sounded like a great idea, so we got some sewing thread and began to tie some strands onto a June bug's legs. It was like having a June bug on a leash. We played with June bugs for hours each day, until they started dying or disappearing. June bugs are around only about one month each year. However, we were as poor as dirt, and June bugs substituted for the store-bought toys we could not afford to buy. To have the June bugs for any length of time was great for us.

Another group of insects that we noticed very quickly in the summertime were the lightning bugs. There seemed to be millions of them flying at all heights, many at just the right height for small children to catch.

At first, we just watched the lightning bugs as they flew around the area. They would light up for about one full second and then seemingly disappear. Then they would reappear a few feet, or yards, from where they were last seen. They were fascinating to watch. It was like watching millions of tiny stars moving around in the sky, and it was a beautiful sight. The proper name for lightning bug is "firefly." Watching the bright, flickering lights of the fireflies was cheap entertainment for us.

We decided to try catching a few when just watching the lightning bugs became boring. We saw one light up and ran toward the spot. When it lit up again, just a short distance away, we attempted to keep it in sight as it went dark. We learned that we could catch one if we got to it just as its light came on, because the light remained bright for about a full second and then there was a dull glow. We caught them while they were in their dull glow phase.

We also learned that we could rip off the tail of a lightning bug the instant it flashed its brightest, and the tail would continue to glow brightly for several hours. I have no idea why the tails worked that way, they just did. We filled our hands with brightly lit lightning-bug tails and pretended that we were carrying lanterns. However, we stopped doing that because it required killing the lightning bugs.

To this day, none of us, especially Mother, have forgotten the night that Mother gave us a wide-mouth gallon jar to hold the captured lightning bugs. All five of us children were chasing lightning bugs all over creation. We managed to catch many, perhaps as many as two or three hundred. We punched holes in the jar lid so the bugs could get air, and we caught lightning bugs until Mother made us go into the house because it was long past our bedtime. We went inside, took our baths, and went to bed.

About half an hour later, William crept outside and retrieved the jar full of lightning bugs. At first, we just set the jar in the middle of the room and observed the bugs as they lit up the room. It was like having a lantern lit. We were laughing, whispering, and just having a good time, but then someone decided to open the jar and let the bugs out.

When the bugs were released, they began flying all over the bedroom. It was a good thing our bedroom doors were closed, or they would have been all over the house. They lit up our bedroom like a Christmas tree. We began to giggle and laugh out loud, and we were also talking well above a whisper.

All of a sudden, our bedroom door flew open. Mother had heard the commotion and had come to check on us. When she saw the lightning bugs, she appeared to be about to have a fit. She acted as if she was going to be very angry, but when she realized what we had done, she burst into laughter. I think she really didn't know what to do. She quickly closed the bedroom door to prevent the lightning bugs from escaping our bedroom, and then she told us through the door to catch every single one of them and get them out of the house. She went back to bed, but we could hear her and Dad talking. They were laughing, so we felt safe for the night.

We didn't jump up and catch the lightning bugs immediately; we waited until the next morning. When we did catch them, it was a lot more difficult than the first time. They were all over everything, including the ceiling. After a couple of hours, we had caught all of the lightning bugs that we could see and released them outside. However, we continued to catch lightning bugs inside the house all day long. After that fiasco, we never carried lightning bugs into the house again.

The good thing about that incident was that both of our parents saw humor in it. We did not get a whipping because they thought the incident was so funny, and they told all of our neighbors and relatives about it. They were laughing every time they told the story, and we still laugh about the lightning bug incident.

One of the first things I noticed when we moved to Fourth Street was that the house was high enough on one side for me to walk under it. Of course, during the summers, my brothers and I explored every inch of the space underneath the house. There were brick pillars everywhere, and there was a very wide chimney base. No one had ever bothered to underpin the house, probably because the prior residents had no money and the mill didn't just give such luxuries to their workers other than the supervisors and administrators. We knew it would not be underpinned while we lived there. Some of the people in our village used the space underneath their houses for storage, but we kept the space under our house swept clean. We didn't have anything to store anyway, so we had one heck of a place to play.

We played hide and seek regularly. Maybe it was because I was young and small, or maybe it was because I was very smart—maybe it was neither—but my brothers and friends always seemed to have a difficult time finding me. In retrospect, I think, because I was the youngest participant, to make me happy they just pretended they couldn't find me. I would hide under the house every time we played hide and seek, and then when the "it" walked away from the base, I would scamper from under the house and run to the base screaming "Home Free." I thought I was really great at that game.

We played other games also, and some of them required us to go under the house. Some of the other children in the village used to come to our house often, and we would go under the house and play grocery store, house, or doctor.

We had only old cans, bottles, and sometimes paper cartons to play with. I can't recall ever having anything with actual food or drink in it. We improvised by filling a can with dirt, water, or grass. We didn't have any real money so we used small strips of newspaper.

We sold more pretend groceries than Kash and Karry sold real groceries. We pretended that our store was Kash and Karry. After all, Grace worked there, and practically all cotton mill workers in Greenville County bought food there. As fast as an item was sold, the buyer replaced the item on the shelf, and he purchased the same item again later. None of our groceries ever left the store. It made sense to us. We just never got around to eating anything.

Playing house was a little different than playing store because we had chores to do. Of course, whoever the parents happened to be gave all the orders and did none of the work. I was never a parent so I must have swept the floor (ground) a million times a day, and I had to dust the furniture (brick pillars) constantly.

We used old tin cans and fruit jar lids that were no longer useful to our parents as cooking utensils, glasses, and whatever else we could think of. We had to sit on the ground because we had nothing to serve as a table, chair, or any other piece of furniture. We must have pretended to eat ten times an hour. To get out of housework, we would usually yell that it was time to eat. We ate our pretend meals, which we made last as long as the pretend parents would let us. The only real thing we had to drink was water that we got from inside the house. We played house often, but once we started playing doctor, playing store and house became significantly less interesting.

Playing doctor was a totally new experience for me. I had several older friends and a couple of brothers who, for some reason, seemed to love the game. I had no idea why, but they always wanted to include the neighborhood girls in our games of doctor.

We always went under the house, out of sight of any adults, when we participated in the game of doctor. Usually, my older friends took the girls behind the chimney base, but they wouldn't let me see what was going on. I knew there were a lot of surgeries being performed, but I was never allowed to participate. Although I don't think the boys ever actually had sex with the girls, I don't know for certain that they didn't either. I did know that one of the primary goals of the boys was to get the girls to take off their clothes. I was quite young, but I could see clearly that there was a difference between the anatomies of boys and girls.

One day when all of my brothers were gone off with their friends and no one else was home but Grandmother and me, a neighbor girl came over to play with me. Of course, when she asked what I wanted to play, the first thing that popped into my mind was doctor. She was two years older than I was, and I was trying to figure out how to get her to participate in a surgery. Just out of the blue, she said that she would show me hers if I would show her mine. At first, I didn't even realize what she was talking about, but as she started to pull at her pants, it hit me. I agreed, and we went behind the chimney base. She pulled her pants off, and I pulled mine off. We must have stared at each other for what seemed like five minutes. Then, unexpectedly, she asked me if I wanted to "do it." I knew immediately what "do it" meant, because my brothers, friends, and I had watched the village dogs "doing it" a lot of times. I knew they were doing it because that's what the older boys called it. I had never heard the word "sex," just "doing it."

The girl lay down on her back on the ground, and I got on top of her. I was too young to have any type of bodily activity, not even an erection, so our version of doing it was lying there motionless, with no pants on, pretending something was happening that was not. We lay there like that for a good five minutes, and then we put our pants back on and continued playing.

I learned a lot that day. The phrase "I'll show you mine if you show me yours" is something I have never forgotten. I also learned to say, "Do you want to do it?" I used both of those phrases several times before we moved away from Poe Mill. However, they never worked for me. I guess the little girl was just smarter than I was. However, even if the phrase had worked, I would not have been any more effective than I was the first time.

If our parents had ever found out what all of us boys had done under the house, they would have killed us right on the spot, especially me, for my little sexual episode. If Grandmother had known that I was involved in such activities while she was sitting in her wheelchair at the front door of our house, she would have found the strength and ability to walk. Grandmother was the most truly religious person I have ever met. She prayed to God every day while we were all gathered around her bed. Although she was in the condition she was, she thanked God for her life. Love of God seemed to be her life. She never would have allowed our activities to go on, not for a second. Thankfully, we never got caught. The girls who participated with us never got caught either. Come to think of it, if Grace had known what was going on, she also probably would have killed us. She was a straitlaced Christian girl who wouldn't have participated in or allowed those activities anywhere near our house. However, she was away most of the time.

I guess we were all lucky to survive those early years, but we did learn a lot from our experiences. One important thing I learned is that parents can't wait until their children are twelve or thirteen to start sex education. By that time, the children can already tell their parents about as much as the parents know, if not more.

Another thing we did under the house was to play with pretend automobiles. We found a small block of wood or a piece of brick to use as an automobile. I don't recall ever owning a real toy automobile, and I also don't recall having any friends who owned real toy automobiles.

We used a brick or a small block of wood to build roads, and we scraped a path in the dirt about three to four inches wide. Sometimes, our roads wound around every brick pillar under the house. Each brick pillar represented a state in the United States, so we traveled all over the country and never left the house. We traveled across the country many times.

While playing under the house, I discovered a really good hiding place for my valuables, behind the chimney base. I carried marbles, rocks I had found, and other assorted items to that location and buried them. I don't think anyone ever thought to look there for my stuff. In fact, there might be some things still buried there today. I don't know whether or not I ever uncovered and retrieved everything I buried. I have a lot of great memories from Fourth Street, but playing under the house provided me with some really special ones.

In addition to all of my good memories of playing under the house, I have many more memories of experiences at other locations. From the time I was six years old, my older brothers and I roamed all over the village of Poe Mill. We also roamed to many places quite distant. The golf course where we caddied, for example, was five and one-half miles from home, and we probably roamed to other places just as distant, or farther. No doubt, we went to places that were both dangerous to travel to and dangerous to visit.

We got up and snuck quietly out of the house as it began to get daylight. We usually found a biscuit or some other food item from the night before and ate as we traveled. I cannot recall ever being stopped from sneaking out of the house when we were going on one of our early-morning excursions. Dad and Mother may have been heavy sleepers because of always being so tired from working in the cotton mill, or maybe they did hear us but just thought we were going no farther than our own yard. Who knows?

My brothers, several of our friends, and I had a hideout in the trees next to the railroad tracks about two blocks from our house. One of the trees at the hideout was an Indian cigar tree—at least that's what we called it. The correct name is Catalpa tree. Occasionally, I would go to the hideout and smoke an Indian cigar, but I also brought some of them home and hid them under the house. I thought I was doing something great. I had not smoked a cigarette since we moved from Cateechee, so having the Indian cigars was a treat for me. However, I did smoke cigarettes again while living on Fourth Street.

One day I was walking along a roadway with one of my brothers and some older friends. One of the older boys picked up part of a cigarette that had been discarded by someone and then pulled some matches from his pocket and lit the piece of cigarette and began smoking it. I asked him what he was doing, and he replied that he was "shooting a duck." From that moment on, every time I saw a piece of cigarette lying on the street that was large enough to smoke, I would pick it up and smoke it. I guess I was just so ignorant of health hazards that I thought shooting ducks was a wonderful thing to do.

However, there was one time that I didn't think smoking was so great, and that was when Mother caught me.

I had been walking all over the mill village picking up cigarette butts, and I had collected at least twenty. I was afraid to take them home because Mother was at home that day, so I went to a neighbor's house where there was a large barn in the backyard. I climbed up into the loft of the barn and sat near the middle of the loft so I could see out the large doorway at the front of the barn loft. I wanted to be able to see anyone who might come toward the barn. I didn't think about the danger of smoking in a barn loft filled with hay, nor did I think about the fact that, because I was sitting in a dark area, the bright red fire on the end of a cigarette could be seen from a long distance by anyone approaching the barn. I was just sitting there nonchalantly smoking one of my cigarettes and not paying much attention to anything else. I didn't even see Mother when she rounded the corner of the neighbor's house and was headed straight toward the barn. By the time I did see her, she had already seen me take at least two puffs of smoke from the cigarette. She yelled at me to get down from there that instant. In a flash, I had extinguished the cigarette and was climbing down the ladder. By the time I got to the next to last rung on the ladder, I felt Mother's hand whacking my bottom. When I got onto the ground, she slapped me all over the head and body. I was screaming and crying, but she just kept slapping. I was wishing I had found a better place for shooting ducks. After that incident, I was always much more careful not to get caught when I smoked cigarettes and Indian cigars.

One day I was walking in the mill village, looking for cigarette ducks, when I found a wad of money instead. I picked it up, but at first I didn't realize what it was because it was all wadded and folded together. When I unfolded it and saw what it was, I became a little frightened. I had never held so much money in my hands before. I'm not even sure that I had ever seen that much money at one time before, other than at the golf course. I had found more than sixty dollars. In the late 1940s, that was a very large amount of money for anyone to have, especially our family. That was close to, if not more than, the combined amount of money that Dad and Mother earned in an entire week. I ran home as fast as I could run, with the wind whistling in my ears so much that I felt as if I were flying.

I handed the money to Mother. She appeared to be shocked that I had found so much money and she told me not to tell anyone about it. She said someone might report the money missing, and if that happened we would return it. However, if no one reported the money missing, we would keep it. I know we never reported finding the money to anyone, but I have never known whether or not the money was returned to the person who lost it or Mother kept it and used it for family expenses. I do know that I never got a cent of it.

I would occasionally walk the streets to look for more money, but I never found any more. However, we had some neighbors who seemed to find a little money almost every day. They seemed to have a ritual of looking for money on the streets of the mill village. We watched them as they left their house to go on a search. The father and one son walked on one side of the street, and the other son walked on the opposite side of the street. They walked down one street, from one end to the other, and then they walked another street the same way. They searched the entire mill village within a couple of hours. We know they were always looking for money because we intentionally walked close to them sometimes so we could hear their conversations. The father was always giving directions to the boys about where to look. When one of them found a coin, it would be reported to the father. We were fascinated by their searches and conversations. They acted as if we didn't exist, even when we walked near them. They were very different from all the rest of our neighbors. We never spent any time with them, but we spent a lot of time with some of our other neighbors. There were children living in almost every house on our street, and we played with almost all of them.

There was one little boy named Terry Lewis who lived two houses from us that I enjoyed playing with. He was younger than I was, so my brothers didn't play with us. We played every conceivable game we could play together, but we enjoyed hunting insects and romping through the high weeds behind his house more than anything else. He seemed to love the outdoors as much as I did.

One day Terry came over to our house to ask whether or not I could

Scene of North Main Street with Ottaray Hotel at top.
Photo Courtesy of Greenville County Historical Society. Greenville, South Carolina.

Streetcars in Greenville prior to trolleys. Old Car in lower center next to streetcar resembles our
A-model. Photo Courtesy of Greenville County Historical Society. Greenville, South Carolina.

go with him and his family to the mountains. He had a grandmother who lived in the mountains of Pickens County, South Carolina. My parents gave me permission to go, so off we went. The drive to the mountains and back seemed as if it were nine hours, although the round-trip ride was probably no more than three hours.

The first thing I noticed when we arrived at my friend's grandmother's house was that a small mountain stream ran right past her house. I was so excited that I couldn't get out of the car fast enough, and the first thing I did when I did get out was to head for the stream. No one scolded us or attempted to stop my friend and me from playing in the stream. In fact, everyone encouraged us to do so. We weren't wearing shoes so we waded in the stream for a good two hours before we were called to lunch. After lunch, we played in the stream for another couple of hours before we had to get out so we could go back home. I think I enjoyed that trip about as much as I have ever enjoyed any trip. After the trip to the mountains, Terry was invited to play with me anytime he wished, whether my brothers played with us or not.

Not long after I went on the mountain trip with Terry, Dad bought the first automobile our family ever owned. It was a 1928 A-Model Ford. Dad couldn't afford to buy anything newer, but I thought we were rich. The automobile was green and black with red wheels and black tires. I remember when Dad drove us on our first trip by automobile to the downtown area of the city

Scene of South Main Street. Photo Courtesy of
Greenville County Historical Society. Greenville, South Carolina.

of Greenville. Greenville County was known internationally as the "Textile Center of the World," but although Camperdown Mill was in the downtown area, I saw no mills in downtown Greenville. I suppose it was because we did not pass the mill. However, I had never seen so many buildings.

I remember seeing the Ottaray Hotel and the Carolina Theatre at the north end of Main Street. I saw several other theatres on Main Street as well, including the Fox, Center, Roxy, and Paris. I saw numerous department stores such as Belk's, Meyers-Arnold, JC Penney's, Woolworth's, and Ivey's. I remember that the tallest building in Greenville was the Woodside Building, which was on South Main Street. I also remember that Thom McAn's shoe store was located at the corner of Main and Washington streets. The Poinsett Hotel was at the south end of Main Street at Court Street. Main Street was lined with stores and other types of businesses. Downtown Greenville seemed to be a thriving business area, and it was like being in another world for a young mill village boy. There were numerous electrically operated trolleys traveling both north and south on Main Street. Electrical wires were the power source for the trolleys, and they were suspended over both sides of the street. The trolleys had long connecting rods on top of them that extended to the electrical wires. I was excited just to see downtown and the trolleys, and I enjoyed every trip I made to downtown while we lived at Poe Mill. I was happy that we had an automobile to drive downtown, even if it was old.

We had some friends who lived across the street who also bought a car. Theirs was a Nash. The only explanation I can give for both families being able to own a car is that World War II had been over for a few years and cars were no longer rationed, plus things were getting somewhat better financially for some people, us included.

One day Dad was having a conversation with the Nash owner about his Ford. He was telling the neighbor about how powerful the Ford was, and the neighbor began to counter that his Nash was even more powerful. After all, the Nash was newer. Well, one thing led to another, and soon the two of them decided that they would just find out which car was the most powerful. To prove which car was the most powerful, they decided to drive their cars over Paris Mountain. The car that made it over the mountain with the fewest problems would be the most powerful.

The neighbor's wife wanted to ride with the neighbor, so Mother decided to ride with Dad. Then Dad said that his Ford was so powerful that he could take his whole family and still get over the mountain easier than the Nash. That didn't sit too well with the neighbor, so he challenged Dad to try it. The next thing I knew, our whole family was in the Ford. All of us children were laughing and having a great time. We loved those neighbors, so it wasn't as if Dad were going to have any kind of terrible confrontation with them. Everything was being done as fun.

We drove to Paris Mountain and began the ascent. When we began ascending the mountain, Dad was in front of the Nash. As we climbed the mountain, the Nash began to fall farther and farther behind, and by the time we reached the summit, the Nash was nowhere to be seen. We turned around and went back down the mountain, and we found the Nash parked on the side of the road with steam billowing from under the hood. We pulled over and parked so we could help our neighbors. We went to a nearby creek and

Scene of Belk's Department Store and Poinsett Hotel. Also shows electrically operated trolley. Photo Courtesy of Greenville County Historical Society. Greenville, South Carolina.

filled a can with water, and then, when the Nash had cooled off enough, we filled the radiator with cool water. The neighbor turned his Nash around and drove it home. I can't recall another conversation in which he even mentioned the power of his Nash. However, our neighbors kept their Nash for several years. It wasn't long before we were without an automobile again. Fortunately, our uncle Hoyt Porter drove a trolley on a route called the belt-line that went to Main Street and to, or near, most mill villages on the outskirts of the city of Greenville. We rode to town and back with him many times.

The same neighbors who owned the Nash also bought the first television set I ever saw. I don't recall the year, but I know it was after our grandmother was no longer living with us. She had lived with us more than a year when she left to live with other relatives. Not long after Grandmother moved away, Dad's father died as a result of a massive heart attack. Although I never got to know him very well, we were all saddened by the death of our grandfather. It was just a few months after our grandfather's death that our neighbors bought their television set.

We were invited over to the neighbors' house almost every night to watch television with them, but I much preferred listening to the radio and pretending that I was one of the characters of each program. I listened to such programs as *The Great Gildersleeve, Fibber McGee and Molly, Amos and Andy, The Lone Ranger, The Green Hornet, The Screaking Door, Boston Blackie, The Shadow,* and *The Grand Ole Opry.* I'm sure there are others that I just don't recall. When I was young, I wanted to listen to the radio until bedtime every night, and then I would go to bed and think about the programs I had just heard until I fell asleep. The radio programs stirred a person's imagination more than any television program I have ever seen. I miss the days of radio programs such as the ones I have identified. However, I must admit that I also enjoyed television. I just preferred the radio.

I know Dad and Mother thoroughly enjoyed some of the television programs they got an opportunity to see, and so did I. We could not afford a television set, so being invited over by our neighbors was a real treat for all of us. Besides, other than watching television, all of us children always received some type of treat when we went over, and I enjoyed that immensely.

A few months after I saw my first television, some really wonderful items began showing up at our house. Although she never stopped using it altogether, Mother was able to set her woodstove aside for an electric stove. She got a new refrigerator and pushed our old icebox out of the way. We really were beginning to think we were in heaven, but things got even better. A few months after we got the refrigerator and stove, we got a washing machine, an electric iron, and an ironing board. Until then, I didn't even know such things existed. I think we were all very excited about the washing machine, more excited than for all the other items combined. The washing machine was a new wringer-type machine. We washed our clothes in it, but it had no rinse cycle. I don't think any washing machine had a rinse cycle back then. After the clothes were thoroughly washed, we ran them through the wringer and into a large tin tub. We emptied the washing machine and refilled it with cold water. The clothes were placed back into the machine, and it was turned on again. That was our way of creating a rinse cycle. The clothes were rinsed free of as much soap as possible. Then, we ran them through the wringer and into the tub again. If necessary, we repeated the rinsing process. Once the clothes were thoroughly rinsed free of dirt and soap, we ran them through the wringer to get as much water out of them as possible, and then we shook them out and hung them on the clothesline to dry.

The washing machine saved us a lot of time and labor. We no longer had to build a fire to wash clothes, so we needed less wood. We had an electric stove that also saved a lot of time and labor because we burned less wood in the woodstove. Even though we still had our chores to do, we had more time in which to do them because we spent less time chopping and carrying wood. Our lives were just getting better and better. Most of our friends and neighbors seemed to be prospering also. We were all grateful for what we had and happy to see our neighbors doing better as well.

Unfortunately, our happiness was briefly interrupted by the death of one of our grandmothers. Mother's mother, Vesta Odella Sanders Thomas, died on my tenth birthday, the saddest birthday I ever had.

There was another sad incident that involved a tragedy for some of our neighbors. I remember being awakened by David sometime in the middle of the night and being told that the house of our neighbors was burning. We went to the window and looked in the direction of our neighbor's house. Flames were shooting high into the air, and the fire was crackling and popping loudly. It was frightening. David and I went outside and walked across the street to the school grounds and watched as the firefighters attempted to extinguish the blaze. The firefighters were scrambling around and working as hard as they could, but the fire was too large to contain. Within a couple of hours, our neighbor's house was completely burned to the ground. None of the family members were injured, but the only possessions they had left were whatever clothing they had been wearing when they escaped the burning house. As poor and financially bad off as we were, they were in much worse circumstances. I remember Mother searching through our possessions to find something, anything, that we could give to that family. The family had to find another home, and I have never known where they lived after the fire.

Another of our neighbors had a son who was drafted into the military because of the Korean War. I remember visiting their home with my brothers almost every day. There were several other boys in that family that we played with regularly. The mother of those boys always talked about her son in the military, and it was obvious that she worried about him constantly. Reports of American military personnel being killed or wounded were being broadcast on the radio daily. My brother, David, always told the lady that her son was coming home safely, and he would be the first one to see him when he came home. I think it was in early 1952 that the boy came home from Korea. He had not been injured, and sure enough, David was the first person on our street to see him when he arrived home.

We also had numerous relatives who lived in the mill village. One family was Bill and Lucille Porter and their four children, Boyce, Cheryl, Michael, and Harriet, who lived two houses from us on Fourth Street. (Bill and Lucille later had another child named Ricky.) The second family was Hoyt and Viola Porter and their two children, Winfred and Kathryn, who lived two blocks from us on Second Street. The third family was Roy and Ollie Mae Stancil and their four children, Randolph, Mary Ellen, Margaret, and Ann, who lived three blocks from us on First Street. The only other relatives I can recall living in Poe Mill village were cousins Phillip and Ellen Smith and their three children, Jerry, Judy, and Dennis, who lived two blocks from us on Sixth Street.

Our uncle Hoyt was a humorous individual who enjoyed joking with and picking at anyone he came in contact with. He always had something funny to say. He had kept me from getting a whipping once when we lived on Third Street, so I liked him for more than just his humor. He loved children.

One day a mouse went scampering across the floor in our house. I decided that I wanted to catch it, but not kill it. I ran to get a paper bag and then came back to try catching the mouse. I don't think anyone believed that I would really catch the mouse with a bag, but somehow I did. I crimped the top of the bag so the mouse couldn't escape and played with it for a few minutes, and then I got the idea that our uncle Hoyt would enjoy seeing the mouse I had caught, so I walked two blocks to his house. When I told Hoyt I had a mouse in the bag, he said something funny and sarcastic. He was acting as though he didn't believe me. Before he could stop me, I had the bag open and out jumped the mouse. The mouse ran under some furniture and then into another room. Although we searched for a couple of hours, we never found the mouse. After that incident, Hoyt always checked to make sure I didn't have anything that was alive when I visited him.

Hoyt got even with me when Christmas came that year. I was sitting near the front of Poe Baptist Church on the last Sunday before Christmas. All of a sudden, the rear door of the sanctuary flew open, and in walked Santa Claus. Everyone turned around to watch as Santa Claus came down the aisle laughing and shouting, "Merry Christmas." He was bouncing all over the church. He looked directly at me when he got near the front of the church. My eyes must have been wide open, probably as big as saucers. He immediately approached me, squeezing between the pews as he came. He started asking me what I wanted for Christmas. I was so frightened I didn't know what to do. I started to back away from him, but he just kept coming, all the time shouting, "Ho, Ho, Ho! What do you want for Christmas, little boy?" Finally, I got so scared that I was about to cry. When he saw that I was about to cry, Santa Claus turned and walked away. He continued to walk all over the church and I watched him in awe, but I was intending to run if he started toward me again. I ran home as fast as I could run when church was over. I didn't learn that our church Santa Claus was my uncle until my brothers told me after Christmas.

Our cousin Randy Stancil had also lived in Cateechee when we did. He was the cousin who swam in Twelve Mile River and went with us almost everywhere we went. His family had moved to Poe Mill about the same time we did. He was about the same age as my brother William, and he was always interested in the outdoors and loved to be involved with any type of wildlife. He also was a collector of Indian arrowheads, which he searched for and found in the nearby mountains where Cherokee Indians had once lived and hunted.

On one occasion, all of us boys went along with our cousin to search for arrowheads. I had no idea how to find an arrowhead; I just wanted to be with my brothers and cousin. We walked along the railroad tracks until we reached a place called Piney Mountain, and then we began to walk all over the territory, constantly looking toward the ground. Our cousin found an arrowhead and showed it to us. I was immediately hooked on searching for them. We spent the rest of the day searching for arrowheads, and we found a few before darkness forced us to return to our homes. Since that day, when I'm in an area where I think Indians might have lived or hunted, I search for arrowheads.

Randy also raised pigeons. I don't know how he came up with the idea, but he decided he wanted to catch some of the pigeons that flew over the mill village all the time. He set some baited traps and managed to catch several pigeons, and then he built a huge pigeon pen in his backyard. Since the pigeon pen was constructed of mostly chicken wire, the other pigeons that flew over the mill village could see the pigeons in the pen. They began to visit the pen, so our cousin constructed a trap door on his pigeon pen. The trap door was designed in such a way that pigeons could get into the pen, but they couldn't get back out. Before long, our cousin had forty to fifty pigeons, but that was not enough for him. He wanted to catch more.

Randy recruited all of us boys to assist him with his pigeon catching. We walked a short distance away from the mill village into the city limits of Greenville. We scoured Stall Street, James Street, and Earle Street because we knew a lot of pigeons roosted in the nooks and crannies of the huge houses.

The large houses were the homes of wealthy people who owned businesses in Greenville. Apparently, they didn't mind a bunch of mill village kids catching the pigeons, because we were never once run off or scolded. We caught a few more pigeons every time we went to that area.

One day I went to visit our cousin to see his pigeons. When I arrived, he was inside the pigeon pen gathering up a group of young pigeons that were about half grown. I asked him why he was catching all the young pigeons, and he said he was going to cook and eat them. I couldn't believe my ears, but I stayed and watched as he killed, cleaned, and cooked all of the small pigeons. He asked me to join him, so I did. He said the meat we were eating was called "squab," which just meant unfledged pigeon. The meat had a very good taste, much like chicken. I don't recall what we ate with the pigeons, maybe nothing.

On another visit to Randy's house, I discovered he had decided to open a small hole in the side of his pigeon pen. I asked him why he put a hole in the pen, because it looked as if the pigeons could escape. He said his pigeons were used to the pen and considered it to be their home. They might fly away, but they would return. He called them "homing pigeons." Sure enough, the pigeons would fly away, stay gone for a while, then return. He said he had taken some of them as far away as forty miles to release them, and they were already back in the pen by the time he got back home. I don't know how long our cousin continued raising pigeons, but he still had them when we moved away from Poe Mill.

All of us boys went to visit Randy regularly, not just to see his pigeons, but because he was one of the most interesting people we knew and we learned a lot from him. One evening, when we went to his house to spend the night, we went upstairs to his bedroom and, using quilts, sheets, and pillows, made what we called pallets on the floor for us to sleep on. We talked and played until late at night, and then we went to sleep.

Sometime later, we were awakened by a loud noise. We rose up just in time to see a man coming through the bedroom window. We were frightened out of our wits. The man started making weird sounds and grabbing at us. I was so scared that I can't really remember exactly what he said, but I think he said something to the effect that he was going to eat us up. We started screaming, and we were just about to begin crying when we discovered the man was our uncle Roy. He had gone onto the roof of the house from the other upstairs bedroom and walked across the roof to our window and climbed in. After we discovered the man was Roy, we all had a good laugh. He even played with us for a few minutes to make sure we were calmed down before he left the room. I think we all slept lightly the rest of the night even though we knew we were safe. Our uncle Roy was typical of all of our uncles. They all loved to play practical jokes on us or create fear in us whenever they got the opportunity. However, they loved us and protected us as well, just as Dad did.

One Sunday, after church, our whole family went with our uncle Roy and his whole family to Keowee River in Pickens County for a riverside picnic. Of course, we children played in the river. The area of the Keowee River that we visited often is now under Keowee Lake. The river was one of the most pristine and beautiful mountain rivers in all of South Carolina. However, it was also very dangerous. There were potholes in the river that a person could not see before it was too late to avoid stepping or falling into them. We went to a beautiful sandy and rocky area adjacent to the river and chose our picnic spot. While our parents were spreading quilts on the ground and preparing food for our picnic, all of us children went into the river. I had not yet learned to swim, so I had to stay in shallow water near the bank. Randy could swim as if he were a duck, so he went into the deeper water. William could not swim, but because he was the same age as Randy, he wanted to follow him into the deeper water, and he did. They were playing in water that was about three feet deep. Then, Randy told William not to come to where he was because he had stepped into a pothole. Randy was treading water, and William thought that he was just on his knees pretending he was in deep water. William walked toward Randy and fell into the pothole. Randy had his back turned so he didn't see William fall into the pothole, and William went under the water. Roy saw what was happening so he yelled at Randy, telling him to rescue William. Randy swam to William and grabbed him before he went under the water again. However, William also grabbed Randy, and they both went under the water. By that time, Dad was watching the rescue effort. When Dad saw both boys go under the water, he knew the rescue was going badly so he jumped into the river. He was still wearing his suit and shoes he had worn to church, but he swam to the boys anyway. He managed to pull both boys from the pothole, probably saving both of their lives. We stayed at the river even though Dad's clothes and shoes were soaked. We thoroughly enjoyed our picnic, but the nonswimmers stayed close to the riverbank the rest of the day.

Roy loved to go fishing about as much as anyone I have ever met, and Dad also enjoyed fishing. I remember one day that Roy asked Dad to go fishing with him. All of us boys wanted to go too, but we were told we couldn't go because the trip would be too rough for us. Dad and Roy left early the next morning and came back late in the evening, after dark. They had caught so many large catfish that they filled up a large tin tub, like the one we bathed in. I could not believe my eyes. I had caught a few fish when we lived in Cateechee, but nothing like the fish they had. I asked Dad what kind of bait they used, and he replied that they didn't use any bait. He said they were "seining." I thought he said they had been "singing." (Some people I knew pronounced "singing" as "sanging"). I asked him what kind of song he sang to catch fish, and he laughed. He explained to me that seining is when people get into the water with a net and drag the net around the bottom and then quickly pull the net up. Sometimes they catch fish; sometimes they don't catch anything.

Dad said they also did some grappling, and that's how they caught the largest fish. Grappling is a method of fishing that requires the fisherman to get into the river and swim along the bank and reach into holes under water in the riverbank to catch fish. The fisherman first feels a fish, then sticks his hand into the mouth or gills of the fish, seizes it by hand, and drags it from the hole. Grappling was a very scary thought for a small boy, and when Dad told me that he sometimes pulled snakes from the holes, I decided I was not cut out for that type of fishing. I would stick to my cane poles. I was happy I had not gone with them.

Dad did not take me fishing very much because I could not fish the way he did. However, I remember going with him several times. Although I'm not sure I have all the facts correct, one trip I went on was very frightening. Dad, my brothers, Roy, Randy, and I went on a fishing trip to a place called the Horse Pasture, which was a large part of a gigantic wilderness area in the northwestern mountains of South Carolina. Most of that area is now covered by Jocassee Lake. We drove on a dirt road as far into the area as we could drive, and then walked what seemed to be a mile to the river. We cut some canes near the river to use as fishing poles. We dug up some worms near the river to use as bait while Dad and Roy rigged the lines and hooks on the canes. As soon as the canes were rigged and bait was on each of the hooks, my brothers, Randy, and I began fishing.

Dad and Roy told us to continue fishing, and they would be back in a little while. They started walking up the riverbank, placing set hooks with cut bait on them every few yards. They went out of sight and were gone for a considerable length of time. When they came back, they started placing set hooks in the other direction. I don't have any idea how many hooks they put out, but neither of them ever picked up a cane pole to fish when they returned.

We fished until it was too dark to see our corks bobbing on top of the water, and we had caught a few fish. Dad called them "suckers" and "perch." Although we did catch a few catfish after dark, we never caught anything large. We gathered up our poles and fish and went to the campsite that Dad and Roy had prepared. We ate and relaxed before time to bed down for the night. We sat there and listened to Dad and Roy talk, mostly about fishing and hunting. Later, Dad said he and Roy were going to check their set hooks. They left, with lanterns in hand, to walk the riverbank. I have no idea what time they got back because I was already sound asleep.

Sometime in the wee hours of the morning, I was awakened by a very loud, piercing scream that seemed to be coming from just a few feet away. It was pitch-black dark, and I could not see a thing. The same noise also awakened everyone else in the camp. Dad and Roy began to build up the fire that by then was mostly just red coals. I heard Randy ask what the noise was, and I heard Dad say that it was a "painter." (That was his way of pronouncing "panther"). I knew a panther was a very large, wild cat, big enough to eat me, and I was as scared as I have ever been in my life. Dad said the panther would not come to the fire, and he kept the fire blazing the remainder of the night. Eventually, I went back to sleep, but only because I was exhausted.

When I woke up, Dad and Roy were gone. It was a very bright, sunny day, but that didn't keep the earlier fear I had felt from returning. I was petrified to be there without the adults. The sound of the panther was still ringing in my ears. It had sounded much like a screaming baby or a woman.

Dad and Roy had been out checking their set hooks, and they returned to camp with their arms full of large catfish. I was happy to see them, but when I saw the fish, I was in awe. They said they had not finished checking all of their hooks, and I knew they would be leaving us in the camp again. I didn't want them to leave, but I tried to be as brave as I could. I didn't cry when they left to check their remaining hooks. When they returned, they had just as many fish as they had the first time, if not more. I didn't know there were so many fish in that river. They had collected their set hooks as they collected their fish so I knew we would be leaving for home soon. I was just as eager to get home as I had been to go on the trip. Dad and Roy cleaned all the fish we had caught and divided them up. Roy and Randy took their share home with them, and we kept what was left. We ate fish for days.

When I was about nine years old, my brothers introduced me to golf. They learned there was a golf course a few miles from our house that allowed youngsters to come up and work as caddies. Back then, caddies were not required to be knowledgeable about the game of golf. However, they had to be strong enough to carry a golf bag full of clubs and accessories while the person he caddied for played eighteen holes or more. The job of a caddy also required the caddy's eyesight to be good enough to watch the flight of a golf ball that was hit by the golfer for whom he was caddying. It was imperative that a caddy observe where the ball stopped, especially when the golfer hit an errant shot. Many golfers hit their golf balls deep into the woods or into one of the many streams running through the golf course. As far as I know, the caddies at that particular golf course, mostly children, knew nothing about choosing clubs for a golfer or giving the golfer the correct distance to a hole from any particular location. As a caddy, I spent a lot of time in the woods, streams, and fairways at Paris Mountain Country Club.

Joe Pelham Traynham Sr. was greens superintendent from 1921 to 1946 at the Greenville Country Club just off Byrd Boulevard in Greenville. It was while he was working at the Greenville Country Club that Mr. Traynham decided he wanted to build a golf course of his own. He purchased land north of Greenville at the foot of Paris Mountain in 1937. He designed and built all of the Paris Mountain Country Club. The first nine holes were completed and open for business as a public golf course in November 1938. Over the years, Mr. Traynham bought additional land and expanded the golf course to eighteen holes. When the project was completed in 1948, there was a clubhouse, driving range, putting green, and an eighteen-hole public golf course that was located in one of the most beautiful areas of the entire state of

Clubhouse – Paris Mountain Country Club. Photo Courtesy of the Traynham family.

South Carolina. Two years later, in 1950, the Paris Mountain Country Club became a private club. Paris Mountain Country Club was five and one-half miles from our house.

I was allowed to go to the golf course because my parents knew I would be safe in the company of my brothers, or perhaps they just enjoyed the free time without children around. Either way, I was thrilled that I could go. I enjoyed being with my brothers wherever they went.

The most amazing thing I remember about going to the golf course is that we hitchhiked or walked to get there. I can't imagine, in my wildest dreams, that parents today would allow their children to hitch a ride with perfect strangers or to walk five miles to get anywhere. When I read or listen to the news today, I cringe when I think of what might have been. However, we were allowed to get to the golf course any way we could. Golfers who recognized us picked us up most of the time. Other times, strangers picked us up, or we walked. However, on Wednesdays, we were picked up at our home by Mr. Allen Morgan, who managed the Center and Paris theatres in downtown Greenville. He always gave us free tickets to attend movies at those theatres. We knew every Wednesday one of us would caddy for Mr. Morgan.

One day when my brothers left home early to go to the Paris Mountain Country Club, I was left behind because I wasn't dressed early enough. However, I was determined I was not going to be left at home alone, so I headed for Poinsett Highway. When I reached the highway, about a half-mile from home, I began to thumb a ride. If a car passed without offering me a ride, I walked in the direction of the golf course until I saw another car coming, and then I stuck out my thumb again.

After I had been hitchhiking for about fifteen minutes, a car stopped to offer me a ride. The car contained a man, woman, and two teenage girls. I climbed in and told them which golf course I was going to. The girls started talking to me. They were talking about how cute I was, and they were making other remarks that were causing me embarrassment. For a boy my age, their flirting was just downright unflattering and humiliating, and I was getting a little irritated. As we drove further away from home, I began to get a little angry. There I was, in a car with people whom I had never seen before and a long distance from home or the Paris Mountain Country Club I was going to. I told the people I had decided to go to a closer golf course, but I really just wanted to get out of that car. Hillandale Golf Course was two and one-half miles from our house. We never caddied there, so I know nothing about it. They stopped at the entrance to Hillandale; however, the woman must have sensed I was nervous or upset because she asked me if I really wanted to get out there or go on to Paris Mountain. She told me she knew Paris Mountain golf course was much nicer. She also said she hoped they hadn't said or done anything to upset me. The lady was very nice, and as she talked I began to feel more relaxed. I jumped back into the car, and they took me to the Paris Mountain Country Club. I was happy to see my brothers when I walked up to the clubhouse. However, that was not the only time I hitched a ride alone, just the first.

There would be no one to caddy for at times when we arrived at the golf course, so we passed the time by playing games in the woods adjacent to the golf course, but we were always close enough to hear the club manager call for us when he needed a caddy. When he needed a caddy, it was usually one of the older boys who got the call. I think I must have gone to the golf course twenty times before the pro shop manager, J. P. Traynham Jr., selected me, and then it was to shag golf balls, not really to caddy.

The driving range on the golf course began at the top of a mountain and ended at the bottom. The golfer's idea of having a caddy to shag balls was to have the caddy stand at the bottom of the mountain while the golfer hit golf balls from the top, and the golfer would attempt to hit the golf balls toward the caddy. It was the job of the caddy to watch the flight of the golf ball, retrieve it when it landed, and put it into a shag bag. Sometimes, the golfer's accuracy was too good, because I had to dodge a lot of golf balls. After I collected all the golf balls the golfer had hit, I trudged back up the mountain to return them. Sometimes, the golfer would choose to hit all of them again. That was fine with me, because it meant an additional quarter every time he hit a bag of golf balls, and I never got tired of collecting quarters.

The one really good thing about going to the golf course was I always had someone to take care of me when I got there. My brothers looked after me until they were selected to caddy for someone, and then Mr. Traynham allowed me to hang around the clubhouse while my brothers were working. I was too young to caddy for some golfers, so I didn't get the opportunity to caddy as much as I would have liked.

One good thing about hanging around the clubhouse was that I could spend a little time with Joel Duncan, who worked in the clubhouse and also caddied. There was also a small Pekinese dog named Pug that hung around the clubhouse frequently, and I played with it a lot. It belonged to the Traynham family. I also had opportunities to see most of the clubhouse visitors. They probably didn't notice me, but I certainly noticed them. In addition to J. P. Traynham Sr. and J. P. Jr., I saw all of the other children of J. P. Traynham Sr. They were named John, Dillard, Wilcy, Winona, Mary, and Iris.

The Traynham Family: Back Row L to R: Gladys Nicholson, Iris Traynham, Ellis Stone, Juanita Traynham, J.P. Traynham, Sr., Winona Pruitt, Mary League. Front Row L to R: J.P. Traynham, Jr., John Traynham, Wilcy Traynham, Dillard Traynham. Photo courtesy of the Traynham family.

All three of the Traynham daughters were very pretty, but I especially noticed Mary and Iris because they were closer in age to me. I loved to watch Mary play golf, but I just loved to watch Iris, no matter what she was doing. She was about the same age I was, and I thought she was beautiful. Of course, I never attempted to talk to her because I was intimidated by her looks and the fact that she was a Traynham. I was afraid she wouldn't talk to me, and I was afraid J.P. would send me packing if she did. I was a caddy, and I needed to work. My brother David also thought Iris was attractive, and he especially liked the name "Iris." In fact, he was so impressed with her name that, years later, he named one of his own children Iris.

I had many opportunities to watch some members of the Traynham family play golf. I never saw Iris play, but Winona and Mary were excellent golfers. J. P. Jr., Dillard, John, and Wilcy were also excellent golfers. The fairway to the number-one hole on the golf course was down the mountain with a sharp dogleg to the right at the bottom. There was a heavily wooded area to the right side of the fairway. I remember watching Wilcy and Dillard tee their golf balls up and hit them over the woods to the number-one hole. Both of them could actually drive the ball to the green on the par-four hole. They were consistently attempting to get an eagle on that hole.

I also remember that George Pruitt and Jack League frequented the golf course, and I saw them in the clubhouse regularly. George married Winona Traynham, and Jack married Mary Traynham. Dillard Pruitt, who is currently a professional golfer, is the son of George and Winona, and Winona's daughter Jan is married to Jay Haas, who is also a professional golfer from Greenville.

I saw many other visitors to the clubhouse, including Jack Long, Frank and Virginia Ulmer, Reese Truesdale, George Blackwell, Johnny Simkins, and Buck Carnes. Paris Mountain Country Club was quite popular back then, and I never had to worry about being alone. That was important to me.

I also never had to worry about being hungry at the golf course. My brothers bought candy and drinks for me when they were around, and Mr. Traynham always gave me drinks and candy when my brothers were caddying for golfers and he thought I was hungry.

The first time I was selected to actually caddy, I caddied for a female golfer. That was a rarity because very few women played golf at that course, so I was lucky. The good thing about female golfers of that era was most of them had lightweight bags. I really had no idea what I was going to do as a first-time caddy, but as it turned out, I had nothing to worry about. The golfer was a very good golfer. She hit her golf balls in the fairways all the way around the course, so I never had to look for them. They were always in plain sight. She was also very pretty, and that helped me to forget I was working. After lugging her bag around eighteen holes, I received a dollar and a quarter from Mr. Traynham, and then to my surprise, the golfer gave me another dollar as a tip. I floated on air the rest of the day. Unfortunately, I don't recall the golfer's name.

I think either Mr. Traynham or the female golfers must have felt sorry for me because, after my first selection, I was selected several more times to caddy for ladies. Perhaps I was selected because I was the youngest and smallest caddy at the golf course. I knew some of the female golfers didn't really need a caddy, but I was always happy to work for them and receive the generous tips they offered. I always spent most of my tips on candy and drinks, and the rest of my earnings were taken home to buy items of clothing or something else I needed. I might have been a tired caddy, but I was a contented one also.

When it came to caddying for men, it was a different story. The men expected the caddies to carry their very heavy bags, watch their golf balls, and find the balls even when they hit them deep into the woods or into a stream. I was not the ideal caddy for men, but I tried hard to please them. I found out early the men were good tippers if they didn't lose golf balls and scored well enough to win. I always wanted my golfer to win, and I would go into the woods or walk in the creeks until I located my golfer's ball. I never gave snakes and other creatures a thought. I had to be successful at finding golf balls if I hoped to be selected to caddy for a man again. Many of the golfers were gambling, and they didn't want a caddy who couldn't find a golf ball, because a lost ball meant a stroke penalty.

I wasn't aware so much gambling took place on a golf course before I started caddying for men. I didn't even know there were people in the world who could afford to lose large sums of money on a single golf shot. I caddied for one golfer who always started the game by betting ten dollars for each nine holes; however, by the time we got to the third or fourth hole, he would be betting ten dollars a stroke. I thought he was betting a fortune on a round of golf. Sometimes he won, but most of the time he lost because he was not a very good golfer; he just had more money than he had sense. I saw him lose over a hundred dollars in one day because he kept pressing his bets with the better golfers—and then he gave me no tip. I always attempted to hide when he showed up after that. I didn't want to ever be selected to caddy for that person again. However, whenever I got the opportunity, I loved caddying for golfers who were opposing him. They always won, and I was always tipped very well.

Caddying for winners was always easier and more rewarding than caddying for losers. I remember one time when I received a dollar and a quarter from the club manager for caddying eighteen holes, and then I received a ten-dollar tip from the golfer I caddied for. He won almost a hundred dollars from the golfer who had previously given no tip to me when he lost. I went home happy that day.

Things were really slow at the golf course on Tuesdays, so Mr. Traynham would allow us caddies to play a round of golf. I learned to play by beating the ball around the golf course when I wasn't caddying. Watching the golfers play when I caddied was one thing; actually playing was another thing. I loved the game of golf from the first time I held a club in my hand and struck a golf ball, and I still play golf today. I also loved the beauty of the golf courses, and I loved the fact that I had to be outdoors when I played golf or caddied. Paris Mountain Country Club was a special place for me, as it was for my brothers.

It was sad news for me when I learned ownership of Paris Mountain Country Club had changed, but it was sadder still when I learned the name had been changed to Summersett. Why the name of such a landmark was changed is beyond my comprehension. However, the hair on the back of my neck raised and I was a little rankled when I read an article giving credit to someone else for the design of the golf course. That's tantamount to someone buying a beautiful dress my mother made, ripping the arms off of it, and stating they designed it. J. P. Traynham Sr. designed and built that golf course. After the Paris Mountain Country Club changed ownership, someone else may have torn down the clubhouse and built a new one in a different place and then altered or rearranged the golf course to make it look different, but he certainly did not design it.

David, James, and I continued caddying until we moved across town. However, William could not caddy as often as we did because he worked in grocery stores. Dad had gotten William a job at Williams Grocery Store on Hammett Street. William delivered groceries for Mr. Williams for a few weeks and then he got a job at the Piggly Wiggly grocery store on Poinsett Highway. He worked there a few months and then got a job at Kash and Karry. After William began working in the grocery stores, he had much less time to spend with the rest of us. We just spent as much time as we could at the golf course, but I also visited Paris Mountain for other purposes.

When we lived on Fourth Street, Dad started taking me to Paris Mountain to hunt squirrels. On the first trip I remember, we went up on Paris Mountain where there were some large oak, hickory, and poplar trees. I was walking and looking for squirrels the whole time it took to reach our destination, but I had not seen one squirrel. In fact, I was beginning to believe there were no squirrels in that neck of the woods.

Dad sat down and leaned back against a large tree. I didn't understand how he expected to find squirrels sitting under a tree, so I told him that I thought we were going to hunt for squirrels. He looked at me with a slight grin and told me to sit down and get quiet. I knew when Dad said to "get quiet" he meant no talking, no rustling of leaves, and no noise. I was about to get upset, thinking he had brought me all that distance to sit quietly under a tree. I knew better than to challenge him, but I didn't understand how we were going to find squirrels. Heck, if I sat still and quiet, I might fall asleep, as I usually did under those conditions. Out of fear, I got still and quiet. After about fifteen minutes of absolute quiet, Dad whispered something to me. I asked what he had said, and he said for me to listen. My ears perked up, but I didn't hear a sound. I asked what I was supposed to be listening to, and he said for me to get quiet. Suddenly,

I did hear something rustling in the leaves straight in front of us. I couldn't see anything, but I knew something was there. Dad raised and shouldered his shotgun very slowly. I put my hands over my ears because I had heard that gun before. *BOOM!* The sound was almost deafening, but I was happy to see that Dad had shot a squirrel. When he told me to go get it, I asked what I should do if the squirrel were still alive, and he said to take a stick with me and punch the squirrel before I picked it up. When I told him that the squirrel might be just pretending to be dead, like a possum, he said to pick it up by the tail. He said to never pick up a squirrel any other way because, if it were alive, it could bite right through my hand. When he said that a squirrel could bite through my hand he scared me, but I went down and retrieved the squirrel anyway. When I returned with the squirrel, Dad told me to get quiet again, which I did. He shot, and I retrieved, five more squirrels that day, and our whole family ate fried squirrel for supper. I learned that squirrel hunting required the hunter to be still and get quiet! Hunting rabbits was a different story.

The first time I went rabbit hunting with Dad, I was not allowed to carry a gun because I was much too young. I watched as the beagles chased rabbits and Dad shot them. Two other men were hunting with us, but they never shot anything. Either they didn't know how to hunt, or they just weren't very good at it. Dad killed five rabbits that day, and the other men acted as if they were angry that they didn't get any. However, they went hunting with Dad and me many times after that day.

The first time I was allowed to carry a gun on a hunting trip, I was rabbit hunting with Dad. He had bought an old, used, single-barrel, single-shot, off-brand, twelve-gauge shotgun from a neighbor, and he gave it to me. I didn't care about all the negatives: I had a shotgun of my very own. I was ready to hunt!

While we were walking along the edge of a field, next to the woods, Dad was attempting to teach me how to find a rabbit in its bed. Suddenly, he stopped, and I stopped beside him. He told me that he had spotted a rabbit in its bed, and pointed toward some roots and vines. I saw nothing but roots and vines. He told me which way the rabbit was facing, and then he told me to look for only the rabbit's eyes. Finally, after straining my eyes to see it, I saw an eye of the rabbit. I was amazed that I had not been able to see it sooner. Once I focused on it, it was just as easy to see as a tree.

I raised my gun and shouldered it. Dad asked me what I was doing. I told him that I was going to shoot the rabbit's nose off. He told me to wait. Suddenly, Dad kicked the brush and the rabbit came out of its bed in a blur. I aimed at the rabbit as it ran away, but I never fired a shot. Dad asked me why I didn't shoot, and I replied that the rabbit was running too fast. He laughed so hard I thought he was going to hurt himself. I was totally humiliated, but I learned to shoot no matter how many times I missed. I would never stand there and watch a rabbit run away again, especially when Dad was along. For the remainder of the day, I never got an opportunity to shoot at another rabbit, although Dad killed four. I guess I didn't see any more rabbits because I was still fuming over Dad allowing the one that I could have shot to escape. I learned that Dad was just attempting to teach me to react quickly when a rabbit jumped from its bed and ran away. I loved spending time in the woods and fields with Dad. He taught me more than he could possibly have ever realized. I have memories of times with him that no one else ever shared, and I will treasure them forever. I will always appreciate the fact that he bought a gun for me and that he taught me to handle it properly. I never placed anyone in danger with my mishandling of a gun, with the exception of my handmade toy rifle that I sometimes used when pretending to be the cowboys and Indians I had seen in movies.

One of the few types of entertainment that my brothers and I actually traveled to and paid for was movies. I recall that a different western was on at some theatre in Greenville every week. Since westerns were about the only type of movies we were interested in, we were always trying to figure out how we were going to get to see one.

Back then, a person could buy a soft drink for six cents, and then return the empty bottle for a refund of one cent. We couldn't afford to buy soft drinks, but if we could just find some empty bottles, we could return them to the company store and collect the refunds.

Fortunately, we knew where the super and all of the boss men who worked in the cotton mill lived. The super was the superintendent, or cotton mill manager, and the boss men were supervisors over individual departments in the mill. We knew that they lived in much nicer houses than we did and they had much more money than we had. We figured they could afford to buy soft drinks if anyone could.

The first time we came up with the idea to look for empty soft drink bottles we decided to look at the super's house. Compared to our house, the super lived in a mansion. At the back of his house was a large screened-in porch. We snuck to the super's house, approaching from the rear, so we would not be detected. We crept up the steps to look into the screened-in porch. There, sitting on the floor, was a whole crate of twenty-four soft drink bottles. We could not believe our eyes. The admission for a movie was only six cents so there was enough money, in bottles, for four individuals to get into a movie. We thought we had found a gold mine. We pulled on the handle of the screen door, but the door was latched with a hook type latch that we could see through the screen. We used a nail that we found to punch a hole through the screen and lift the latch. We got the bottles, crate and all, crept off the porch, and walked away as quickly as possible.

We carried the crate of bottles home, two blocks away, and went under the house. We couldn't let our parents discover what we were doing. Each of us took six bottles and stuffed them into our pockets and other places in our clothing. Bottles were sticking out everywhere. In my mind, that is still a comical sight.

We carried the bottles to the store and, sure enough, we got the twenty-four cents. However, we were not finished. We went to one of the homes of a boss man, where we found two cartons containing twelve empty bottles, and then we hurried to the store to get the refund for them. However, we still were not satisfied. We wanted money for popcorn, candy, and drinks. Each of those items cost five cents each, so we needed a few more bottles. We decided to visit the homes of the other boss men. By the time we had raided the homes of all the boss men, we had an additional fifty-three bottles. We decided to stop looking for bottles because we were beginning to get scared that we were going to get caught. We figured that we could get into the movie and spend the other sixty-five cents on candy, popcorn, and drinks that we could share, but then someone in the crowd announced that he already had a little money before we started collecting bottles, so we had more money than we thought. Riding a trolley to town was six cents, but the theatre was only about two miles away so we walked to save our money. We thoroughly enjoyed our day at the movies.

We repeated the act of collecting bottles over and over. However, we discovered other places to get bottles also. We didn't want to go to the super's house and the homes of the boss men too often; otherwise, we would get caught. Even so, I wonder whether or not some of the people from whom we were taking bottles knew what we were doing and helped us by placing their bottles where we could get to them easily.

We watched movies about *Roy Rogers, Gene Autry, Tom Mix, Lash Larue, Hopalong Cassidy, John Wayne, The Cisco Kid, Billy the Kid, Red Ryder and Little Beaver*, and any other cowboy who happened along. We also watched movies about *Tarzan* and *The Three Stooges*. Sometimes, we would hide under our seats when a movie ended so we could get back into our seats when the next showing of the movie started and watch it again. We weren't afraid because back then the theatre was cleaned only at the end of the day because the projector operator also had the task of cleaning the theatre. We figured the projector operator wouldn't leave the projector to search the theatre and, even if he did, the only thing he would probably do was make us leave the theatre.

After watching a western and leaving the theatre, we became the cowboys we had just watched. We would go home and play cowboys and outlaws or cowboys and Indians for hours.

We rarely had money to buy toy guns and cowboy outfits so we each pretended to hold guns in our hands and pointed index fingers at our intended targets. All a person could hear all day long was "Bang, I gotcha!" Then, the intended victim was heard to say, "No, you didn't, you missed me!"

Week after week, we played our Wild Western games of cowboys, outlaws, and Indians. We eventually grew tired of hearing the phrase "You missed me!" We decided we needed to do something about that. We had one kid in the neighborhood who would never admit to being shot: he was always missed, no matter how close we were to him when we shot him.

Since we could not afford to buy toy guns and a toy gun would have been useless against that particular kid anyway, we decided to use something a little more realistic. We wanted a weapon that actually fired something a person could feel when it hit him and we could see when it struck its target. One of my brothers came up with an idea for a rubber gun, a gun that propelled a strip of rubber. The premise was: if a gun could fire a rubber strip hard enough it would travel to its intended target, within a reasonable distance. If the target were a person, the person would feel the impact of the rubber strip and could not deny being shot.

We gathered several one-half-inch-thick boards from somewhere in the neighborhood, and then we got a saw from our house and began to saw out square-cornered replicas of guns. In our minds, we were making pistols like those the cowboys in the movies used. Once we had carved out the gun replicas, we took old clothespins we had taken from our mother's clothespin bag and disassembled them. We nailed the sides of the clothespins with the springs attached to the back of the handles of the guns. Then, we placed the other sides of the clothespins onto the sides already attached to the guns. We then had firing mechanisms for our guns. Of course, our guns were just crudely made rubber guns; however, in our imaginations, they were real.

We found an old red-rubber inner tube from a car tire and cut it into slender strips, and then we folded the strips and placed the folded ends over the ends of the gun barrels. After that, we stretched the rubber strips as tightly as we could and placed the loose ends into the clothespins. If the springs of the clothespins were strong enough, they would hold the rubber strips until we pressed on the clothespins to release them. To our amazement, our guns worked.

We gathered a group of our friends for a game of cowboys and outlaws. The game became more realistic because a victim of a shooting had to drop out until all of the members of one team or the other had been shot. There was no doubt about who had been shot either. The rubber guns were powerful, sometimes leaving a red mark on someone for an hour or so. Unfortunately, our friend who never died was not present for that first game. However, his time did come.

One day when we were playing with our never-say-die friend, sure enough, after being struck by a rubber strip, he still claimed to have been missed. After a short fight, a real fight, he went home crying.

I decided that if I ever played with that friend again, I wanted to make sure he knew, beyond a shadow of a doubt, when he had been shot. I got out the saw and a fairly long board, and then I sawed out a rifle instead of a pistol. I put a clothespin on it and tried it out. I stretched the red rubber strip as hard as I could stretch it and placed the ends into the clothespin. It held. I took the rifle to a nearby tree, where I fired it at a large leaf. The rubber strip tore right through the leaf and ripped it from the tree at the same time. I figured I was ready for my never-say-die friend.

I went to my friend's house and got him to go back to my house to play, but I had not told him what we would play. When I got home with my friend, some other friends and one or two of my brothers were already engaged in a game of cowboys and outlaws. I chose to be on one side and told my friend he had to be on the other side. He agreed, and I gave a wooden rubber pistol to him, and then I ran to get my rifle.

We must have dodged and ducked for a good twenty minutes before I looked around a corner of the house to see my never-say-die friend headed straight toward me. I waited until I could hear the sounds of his feet striking the ground just around the corner, and then I stuck the barrel of the rifle around the corner and fired. I saw the rubber strip as it hit my friend just below his left eye, but as the rubber strip was traveling in his direction, I yelled, "Bang, I gotcha."

When the rubber strip struck my friend, he screamed and fell to the ground crying. You would have thought he was really dying. The rest of the cowboys and outlaws came running to see what was wrong, and by the time they arrived my friend had a welt under his eye. One of my brothers thought I had hit my friend with my fist. When I explained what really happened, my brother looked at my friend and said, "You mean he didn't miss you?" Everybody laughed! Well, my injured, or dead, friend didn't laugh. I apologized to my friend for hurting him, but I also warned him that he should never claim he was missed when he knew for a fact he had been hit.

We played cowboys and outlaws many times after that, and my former never-say-die friend played right along with us. He was still my friend, just no longer a never-say-die friend. When someone pointed at him and said, "Bang, I gotcha," he always fell out, pretending to be dead. I guess he was afraid that my rifle might reappear. However, I put my rifle away and quit playing cowboys and outlaws, because there were many other more exciting games and adventures for me to be involved in with my brothers and friends. One such adventure involved the making of cog-wheel wagons.

I had never heard the adage, "One person's junk is another person's treasure." However, between the ages of seven and eleven, I could have applied that adage to the ramblings and findings of my brothers and me many times.

One of the destinations we had when we walked the railroad tracks near our house was a junkyard on Poinsett Highway. The junkyard was located adjacent to the railroad tracks on one side and adjacent to Poinsett Highway, one of the busiest highways in the county, on the front side. It was also diagonally across the railroad tracks from Bruce's Auction Barn, a place we visited frequently to ride every animal we could find. I don't know which we discovered first, the junkyard or the auction barn.

We got up very early and set out for the junkyard, sometimes before the sun actually appeared in the eastern sky. We walked down Fourth Street, crossed the road that ran in front of the cotton mill, walked across the mill village pasture to get to the railroad tracks, and then we walked approximately a half-mile to reach the junkyard.

We climbed the red clay railroad embankment and stood outside the fence for a few minutes to determine whether or not someone was on the premises, like the owner or a guard. There could have been a guard dog, but I don't recall ever seeing one.

Once we determined that no one was present, we pulled the bottom of the fence out far enough to crawl under it. We knew very well we were not supposed to be inside the junkyard fence. We went under the fence rather than over the top to prevent our detection. We knew that going over the top of the fence would expose us to anyone who might be traveling on the adjacent highway or to anyone who just happened to be inside the junkyard. The junk was piled high, so we could stay low and browse for a long time without the possibility of anyone seeing us. We also knew very well that we had no intention of paying for any treasure we might find. We went there with full intentions of stealing whatever we could find that was useful to us. We knew it was wrong, and we knew if we got caught we would be in big trouble with our parents and law enforcement authorities.

One of the first things I recall finding in the junkyard that caused my imagination to go wild was a cogwheel. I had no idea what a cog was, nor did I have any idea what a cogwheel was. I just listened to the others calling them "cogwheels," and I figured they knew what they were talking about. I never questioned whether or not they were right or wrong. I do recall, however, that we all had the same vision in our minds, cogwheel wagons!

I found out later that a cogwheel is a very large type of gear for heavy machinery. The cog is one of a series of teeth on the rim of the wheel which engages with the teeth of a corresponding wheel to transmit motive force, similar to the tiny cogwheels in an old watch.

Because the cogwheels we took were made of some type of heavy metal, probably steel or iron, they were so heavy that I could carry only one, but my brothers were strong enough to carry two each.

We took seven cogwheels on our first visit to the junkyard. We scampered to the fence, put the wheels under the fence to the outside, and then crawled under. We rolled the wheels to the bottom of the railroad embankment and followed them down, and then we picked the wheels up and headed for home. We had to stop and rest several times along the way. We had to carry those wheels close to a mile because there was no way to roll the wheels along on the bed of a railroad track. By the time we arrived home, we were absolutely exhausted, and we were also covered with black grease from the cogwheels.

I recall being asked by our parents where we got the cogwheels, but I don't recall our answer. I think we said something to the effect that we just found them. I don't recall any further questions or interrogation from our parents, just the one question. I remember how excited we were when we told our parents that we were going to build a cogwheel wagon. They didn't express any objections, so we were in business.

The first thing we realized was that we had only wheels, no other materials, so our wagon-building project was put on hold for just a short time. We had no money to buy materials, so we started scouring the entire mill village looking for anything we thought might be useful for wagon building.

We came across an empty mill-owned house that was being repaired for occupancy. Short pieces of two-by-fours and small pieces of wide boards were just lying around to be taken, so we took them. We also found some new nails in a container inside the house. We didn't take just enough nails for our project; we took the container. When we thought we had enough materials to build a wagon, we headed home.

There, we began to lay the materials out on the ground. We sawed the pieces of two-by-fours into the correct lengths for cross-boards, to which we intended to attach our axles that we didn't even have yet. Next, we cut the wide boards into the shapes we needed for the sides. It was our intention to build a fully enclosed wagon, much like a car. Then we used a two-by-six for the centerpiece that ran from the front to the rear. One two-by-four cross-board for the rear axle was nailed securely to the two-by-six centerpiece. The front cross-board was attached to the two-by-six with a large bolt. The bolt held the cross-board firmly but allowed it to rotate so the wagon could make turns. We discovered that one two-by-six was not wide enough to sit on, so we constructed a box-like seat from the wide boards and nailed it securely onto the two-by-six. We had a skeleton for a wagon.

We had wheels, but no way to attach them to the wagon without axles. Even if we had axles, we had nothing to use for a steering mechanism. We needed a steering wheel and a steering rod, and we needed something to use for brakes. We had worked all day just to get to that point and we were tired, so we decided to wait until morning to make another trip to the junkyard.

The next morning at the junkyard we knew exactly what we needed, so we began our search very quietly but with the intensity of professionals. Eureka! We found a whole pile of steering wheels from wrecked automobiles, and we took the best one we could find. Next we discovered some steel rods that looked as though they were made for cogwheel wagon axles, and we took several. We left the junkyard as fast as we could run, and we never stopped to rest until after we were out of sight of the junkyard and highway.

It was so early when we arrived home and began working that we might have awakened some of our neighbors with all the hammering we were doing. We placed an axle on one of the two-by-four cross-boards and then drove nails into the boards and bent them over the axle. We did this every two inches along the axle to secure the axle tightly enough to ensure that it would not wiggle. When we had both axles secured, we placed the wheels onto the end of the axles. The axles had holes through them, at each end, and we put nails through the holes and bent them so the wheels could not slide off. On the other side of the wheels we had no way of securing them, but we knew if they did slide, they could slide no further than the end of the two-by-four cross boards, so they were fine.

Once the wheels were on, we had a wagon. However, we still could not use it because we had no way to attach the steering wheel. Even if we could attach the steering wheel to one end of the steel rod we had, what kind of mechanism could we use to cause the wheels to actually turn? It was brainstorming time.

One of my brothers—I don't recall which—came up with a most ingenious idea. We could use a broomstick or a mop handle as a steering shaft and we could attach one end of a rope or a strip of leather to the steering wheel shaft and the other end to the outside end of the front two-by-four cross-board. When the steering wheel was turned, the rope or leather would coil around the shaft, thereby pulling the front wheel around. This, in turn, would cause the wagon to turn. We did exactly what my brother said to do. However, we quickly discovered that the wagon would turn in only one direction. My brother had another idea. If one rope or leather strip would turn the wagon in only one direction, we needed two such devices to turn the wagon in both directions.

The problem was how to attach two devices to the steering shaft without the two of them getting entangled. To my brother, it was simple. We attached a short length of leather to the front cross-board on the left side and attached the other end of it to the lower end of the steering shaft. We then attached a longer strip of leather to the cross-board on the right side and attached it to a higher place on the steering shaft. It worked. We had our wagon.

We took the wagon to the roadway. We lived on a corner lot, and both streets were running downhill. We chose the street beside the house because the hill was longer and we wanted to travel as far as possible. Of course, one of my brothers would get the first ride. He got into the wagon and was pushed by the rest of us until he was going too fast for us to keep up. We thought he was just going to ride to the next corner and come back but he kept going. We could hear him yelling something, but we could not understand him. He went all the way to the end of the hill, crossing several cross-streets as he went, before he stopped about three blocks away. We saw him jump from the wagon and then he began pulling it back. When he got back to our location, we found out what he had been yelling about. In our excitement, we had forgotten all about brakes.

We took the wagon back into the yard to construct a braking system. We took a piece of two-by-four and nailed one very large nail through it, attaching it to the body of the wagon. Because it had only one nail through it, it was movable. When the driver pushed the top of the two-by-four forward, the bottom of it came back and rubbed against a rear wheel. *Shazam!* We had brakes. By bending the nail, we made sure the brake handle would not come off.

We took our completed cogwheel wagon to the streets. We pushed the person who was driving all over the mill village, and we had friends from everywhere coming to join us. I guess the sound of those heavy, metal cogwheels rolling on the asphalt surface just naturally attracted the attention of everyone within hearing distance. We took turns driving, first among us brothers, and then among our friends. We quickly saw the need for more cogwheel wagons.

Before any of our friends discovered where we had gotten the cogwheels, we visited that junkyard numerous times, collecting everything we needed to build more wagons. We also got plenty of spare parts.

After we told some of our friends where the cogwheels came from, we seldom went back to the junkyard. We figured if people were going to get caught, it would be them, not us. However, I don't recall anyone ever getting caught. Perhaps the junkyard owner knew what was going on all along. He might have been enjoying watching us as much as we were enjoying ourselves. If that's the case, I really appreciate his generosity. If not, I'm glad we never got caught.

As time went by, we became more and more proficient at building cogwheel wagons. When one of our wagons fell apart or was no longer in style with our newer wagons, we just built a new one. We no longer needed to travel to the junkyard for wheels, axles, or shafts. The wheels and other parts we had collected from the junkyard would last a lifetime.

We also became more proficient at driving our wagons. We discovered if we turned the front wheels quickly when we were traveling really fast, the wagon would go into a skid. Sometimes, it would rotate several times before it would come to a halt. We rode our wagons in that fashion for weeks, putting them into skids regularly, and then we taught that maneuver to every kid in the mill village—if he or she were brave enough to try it. There were times when we skidded off the roadway into a ditch, but other than a few minor bruises and abrasions, we never got hurt. Certainly, no bones ever got broken. Anyway, the rougher and more frightening the ride, the better we seemed to like it.

When we moved from Poe Mill, I was eleven years old. We had to leave our cogwheel wagons behind, but my brothers had already gotten too big to ride them anyway. Although I did build another cogwheel wagon when I was twelve, I rode it only a few times. I guess not having my brothers to enjoy it with me caused me to lose interest in it, so I gave it to a friend.

I was thirteen when I first saw *The Little Rascals* on television. Some of the wagons the kids in *The Little Rascals* were playing with looked very similar to ours, except they didn't have cogwheels. Some of the children in that show even dressed like some of us. Also, some of the activities they were involved in were very similar to some of the activities we had been involved in. We even allowed girls to come into our hideouts and other places of play just as the Little Rascals did. If I had not known better, I would have sworn that someone observed us building and playing with our cogwheel wagons and while we were engaged in some of our other activities and decided to make films about our adventures. Maybe someone did!

Just as we walked the railroad tracks and sometimes actually rode trains to get to the junkyard to get parts for our cogwheel wagons, we also walked or rode to Bruce's Auction Barn, a livestock auction barn on Poinsett Highway that we called the Jockey Lot.

The Jockey Lot was about one mile from home by way of the railroad tracks. We would go there and watch people bring in their animals to auction, and sometimes we would be there early enough to see the first animal arrive at about 7:30 in the morning.

As the animals arrived at the auction barn, we would walk up and down the aisle in the center of the barn and look at every animal. I especially wanted to look at the horses.

When the auctioneer took his position, we knew that was our cue to get to a safe place from which to watch the auction and the action. If we didn't get to a safe place, there was a fifty-fifty chance that some type of animal would

P.L. Bruce's Auction Barn. Photo Courtesy of Greenville County Historical Society. Greenville, South Carolina.

trample us. Many different types of animals were brought in for auction. I recall seeing horses, ponies, donkeys, mules, bulls, cows, goats, sheep, and pigs. I think I even recall seeing one llama, and there might have been some chickens and roosters.

The auctioneer would call for a particular animal, and the owner would bring it out. Sometimes, the animal would resist, and we would see big men tossed around as if they were small children. To us, that was exciting. Most of the animals were led out without incident though. We got every chance to see up close every type of farm animal there was, in our area anyway. We could smell them and touch them, and that was even more exciting because touching them was what we went for.

One of the benefits of being at the auction barn early was that we would get to see and hear the animal owners bargaining over the breeding of some of the animals, especially the horses and cattle. We loved that because we knew we might get a chance to see the animals in action. It's one thing to see a stallion in a movie when he is rearing up like Silver (the Lone Ranger's horse), or running full speed across a meadow, or making noise for the microphones, but it's something altogether different to watch the real wildness come out in a stallion when he sees and smells a mare in heat less than twenty yards from him. He goes crazy! The stallion makes almost deafening sounds as he is attempting to shed his human handlers and race to conquer the apprehensive mare. Once the stallion is allowed to enter the ring with the mare, he quickly battles her into submission, and then he mates with the mare with such intensity that it is absolutely frightening. I have never seen a more exciting scene. However, I have always felt sorry for the mares. It seems to be a little unfair that the stallions are allowed to kick, bite, and pummel mares the way they do. I guess that's just the natural way for horses, but I would prefer to see breeding done in a more gentle way.

After the auctions were over, some of the animals were stalled and kept overnight, and that was what we were always waiting for. We would hide on the railroad embankment adjacent to the auction barn property until everyone was gone, and then we would crawl under the railings to look at the animals that were left behind. Usually, there would be some type of animal we could ride up and down the center aisle of the barn. We would try to find at least two animals we could ride because we always wanted to race. I would get on the back of an animal, and one of my older brothers would get on behind me. Riding double was safer for me because I was the youngest and smallest. I had someone to protect me, or so I thought.

One Sunday when the auction barn was closed, we decided to visit it to attempt to ride some unsuspecting animals. We found a mule and a horse that looked as if they could be easily ridden. We led them to the center aisle, holding them by their manes. We didn't even have a halter rope. I climbed up onto the stall rails and slid onto the back of the mule, and James got on behind me. William and David got onto the back of the horse. We counted to three and kicked the animals in their sides as we had seen the cowboys do in the movies. Both animals took off like bolts of lightning. The ride wasn't at all smooth like it looked when the cowboys were doing it. Although the mule was out-running the horse, I was bouncing around like a football, going in every direction. Suddenly, I started sliding off. I was yelling for James to help me, but he was holding on to the mule's mane for dear life. Needless to say, I fell from the mule. I guess it was a good thing that we were riding the mule because it stopped dead in its tracks when I fell underneath it. I didn't get hit, or stepped on, by one hoof. However, I was not totally uninjured. I fell on my back and had the breath knocked out of me, and I was writhing on the ground and attempting to suck in air. I recall that I was making some pretty weird sounds too. When I was able to breathe again, I was ready to go home. I was filthy, with dirt all over my best church clothes, and William, James, and David were almost as dirty as I was.

When we got home, Mother fussed at us for getting our best clothes in such a mess, but we did not get punished. Mother washed our clothes and then prepared food for us. We ate a hearty meal.

We went back to the auction barn every chance we got. One time I got onto the back of a hog and the hog took off and just ran right out from under me. I tried and tried to ride that hog, but I could never stay aboard. There is nothing to hold onto, and I believe hogs must be the hardest animals alive to ride. Hogs have no mane, and their ears are located too far away from a rider. A person can't dig in his heels because hogs are too short and fat, and if a rider picks up his feet, he is practically lying down. In addition, the hair on a hog's back is too short and greasy to grasp it firmly. One day of attempting to ride a hog was enough to last me a lifetime.

On another Sunday when we knew the auction barn was closed, we walked up there. I was walking around looking at cows when I decided I would attempt to ride a cow. Instead of a cow, I found a big bull that looked as if it had a large deformity on its back. The deformity was a large hump right up next to its shoulders. I was sure I could ride a deformed bull, so I climbed onto the top railing and slid onto the bull's back. I figured I could hold on to the hump on its back. I didn't get onto the bull's back good before he let out a bellow and went stark raving mad. I was just about to tell one of my brothers to open the stall gate when the bull threw his rear end up into the air, in a twisting motion, and off I flew. Yeah, the word is *flew*! If a person had seen this spectacle, he or she would have thought I had wings. I landed about eight feet away, in the center aisle of the barn. I had the breath knocked out of me, so I lay on the ground until I was finally able to suck in some air. By the time I could breathe again, I had already decided to leave that bull alone. I figured he was grumpy because he was deformed, so I found something else to do the rest of the day.

A couple of months later I saw another deformed bull, and I asked its owner why it was deformed. He told me that the bull was not deformed; it was a "Brahma Bull." I learned that I had attempted to ride one of the meanest and most dangerous critters alive. I was lucky to still be alive. I never again attempted to climb onto a Brahma Bull, but my brothers and I continued to ride other animals.

Bruce's Auction Barn was the place where I first rode horses and other animals, but it was not the only place where I found animals to ride. We had relatives who lived on farms, and we visited the ones who owned horses or mules as often as we could get our parents to take us.

Mother's side of the family had family reunions regularly. The extended family was large because Mother had eight siblings, all of whom had children. There was always a need for a large place to hold a reunion, so we just naturally traveled to the farm of one of our relatives in Pickens County, where that particular uncle owned a mule. That uncle was King Nix. He was married to my mother's sister Iola, and they had two children named Mildred and Margaret.

On one occasion, the entire extended family was present for a reunion at the farm, and everyone was having a very pleasant time. We had eaten until no one could possibly hold another bite, so after-dinner conversations were going on. It seemed as if there must have been at least twenty separate conversations going at once; however, I was interested in only one. I was interested in the conversation our uncle was involved in about his mule. Our uncle was discussing whether or not he should get his mule from the barn to let all the children ride it. I was all for that, and so were all the other children. We began to ask him to please get the mule out, so he did.

The older boys were called forward to get the first rides, which I thought was a little unfair. I thought that allowing the younger and smaller children to ride first would have been a better idea. Anyway, the big boys began to ride the mule, one at a time, in the area designated by our uncle, and everything was going smoothly. The big boys rode for about an hour, mostly with the mule just walking slowly from one side of the yard to the other. I actually got a little tired and was becoming bored with watching them ride.

Finally, I got my turn to ride, but to my disappointment, I was not going to ride alone because our uncle decided that it would be better to put two of the smaller children on the mule. I guess he did that to get the rides over more quickly. He helped me onto the mule's back, and then he helped one of my cousins get aboard, but in front of me. I couldn't reach the mule's mane, and we had only a halter rope that my cousin was to use to guide the mule. We were riding bareback, so the only thing I could hold onto was my cousin. I put my arms around his torso and prepared for the ride. When our uncle told us to go, I kicked the mule in its sides. Either the mule was tired or I wasn't strong enough to impress it, because the mule just stood there. I wasn't happy with the mule for standing still, so I kicked it again and yelled "Giddy up!" The mule just continued to stand still. Our uncle was standing behind the mule, but to one side. When he saw the mule wasn't moving, I guess he decided to give us a helping hand. I didn't see him approach the mule, but I heard the loud slap he placed on the mule's rump. The next thing I knew, the mule had leaped forward and was running at a full gallop. Needless to say, I was not a great horseman and neither was my cousin. As the mule ran, my cousin was yelling "Whoa," and he was pulling on the halter rope with all his strength. The mule wasn't even slowing down, and then we started to bounce all over the mule's back. A short distance from where we started, we both started to slide from the mule's back. I was holding onto my cousin as tightly as I could, and he was holding onto the halter rope as tightly as he could. However, holding didn't help, and we fell off. When we landed, both of us had the breath knocked out of us, and I'm sure that our attempting to get a breath of air stopped every conversation on the whole farm. The women and girls began to scream and run toward us but the men and boys just walked. It took a minute or so to regain the capacity to breathe normally again, and then we got up from the ground. By that time our uncle had caught his mule, which had stopped running immediately when we fell off. We were ready to get back onto the mule and our uncle was ready to put us back on, but Mother and my cousin's mother prevented us from riding anymore. Our ride had lasted all of about six seconds! I was a very disappointed boy when I left the farm that day, but I knew I would go back another day and ride that mule if it was still there. Meanwhile, we went to other locations to ride animals. Sometimes, I got to ride; other times, I didn't.

One day our whole family went to Oconee County to visit some relatives that Mother had not seen in a long time. We had no idea what to expect when we got there because we had never visited their farm before. I know the name of the man was Leroy Gilstrap, and I think he was a distant cousin, but I don't recall the names of his wife or all of his children. I only remember that one of them was named Oneal. To my knowledge, I had never even met any of them. However, I was surprised by their hospitality. Also, to my surprise, their farm was full of adventurous places to go and things to do.

We went to Leroy's farm pond and fished for a while. While we were fishing, we learned Leroy had a mule, and we immediately asked whether or not we could ride it. Leroy gave the okay.

We put a halter on the mule and brought it out of the barn. James and one of our cousins got onto the back of the mule and rode away, and in a short time they went out of sight. A short time later, we saw the mule running very fast toward the barn, with both boys still aboard. As the mule approached the barn, it ran around the back of it, out of our sight, and headed toward the front of the barn. The rest of us ran around to the front of the barn just in time to see the mule make the last turn to the front of the barn, but there was no longer anyone on its back. The mule went into its stall, and we ran around the barn to see where the boys had gotten to. There they were, on the ground beside the barn. They were not injured, but they were very upset. A large board protruding from the corner of the barn had swept both boys from the back of the mule.

Apparently, Leroy had seen what happened because he came down and put a quick stop to our planned day of riding his mule. He said he had forgotten the mule didn't like being taken so far away from the barn. He also told us the mule had run under that board to get people off its back before. He had been meaning to saw the board off, but he just hadn't thought of it before we came. I left Leroy's farm without getting a ride on his mule, but for over fifty years I have laughed about James and our cousin getting swept off the mule's back. However, James and the rest of the family laughed just as heartily at me because of one of my wild and scary rides that occurred a few months later.

For two weeks one summer, I visited an uncle named Clyde Thomas who lived at Easley with his wife Bertha and their two children, Lester and Larry. I was always afraid of that particular uncle because he was a big man, with a booming voice. He also had a way of looking at someone when he was angry that made the hair on the back of my neck stand up. However, I had no real reason to be afraid, because he was not a menace at all. He was always very kind to me, and when I was older, he became a friend, as well as a beloved uncle.

In Clyde's barn, I discovered that he had bought a horse. Until that day, although I had seen him many times since he had moved from the city to the country, he had never mentioned that he had a horse, so I was somewhat surprised. Not only did he have a horse, he also had a saddle and bridle. Of all the animals I had ridden over the years, I had never had an opportunity to sit on a saddled horse. I was so excited by the time I got back to his house it must have shown. I asked him if I could ride the horse, and he walked down to the barn with me to saddle it up and put the bridle on it. Clyde told me that the horse's name was Buck. I climbed onto the horse's back as quickly as I could, and the feel of the saddle was very different than anything I had even imagined. It was wonderful. The saddle was western, with a saddle horn and stirrups. I placed my feet into the stirrups and took hold of the reins, which were split-reins, one rein on each side of the bridle, and they were not tied together. I just held one rein loosely in each hand.

I got the horse moving by just telling it to go. It walked at a pretty fast pace, so I decided there was no need to kick him or to use the reins to speed him up. I let the horse walk to the paved road that ran in front of Clyde's house, and from the edge of the paved road I could see a dirt road that branched off of the paved road on the opposite side. I yelled to my uncle to get permission to ride the horse down the dirt road, and he said it would be okay.

I rode about a quarter of a mile before I came to a small, shallow stream that flowed across the road. I figured I would just let the horse walk through the water and continue on down the dirt road. Wrong! As I started to walk the horse into the stream, the horse decided it wanted to drink some water. Just then a water snake swam right under the horse's nose, and when the horse saw the snake, it reared up just as I have seen Silver rear up just before the Lone Ranger said "Hi Ho, Silver, away!" I was holding on as tightly as I could. In fact, I had let go of one rein so I could grab hold of the saddle horn. When the loose rein fell, it struck the horse on its foreleg, and I think the horse must have thought the rein was the snake. The horse reared up again, and all in one motion turned around and took off running as fast as it could run toward the paved road. I was hanging on to the saddle horn with one hand and the one rein I still had in my hand with the other. I was trying to reach the loose rein, but I wasn't having much luck. I stood up in the stirrups and leaned forward onto the horse's neck in an effort to reach the loose rein. Just as I thought I was about to get the rein, the horse reached the paved road, and the horse did not even slow down. It ran across the paved road at full speed, jumped over the small embankment, and began to gallop across a freshly plowed field.

Several dangerous things were happening at one time. A person cannot guide a frightened horse with only one rein as I was attempting to do. A horse crossing a paved road in such a manner could have run into an automobile. It is also highly dangerous to be on a horse's back when it is running across a freshly plowed field because the chances of a horse stepping into a hole and breaking a leg are very real. I was quite frightened.

In the distance, off to my right, I could see Clyde and Larry sitting in chairs in their yard. I began to yell at the top of my lungs. I was attempting to tell them that I was on a runaway horse. They began to motion for me to come in their direction, but the horse had another idea. The horse just continued to run, full speed, across the plowed field. I was yelling for help and still trying to reach the loose rein. Finally, I was able to reach the top of the rein where it connected to the bridle, and I pulled it back and let it run through my hand until I had a firm grip on it. When I had both reins in hand, I began to pull back on them in an effort to stop the horse. I got the horse to stop by pulling on the reins and yelling, "Whoa." Once the horse stopped, I let it stand still while I tied the two reins together. I certainly didn't want to lose a rein again.

I rode the horse as it walked back across the plowed field and into Clyde's yard. Clyde immediately began to chastise me for being such an idiot that I would gallop a horse across a plowed field. As soon as I could get a word in, I explained to him what had really happened. He thought I was showing off. When he realized what had really been going on, he began laughing. He laughed about my wild ride for the rest of my two-week stay. I had never seen Clyde laugh so much, and it made me feel good. He let me ride his horse every day of my visit, and the visit was one of the most pleasant experiences of my life. Riding the horse was really my biggest adventure at Clyde's house, but after two weeks, I was happy to return to the mill village.

Freight train passing behind Poe Mill – Poe Elementary School at lower left.
Photo Courtesy of Greenville County Historical Society. Greenville, South Carolina.

Type of Locomotive we often saw at Poe Mill. Photo Courtesy of Greenville County
Historical Society. Greenville, South Carolina.

Living in a cotton mill village was a little bit like living in Disney World: there were places of adventure everywhere. We didn't see a lot of cartoon characters, but we saw a lot of characters that could have passed as cartoon characters. We might not have seen a lot of cartoon animals, but we saw a lot of real animals. We didn't need to see Adventure Land because we had our own, and we enjoyed it to its fullest. We even had our own adventure rides.

One adventure ride passed through our mill village every day. However, we had been told time and again not to get too close to it. Still, we got close to it every time we walked to the livestock auction barn, the junkyard, and many of our other destinations. We even rode it occasionally. The adventure ride was a freight train.

We walked along the railroad tracks to many of our destinations, and the train came by almost every time we got on the tracks. We just stepped to the side of the tracks and let it pass and then got back on the tracks and continued on our journey.

We had a hideout, at least that's what we called it, among the trees in the mill village pasture and adjacent to the railroad tracks, and we went to the hideout to play regularly. In fact, some of our best games of cowboys and Indians were played in and around the hideout.

From the hideout, we watched the trains go by and, in the summertime, we were at the hideout practically every day. We especially enjoyed being there when a train passed by. For some reason, there was a certain fascination about watching the huge steam locomotive pulling the passenger and freight cars and the little red caboose. We just loved seeing the red caboose—for what reason I have no idea. I guess it was because it was always the last car on the train, or it could have been that there was always a railroad worker hanging onto the ladder of the caboose with a lantern in his hand. He would wave the lantern one way and the train would move forward. Then, he would wave the lantern another way and the train would go backwards. We could have watched that action all day. Sometimes, it seems as if we did.

It was about that time in my life that I read the story *The Little Engine That Could*. If I am not mistaken, there was also a story titled *The Little Red Caboose*.

A steam-driven locomotive usually pulled the train. The steam was apparently provided by the burning of coal in the engine furnace to heat water in the engine boiler. We sometimes saw engine operators shoveling coal into the furnace. It appeared that the engineers had access to coal from a railcar loaded with coal that was connected to the rear of the locomotive. The sound of the train as it moved along on the tracks sounded like "choo-choo" to us. As the trains traveled by, we could see large plumes of smoke billowing from the smoke exhaust chimney on the top of the front portion of the engine. We could see the large piston on the side of the engine moving back and forth, and steam was constantly escaping, or being released, which made a very loud hissing sound. Just to hear the sounds of the engine was enough to satisfy us for hours.

The train had regular schedules, but I'm not sure what they were. I think there were two trains in the morning and two in the afternoon. Each time a train left going north, one would come south within thirty minutes or so.

We always knew when the southbound train was coming because, when it reached a particular location, the engineer would sound the whistle that was operated by steam like the locomotive engine. The whistle would start off with a low whining sound and build to a higher-pitched whining sound. It sounded as if it were attempting to speak. Four very distinct tones, or notes, came from the whistle.

Mother told us a story about a woman named Lucy who had been killed on the railroad tracks several years before. She said that every time the train whistle blew, it was saying "Poor old Lucy." The way Mother said "Poor old Lucy," using two clearly separate and distinct sounds for the word "Lucy," she made us believe the four sounds we were hearing from the train whistle were, undoubtedly, those very words. It was spooky to say the least. We enjoyed stories that made the hair on the back of our necks rise, so we loved to hear the train whistle. We even repeated the Lucy phrase every time the whistle blew, and it became a ritual.

We were also able to observe the passengers who were riding in the passenger cars of some of the trains. They always looked rich to us, so we just assumed they were. We certainly didn't know any cotton mill workers who could afford to ride a train. Later in life, I learned that a lot of the passengers had indeed been cotton mill workers. We just didn't know any of them.

There was another class of passengers we observed on the trains that the railway operators didn't know they had. At least, they didn't want to have them. They were hoboes, and we would see them almost every day, hanging onto whatever they could, sometimes underneath the train. Sometimes we saw them as they moved from underneath the train to an open freight car. We even saw some of them climb into coal cars. The movement of the hoboes looked very dangerous to us.

Most of the hoboes were thought to be tramps or vagrants. In fact, most of the hoboes were good, hard-working people who just happened to be on hard times. Even as small children, we understood that. Jobs were hard to find in the 1940s, and the hoboes were traveling from town to town, looking for work. At one time, even Dad had been a hobo for a couple of trips. If they had no money to pay the fare, they would get to some location to find work any way they could. If my family were in such dire straits as some of those hoboes' families were, I would do the same thing if necessary. I don't especially care for tramps and vagrants, but if a person is doing the best he can to support his family, I don't consider him to be either a tramp or a vagrant.

We had hoboes visiting our hideout almost every week because they had learned the train traveled very slowly as it passed by. There was a reason for the slowness of the train at that location. When the northbound train left the depot, it did not have time to pick up much speed before it reached our hideout. When the southbound train reached our hideout, it was already traveling at a slower speed in preparation to stop at the depot. The hoboes would hide in the bushes adjacent to the railroad tracks, and as the train passed they would watch until the engine was out of sight and then jump from the bushes onto the train. Some would jump through open doors of the freight cars; some would actually go underneath the train while it was moving so slowly and cling to something; others would simply jump onto one of the ladders that were on almost every car. As I watched them, I knew if I ever hopped onto a train, it would be on a ladder. The ladders almost reached the ground so it would be easy to get on one, even for a small child.

One day we were on our way to the livestock auction barn when a train started to pass by our hideout. It was moving very slowly, as we had seen the longer trains do many times, and someone in the crowd suggested that we should hop the train and ride to the auction barn. That's all it took. As soon as the engine was out of sight, we ran for the train. Every one of us hopped onto the train, each one on a different ladder. The train moved slowly toward the auction barn, about half a mile away. That was my very first train ride, and it was exhilarating. The train didn't seem to pick up any speed, and when we reached the auction barn we just jumped off and scrambled up the railroad embankment. By the time the caboose with the railroad worker in it got to that point, we were long gone. We had traveled to the auction barn to ride animals, but riding animals seemed a little less exciting after the train ride.

After that first train ride, we were hooked. Why walk to the auction barn when we could ride? We jumped trains many times after that. We always avoided the Pacific and Northern passenger trains because we would have been noticed too easily by passengers. Instead, we rode freight trains. The freight trains usually moved slowly because they consisted of so many heavy freight and cattle cars. There were times when we actually counted more than one hundred freight cars in one train. Sometimes, the trains were so long and heavy that they were pulled by two engines and pushed by a third engine behind the caboose. The trains were always interesting. In about 1950 or 1951, we began to notice that a new type of engine was pulling trains. We asked about the new type of engine and learned that some of the newer engines were diesel-operated. The diesel engines seemed to be stronger and faster than the steam locomotives. In fact, there was one diesel-engine train ride with an older friend that I will never forget. We waited at the hideout until the train came along and then hopped onto the ladders. Our plan was to jump off at the auction barn, but the plan turned out to be badly flawed. Unexpectedly, the train rapidly picked up speed, and by the time we realized we could not safely jump off at the auction barn, we were already passing it. All we could do was hang on until the train slowed down, and we hoped it would be soon. After we had been on the train for what seemed to be more than an hour, I was getting both scared and tired. The train roared along at a very fast pace for quite a few miles, with us hanging onto ladders. Eventually, the train began to slow down because it was about to enter a station or some other town. When the train slowed enough for us to jump off, we did. We quickly found a place to hide before the caboose got to us, because we certainly didn't want the railway workers to see us, especially that far from home.

After the train passed, we came out of hiding. Our first thought was *How are we going to get back home?* We were too frightened to tell anyone who we were or how we got there. We were too scared to even let anyone know we were there. I don't know how we managed to remain calm, but we did, and we began to think of ways to get back home. We decided we would just have to jump on the southbound train and ride it back, so we walked to a curve in the tracks and waited in the bushes. We figured the train would be traveling slowly because it would be leaving the station the northbound train had just pulled into. Sure enough, we heard the train coming long before it arrived because it was quite noisy. We hopped aboard as soon as the engine was out of sight, and we hung on until the train reached our hideout. We didn't even consider jumping off at the auction barn. When I jumped off the train, I hit the ground running, and I ran all the way home. I was happy to see our house, and I never told any of my family members about my trip to wherever. Later, I was told by my friend that we had traveled all the way to Spartanburg, South Carolina. According to him, our round-trip ride was approximately sixty miles. What a wild, frightening, and tiring ride for such little hoboes.

Although I did ride many more trains after my frightening train ride, I didn't ride trains or venture too far away from the mill village for awhile. I just played games at the school yard or at our house. One of our favorite games to play was marbles. We had several different marbles games, such as ring, pig's eye, chase, and throw to the line. We always played for keeps, which meant that we kept any marbles we won from our opponents, and our opponents kept any marbles they could win from us. Regardless of which game of marbles we played, the idea was basically the same. Each player put the same number of marbles into the game as each of the other players. When the game started, the first player to shoot his toy into the marbles could possibly never lose his turn. He could win all of the marbles or miss a shot, and the next player would take a turn. When the game was over, someone usually had won some marbles, if not all of them.

James emerged as the best of the marbles players in our family. He had a technique for shooting a steel ball bearing, which he called his toy, into a ring full of marbles, knocking a marble from the ring and sticking at the very spot at which the marble was struck. That meant that he could continue shooting until he missed a shot. He was so good that he played marbles with adults and won. On one particular day, James left early that morning and came back the same afternoon carrying a flour sack that was made to hold twenty-five pounds of flour completely full of marbles he had won from a neighborhood adult. I could only dream of being so good, but as a result of his winning, we had lots of marbles any time we needed some.

I enjoyed playing marbles, but I preferred contact games because there was always a little more excitement than playing marbles. When we lived in the mill village of Cateechee, we observed some older boys playing a game they called ring-a-leebo. I'm not sure about the spelling of ring-a-leebo, but we still remembered the rules after we moved to Fourth Street at Poe Mill so we described them to our friends. However, we wanted the game to be tough, so we added a few rules of our own. We began soon afterward to play ring-a-leebo with our friends.

The game was similar to tag, but it required a lot more strength, speed, and agility. Unfortunately, it also required the ability to fight sometimes. Instead of having one person to be the search person (it), the game was made up of two teams. One was the search team (it), while the other team hid and was later hunted by the searchers.

Usually, at least ten people played in a game of ring-a-leebo. There was a captain of each team, but only for the purpose of choosing teammates. All team members were equal once the team selection was completed. The team selection began with the flip of a coin, and the captain who won the coin toss selected the first teammate. Then the other captain chose a teammate. That alternate selection process continued until everyone who wanted to play had been chosen to be on a team. Each captain attempted to get the biggest, strongest, fastest, and meanest team members he could find. Sometimes, a team might consist of ten people, but the more team members we had, the more fun we had.

We drew a large ring in the dirt to serve as the area the search team had to stay in while the opposing team ran off somewhere and hid. The ring also served as a prison for captured hiding team members once the hunt began.

A coin toss also decided which team hid first. The winner of the coin toss usually hid first, but not always. Once a decision was made, the search team stood inside the ring for a minimum of three minutes. Then the search team left the ring in search of opposing team members.

When an opposing team member was spotted, he had to be chased and caught. He might escape if he were fast enough. If he were not fast enough to escape, he would still have the opportunity to resist capture. The search team was required to catch and hold onto an opposing team member while tapping him on the head three times and yelling, "ring-a-leebo." If the person could fight the search team off before they managed to go through the entire process, then he could escape. The game sometimes became rough and dangerous while players were attempting to complete the process. However, once the search team was able to complete the process, the opposing team member, regardless of how angry and beat up he might be, was required to stop resisting and go to the ring to be held prisoner.

The search team had to leave at least two guards at the ring with the prisoner. Otherwise, a team member of the hiding team who had not yet been captured could run through the ring and yell "ring-a-leebo," and the captured teammate was free to escape, if he could.

The guards were usually the biggest and roughest of the team members. They were supposed to be alert at all times, and they were supposed to prevent anyone from running through the ring. The guards attempted to stop escapes by capturing any teammate of a prisoner before he could reach the ring; however, if they could not stop him from reaching the ring, they attempted to capture him even if the other prisoners escaped. When the biggest and strongest of the hiding team were not yet captured, the number of guards was sometimes increased to prevent escape. If the big, strong, and tough had been captured, the number of guards could be decreased to provide more team members for the search for the remainder of the hiding team. Once an entire team was captured, the search team then became the hunted team, and the captured team became the search team. Each game could last for many hours.

I remember one occasion very well when I did not want to be captured. I climbed to the very top of an oak tree. I must have been at least sixty feet off the ground. I was one of the smallest of all the team members, and I could not resist capture by fighting, so I climbed onto the smallest of branches in the treetop. I thought I was well hidden among the leaves; however, James spotted me. James was four years older than I, but he wasn't much larger than I was. He came up that tree like a squirrel, and he was determined to capture me. I kicked him on the head and shoulders numerous times, but that didn't slow him down. He climbed right onto the tiny limbs and captured me. It's a thousand wonders both of us didn't tumble to the ground during our struggle. James was not too happy about being kicked a few times, so he didn't hesitate to "tap" me on the head pretty hard. We had a good fight in the treetop, but I lost, so I had to climb down and submit myself to the humility of being placed in the prison ring.

I always enjoyed playing ring-a-leebo even though it was a tough game. If anyone thinks organized sports, such as football and hockey, are rough and dangerous games, he should just try ring-a-leebo. Almost every capture begins or ends with a fight.

Playing contact sports such as ring-a-leebo, baseball, and football was always fun and exciting, but we occasionally received minor injuries. Sports injuries, however, were not the only type of injuries we received. I remember one injury I received while playing on a school playground that had nothing to do with sports, and Dad almost received an identical injury. I still wonder if poetic justice was at play.

When I was three years old, I lied, convincingly, to save myself from getting a whipping I probably deserved. As a result of my lying, all three of my brothers took a whipping that should have come my way. When I was somewhat older, I took a whipping from Dad for something someone else did, and I was totally innocent. Some people might call that poetic justice. Perhaps they are right, but I recall another incident that might also be considered poetic justice.

Not long before we moved away from Poe Mill, Dad decided he wanted to go to a town called Clinton and get a job. The town of Clinton was about forty miles away in Laurens County, South Carolina. Dad traveled there, began living with relatives, and got a job in a cotton mill.

Mother refused to quit her job at Poe Mill and move to Clinton; however, she took all of us children there to visit for a few days. I think she was really thinking about moving to Clinton, but she wanted to see what the place was like before she quit her job at Poe Mill. By that time Poe Mill had sold the mill village houses, and Mother and Dad were buying our house on Fourth Street. They were allowed to pay just a few dollars per week for the house, so moving could have meant a big loss to our family.

When we arrived in Clinton, we discovered Dad didn't even have a place for us to stay. Our relatives lived in a small, four-room house, and they had three children. We could not just turn around and go back home, so we were forced to pack ourselves like sardines into the house with our relatives. All of us children, including the children of our relatives, had to sleep on the floor.

The second day we were in Clinton, we quickly discovered the mill village was covered with ants. It didn't matter how careful we were, ants were all over us all the time. We suffered from a lot of ant bites, and Mother was not happy with the situation at all. Living in such cramped quarters with absolutely no privacy was a little irritating, but being assaulted by ants made things much worse.

Within a few hours after arriving in Clinton, my brothers and I had already roamed all over the entire mill village looking for places to play. Just a couple of blocks from our relative's house, we found a school playground. About a week later, we were playing at the school playground when I injured myself while attempting to run up a stainless steel slide. I had gotten bored with climbing the slide ladder over and over, so I thought I could just run up the slide and then slide down it. As I was running up the slide, my feet slipped from under me and I struck the side rail of the slide with my forehead, just above my right eye. The sound was like an explosion inside my head, but I didn't realize I was injured. I jumped up and began to continue running up the slide, but then I saw the dripping blood. I immediately panicked and began calling for one of my brothers. One of them walked with me back to our relatives' house. When Mother looked at the injury, she immediately told Dad we had to get to a doctor. Our relatives told them we should just go to the mill clinic because there were no other doctors around.

As we walked from our relatives' house to the clinic, Dad began to lecture me about watching where I was going. The intensity of the lecture I was getting never lessened during the four-block trip to the clinic. It was obvious Dad was highly upset that he had to take me to the clinic. He didn't seem to be concerned about my injury at all, and I don't think he even knew what had happened to me. I think he just thought I had not been paying attention to where I was going. All he talked about was I should watch where I was going.

As we entered the gate to the cotton mill property, Dad was still fussing at me and Mother was attempting to get him to calm down. Suddenly, I heard a loud *thud*. Dad immediately fell to the ground, and Mother bent over him and called his name several times, but he was unconscious. I looked up and saw a metal pipe sticking out from the brick pillar of the fence just at the right height to strike Dad on his forehead. Amazingly, Dad was struck at about the exact location on his head as I had been on mine. He wasn't cut, but he had a whopper of a knot on his head!

When Dad regained consciousness, Mother and I helped him to his feet. We went into the clinic, where the doctor treated Dad first, and then me. He gave Dad something for pain, and he had to use two clamps to close my wound.

All the way back to our relatives' house, Dad was stone cold silent. In fact, he was so silent that I was a little frightened by it. He never mentioned watching where I was going again, not even until the day he died. Was that poetic justice? Mother and all of us children have talked and laughed about that incident for many years.

Within two days of my accident, we had packed up and gone home to Poe Mill. I have no recollection about how we got home; I just know we did.

My siblings and I were injured numerous times while we lived on Fourth Street. Most of the time we were not injured badly enough for professional medical care. We were also sick on numerous occasions. By the time we moved into the large house on Fourth Street in the mill village of Poe Mill, all of us children had already been through such illnesses as chicken pox, mumps, and whooping cough. We had also had head lice and the itch. Less than a year after we had moved to Fourth Street, all five of us children were infected with the red measles. In each of those instances, Mother had called a doctor, and a doctor treated us in each instance. However, there were numerous times when we had head colds, chest congestion, influenza, stomach viruses, or just complained that we didn't feel good. In those instances, Mother treated us.

We learned very early in life not to complain about anything remotely relating to illness, unless we were so sick that we had no choice. If we said anything within earshot of Mother about not feeling well, she would go into action with what she thought were the ultimate cures for all illnesses. If the television program titled *The Beverly Hillbillies* had wanted a real-life character to play the role of Granny as a doctor, they could have used Mother. Among the many medicines Mother used were Vicks Salve, turpentine, kerosene, pine oil, sugar, castor oil, honey, whiskey, mustard, and baking soda.

When one of us complained about having an upset stomach or a cold, all of us received treatment. I never understood why, but the first thing Mother always thought she should do was to get us cleaned out. In order to clean us out, she gave each of us a large dose of castor oil. Castor oil was the most God-awful stuff we ever had in our mouths, and all of us had difficulty swallowing it. She would pinch our noses together while she forced the castor oil into our mouths. Then she would attempt to hold our mouths shut to force us to swallow the awful-tasting stuff. If we managed to swallow it, she would immediately give us a glass of orange juice to counter the awful taste and feel of the oil. I never understood how forcing me to swallow something that was going to make me much sicker than I was already was going to make me feel better. Mother knew I always gagged and threw up when she gave castor oil to me, but that didn't deter her at all. If the others had to take it, so did I. As soon as I had finished puking my guts out, Mother had another spoonful waiting. She would force me to swallow it, and then give me some orange juice. Eventually, I would manage to keep a dose of the oil down. Within a short time, all of us were cleaned out.

Once we were thoroughly cleaned out, we would be so weak we thought we were going to die, and then Mother would bring each of us a bowl of chicken soup. I never understood how she expected us to eat anything after she had just made us so sick we had no appetite. However, she made sure that each of us ate the soup before she would leave the room. Whether we felt better or not, we would say we felt better. None of us wanted to go through that routine again. I think the thought of going through the routine again was probably what cured us of the illness. At least, it stopped us from complaining. Although I think castor oil was made for the purpose of punishing kids who were not feeling well but not sick enough for a doctor, Mother must have thought it was a miracle drug. As soon as she reached for the bottle, I always got well!

If we came down with deep chest colds, Mother applied miracle cloths to our chests. She used large, soft cloths onto which she applied a mixture of stuff, such as Vicks salve, turpentine, pine oil, kerosene, mustard, flour, water, and anything else she thought might work. Sometimes, she called the cloths "mustard plaster"; at other times she had no name for the cloths. Once she had all of her ingredients applied to the cloths, she placed them close to our heater to get them warm, and her version of warm was hot. When they were warm enough to suit her, she placed the cloths on our chests. OUCH! The cloths were always too hot, so in the process of being cured, we suffered a few minor burns. I always thought the pain was a part of the cure, and I also always thought I would have gotten well just as quickly without the cloths, but Mother gave full credit to them. I was not about to argue with her for fear I might be recovering from an injury rather an illness.

Although I could be mistaken, I think I recall that Mother gave sugar mixed with turpentine or kerosene to us for the purpose of breaking up congestion in our chests when the cloths failed to work. Sometimes, she applied the cloths and also gave the mixture to us. Mother filled a spoon with sugar and then added a couple of drops of kerosene or turpentine, and we had to eat the mixture slowly. I didn't like the taste of the mixture at all, but I could swallow it much easier than I could swallow castor oil. The mixture never caused vomiting, so I didn't resist it so much. However, I have wondered since childhood whether or not the mixture had any real curative powers. I just always figured Mother was determined to either cure us or kill us. I feel very lucky I am still alive.

Although I don't recall ever having a toothache when I was growing up, I do recall having a few loose teeth that needed to come out. Mother was just as good a dentist as she was a doctor. The only method she had was simple; she used sewing thread and a doorknob. She doubled the sewing thread and attached one end of it to the loose tooth and then she attached the other end to the doorknob of an open door. When I least expected it, she quickly slammed the door shut and, as the door was slammed, the string jerked the loose tooth right out of my mouth. I usually didn't even realize the tooth was gone until I felt the hole it left behind and tasted the blood coming from the hole. I don't recall ever crying as a result of a tooth being jerked out. I think it occurred so quickly I was just totally numbed.

If we ever had bruises, abrasions, or minor cuts, we could always expect to submerge the injury in a container of water and Epsom salts. Mother said the salts would draw out anything that might cause an infection, and if there were no chance of infection, the salts would still draw out the pain. I never understood how the salts were supposed to work; I just did what Mother said to do. I thought I probably would have healed just as well without the salts, but if I argued with Mother, I might have had another bruise or two to apply it to. To heal or not to heal—that was the question!

I tried never to tell Mother when a bee or wasp had stung me. Although I never received any treatment from her for a sting, I know she talked about snuff juice being good for bee and wasp stings. Snuff is tobacco that has been ground into a powder. People dipped snuff by placing the powder into their mouths, usually between their cheeks and gums. Snuff juice was nothing more, or less, than a thick, horrible-looking spit containing snuff and saliva. When I was young, Mother was a snuff dipper. Although she usually spit into a container, I have seen her spit as far as ten to fifteen feet while she was dipping snuff, and when it landed, the spit looked absolutely awful. I knew I never wanted any of that filth rubbed onto my skin, no matter how many times I got stung. I was also very careful not to step into any snuff spit. Thankfully, I was not allergic to bees, because I did get stung many times. I just pulled the stingers out and licked my wounds. Five minutes later, I was trying to catch another bee.

In fairness to Mother, she did call a doctor when we were so sick that she couldn't cure us. Back then, doctors actually made house calls, and I remember a doctor coming to our house on numerous occasions. It's just too bad he didn't advise Mother to discontinue her practice. He didn't, so we learned early that if we weren't really sick, we didn't complain.

During the years we lived on Fourth Street, I heard Dad tell a couple of stories that I have never forgotten. I don't know whether I didn't forget them because the stories were that good or whether he just told them so many times over the years that I have practically memorized them. Dad was a very good storyteller, and he told some stories so many times we actually got to the point that we knew them as well as he did. I remember one story he told about an incident that happened while we lived on Reid School Road. The story was as follows: Dad was an avid hunter of small game. One day he went rabbit hunting, caught a possum, but came home with a chicken. He said he knew it sounded incredible, but it was absolutely true. He left home to go rabbit hunting, and after searching for rabbits for a long time, to no avail, he spotted a possum. He ran the possum down, caught it, and started home. As he was walking by a neighbor's house, the neighbor asked if he could see the possum. He readily showed the possum to the neighbor, and the neighbor offered to trade a chicken for the possum. Dad gladly traded the possum for the chicken, which he carried home to be cooked for supper that very night.

Another story Dad told also involved hunting: One day when Dad was still a teenager, he and one of his brothers went rabbit hunting, although neither of them had a license to hunt. While they were hunting for rabbits, they also had to be on the lookout for the game warden.

They had been hunting for only a short period of time when, sure enough, the game warden showed up. They separated and ran away from the game warden as fast as they could run. The game warden, apparently thinking he could catch Dad, chased him. As Dad ran, he began to put some distance between himself and the game warden. He ran to the edge of a very wide, deep ravine, and was trying to decide whether to run alongside the ravine or cross it when he spotted a rabbit in its bed on the other side of the ravine. He ran down the embankment into the ravine, shot the rabbit, and then ran up the embankment on the opposite side of the ravine from the game warden. He looked back and saw the now-tired game warden approaching the ravine. He held the rabbit high in the air and shook it at the game warden and continued to run and escaped capture.

The next day Dad went into town to get a haircut and had just sat down in the barber's chair when the game warden walked into the barbershop. Dad, being somewhat quick witted, told the barber that he wanted a shave before he got his hair cut. The barber lathered Dad's face and, while he was shaving him, the game warden told the story of the hunter that got away. In concluding the story, the game warden said he believed he would recognize the hunter if he saw him again. He also said he was determined to catch him. Dad just sat there quietly and listened. Before the barber had finished shaving Dad, the game warden left the barbershop. Dad got his haircut and went home, and he was never captured by the game warden. Dad told those stories over and over, and we laughed with him every time.

Telling these stories reminds me of where I came from and of all the fun my siblings and I had at Poe Mill village in the midst of our struggles—a time when the sharing of our work, imaginations, ingenuity, and mischief began the development of all of us into well-rounded and determined individuals. I am happy that I remember so much from Poe Mill because I can pass these stories on to my children and grandchildren just as Dad passed his stories to us. When we left Poe Mill in 1952, we moved across town to a place named Mills Mill.

We lived at 15 Fourth Street in the village of Poe Mill for about five years. Harry Truman was still president of the United States, and J. Strom Thurmond was the governor of South Carolina from 1947 to 1951. Strom Thurmond actually ran for the office of president of the United States against Harry Truman in 1948 while Strom was serving as governor of South Carolina. Strom ran as a Dixiecrat, but he lost the election. James Francis Byrnes became the governor of South Carolina in 1951.

An industrial revolution was taking place all across America during the whole time we were living on Fourth Street at Poe Mill. In South Carolina, a Greenville resident and businessman named Charles Daniel was serving as chairman of a newly created Research, Planning, and Development Board. The board's primary goal was to increase the industrial base in the state. The state was growing, and business in South Carolina began its move toward diversity. Although the textile industry was continuing to grow, work choices in South Carolina were offering workers many avenues away from textiles and farms. Many people in South Carolina were pleased with the progress of the industrial revolution and thankful for new job opportunities.

The city of Greenville was also growing rapidly. The Augusta Street section was annexed in 1946, and in 1948 the Lewis Plaza Shopping Center opened on Augusta Street. It was also in 1948 that the areas of West Greenville, Overbrook, Eastover, Laurens Road, and a section of Highway 29 were annexed into the city of Greenville. Greenville was designated a metropolitan area by the Census Bureau in 1950. A city manager style of government began in the city of Greenville in 1951. The mayor was J. Kenneth Cass, and the new city manager was Gerald W. Shaw. I visited the city of Greenville many times while I was a resident of Mills Mill.

Mills Mill

*M*ills Mill was built in 1897 by Otis Prentiss Mills and his son-in-law Walter Moore at the intersection of Mills Avenue and Guess Street on the banks of Brushy Creek just south of the city of Greenville. The village was small to begin with, but eventually contained 215 houses, a gymnasium, a baseball park, two churches, and an elementary school.

Dad began work at Mills Mill as a doffer in the spinning room, and Mother began work as a spinner. As far as their work was concerned, nothing had changed. They continued to work at the same type jobs they had worked at since they each left school at the end of the sixth grade.

Mills Mill. Photo Courtesy of Greenville County Historical Society. Greenville, South Carolina.

We moved into a small four-room house at 55 Ridge Street in the mill village, and for the first time we had a bathroom that had a commode, bathtub, and sink. We also had hot and cold running water for the first time. We bought an oil-burning heater so we no longer had to buy coal or chop wood.

However, one of the first things I took notice of was the fact that Grace had no bedroom again. She was already a junior at Parker High School. Our move was a step backward for Grace. All of us boys were ranging in ages from eleven to sixteen, and Grace could no longer be expected to share a bedroom with us. She was forced to sleep on a bed that had been placed in the living room. I felt sorry for Grace, but there was nothing I could have done to change things. However, Grace was very busy with school studies, her after-school and Saturday job, church, and dating. She didn't spend a lot of time at home.

We moved to Mills Mill in March 1952. In September 1952, Grace began her senior year of high school; on November 22, 1952, she turned eighteen; and in December 1952, she was married.

I don't know whether or not our moving to Mills Mill when she was a junior in high school and being taken away from all of her many friends at Poe Mill had anything to do with her decision to get married at such a young

Grace and Carl Satterfield – December, 1952.

age. However, I do know I rarely saw Grace during the summer before her marriage. Maybe her decision was based solely on love and her desire to be married to the person with whom she was in love, but I sometimes think Grace had just had enough of our parents' uprooting and moving ways. Maybe she felt that getting married would put some stability into her life. She married a great guy, Carl Satterfield, who became just another big brother as far as I was concerned. Carl worked for Ray Miller Tile Company in Greenville County when he and Grace got married. However, he eventually started his own tile business that was very successful right up until the day of his retirement many years later.

Grace and Carl moved into a house at Poe Mill, the village we had just moved away from. She continued going to school even though it was against the rules for a married person to attend Parker High School at the time. She kept her marriage a secret from school officials, and she graduated from Parker High School in June 1953. We were all very proud of her. She had begun working for a stockbroker named Joe McAlister in the city of Greenville before she graduated from high school, and she never looked at a cotton mill as a probable way of life for her. She had loosened her shackles of cotton mill dependency when she began working at Kash and Karry at the age of fourteen; now she had broken her chains. One of us children had attained freedom to find a different way of life. I think Mother and Dad were proud of Grace; I know I was, and I was planning not to be far behind her.

As far as all of us boys were concerned, Mills Mill offered a totally different lifestyle than Poe Mill. There were no golf courses, no junkyards, no livestock auction barn, no fields of insects, and no nearby railroad tracks; and we had to leave our cogwheel wagons behind. It was as if we had to start life all over again; however, we still had our imaginations and ingenuity. We would discover things to do and build things to play with. After all, we were in a mill village. There must be some adventure and excitement somewhere; we just had to find it.

William was halfway through the tenth grade and James was in the ninth grade at Parker High School. David and I began attending Mills Mill

175

Elementary School. David was in the seventh grade, and I was in the fifth grade. We had only three months left in that school year.

Because William and James were in high school and David and I were still in elementary school, we developed different friendships with classmates and village residents. James joined the Red Shield Club and spent quite a bit of time there, so he wasn't around nearly as much as he had been before. I never knew what the Red Shield Club was all about because David and I were too young to attend, and we never joined when we got older. David and I began to play and travel together more than ever. Sometimes James would be with us, but William rarely was. William had maintained strong relationships with several of his friends from Poe Mill so he visited them or they came by to pick him up frequently. William also went to work at Dixie Home grocery store. Dixie Home later merged with Winn and Lovett and is now called Winn-Dixie.

The store William worked at was on Augusta Street. Shortly after we moved to Ridge Street, William no longer had ample time to do some other things the rest of us did. He also had begun to date; however, when he was not in school, working, dating, or with some of his friends from Poe Mill, he

Dixie Home Grocery Store. Photo Courtesy of Greenville County Historical Society. Greenville, South Carolina.

did spend some time with us. Whether William was around or not, the other three of us explored the mill village and played together.

I will never forget one of our first explorations of the mill village, but I don't recall whether or not William was involved in it. I don't think he was. Anyway, a small creek was located about a hundred feet from our house, and we went there to play. In the stream, we noticed some large drainage pipes that appeared to run from the stream under the roadway. The pipes were open and big enough for even the largest of us to crawl into. The pipes looked inviting, so we all just crawled into them. We crawled through the first drainage pipe from the stream all the way to the next roadway intersection. At that location, pipes ran in three directions. We were interested in finding out where and how far we could travel by crawling through the drainage pipes, so we crawled and crawled. At times, we came to what appeared to be a dead end because the next pipe section appeared to be too small to crawl into. However, we just lay down and scooted along on our bellies until we came to another larger section of pipe. We never gave a thought to the danger of our being inside a drainage pipe. However, if a rainstorm had come up while we were inside a long stretch of drainage pipe, we could have been drowned before we could have gotten out. We toured about half of the mill village by way of drainage pipes. Occasionally, we would come out at an intersection or a culvert to see where we were. Although we were doing a dangerous thing, none of us ever got hurt. After a few days, we discontinued our drainage pipe explorations and decided to further check out the creek.

There were many trees, hedges, and other understory plants growing along the banks of the creek, and the growth was so thick it was practically impossible to walk through. We decided to get into the water and walk under the heavy growth, and it worked perfectly. From the creek bed, it appeared that we were walking inside a tunnel of heavy vegetation. We could see practically everything in the heavy growth, especially if it moved.

The first thing we noticed was the high number of bird's nests in the understory. The nests were in all different shapes and sizes and built with varying materials, so it was obvious to us that birds of many species shared the thick growth. We saw opossum and raccoon tracks in the sand along the creek bank, so we knew they were there also. We saw minnows in the water, but there were no fish large enough for us to attempt to catch and eat. We also saw crawfish and salamanders. We saw quite a few squirrels' beds high up in the trees. We also spotted some rabbit tracks on the ground. There might have been a great deal of difference between Poe Mill and Mills Mill, but we had just discovered a wonderful new paradise.

The first thing we thought of was hunting. To some people, killing birds and animals is just absolutely wrong, regardless of the reason. Today, I have bird feeders in my yard and I love to watch birds; I don't hunt for or kill birds anymore. However, I also have deer and other animals on my land that I do hunt. I don't kill anything anymore unless I intend to eat it or give it to someone I know who will eat it, but when I was young, hunting and killing anything in the wild that moved were the biggest thrills of my life.

We had only a shotgun, and that was illegal to use in an inhabited area like a mill village, so we had to come up with a different way to hunt. We could not afford to buy a BB gun or a pellet rifle, so we had to rely on our imagination and ingenuity to think of something to use as a weapon and then make it. The only thing we could think of to hunt with was a slingshot. Back then, slingshots were not sold in stores, at least not in any stores that we ever visited, so we knew we would have to make our own.

We carried a knife into the heavy growth in search of a tree or bush with forked limbs. We were looking for a limb with two other limbs branching off in such a way that the three limbs formed a perfect *Y*. We wanted the bottom of the *Y*, which would be the handle, to be larger than the two limbs (prongs) that branched off. Once we found what we considered to be a good set of slingshot prongs, we cut them from the tree or bush, and then we trimmed off all of the bark. We cut notches completely around each prong, near the top of each, where we later attached our rubber strips. Once the notches were cut, we placed the prongs into our oven and baked them until all of the moisture within them was gone. After baking dry, the prongs were no longer flexible. When that procedure was finished, we were ready to complete our slingshot.

We searched for old shoes and cut the tongues out of them to use as pockets for our slingshots. We cut a small hole through each side of each pocket and put one end of a strip of rubber through each hole. We then folded each rubber strip so that about an inch of the rubber strip folded back onto the longer end. Using sewing thread, we secured the rubber strips to each side of the pockets. We then attached the opposite ends of the rubber strips to the prongs by folding the ends over the top of the prongs and securing them with sewing thread. The notches we had carved into the prongs earlier helped us to get the thread tight enough to ensure that the rubber strips could not slide off of the prongs when tension was applied by stretching the rubber strips. Once all of those procedures were finished, we were ready to hunt.

A slingshot is useless if a person has no ammunition for it, but we were all very good at playing marbles and each of us had a large number of marbles we had won over a period of about four years. In fact, James still had more than his flour sack full. We stopped counting at two thousand. David and I had several hundred marbles between us so we had plenty of ammunition. We also still played marbles often, so we knew we could win back more than all of the marbles we would lose while hunting.

We were also fortunate to have a lot of gravel lying along the village roadways. Gravel did not travel as accurately to a target as a marble, but it worked well once we got used to it. We collected a large stockpile of gravel just in case we ran out of marbles. We often used gravel just so we could save marbles.

Once we had our slingshots completed and had ammunition in our pockets, we headed for the creek. We walked barefooted in the water, looking for anything we could attempt to shoot. The first thing I saw to shoot at was a bird, a blue jay. It was about twenty feet above me, and it was making a very annoying sound, probably sounding an alarm to the other birds. I didn't care for blue jays anyway because I saw them as bullies toward other birds and as pests for humans. I already had a marble in the pocket of my slingshot so I took careful aim and fired. I missed!

The blue jay flew to another limb just a little bit farther away. I loaded another marble into my slingshot, took aim, and fired again. That time, the blue jay did not fly away; it fell into the creek. The blue jay was dead as soon as the marble struck it because I had hit it squarely on the head, knocking out one of its eyes. Although I had practiced before we had actually begun to hunt, I was both surprised and elated that I could really hit a bird with a marble from a slingshot. I had just realized that I could hunt with either a gun or a slingshot, depending on where I was hunting at the time and what I was hunting.

My brothers and I hunted along the creek as often as we could, killing all sorts of birds. Both David and I learned to shoot our slingshots well enough to be considered experts. I thought I was ready to hunt animals with my slingshot, so I began to look for small animals.

Our yard had numerous water-oak trees in it that produced acorns. Squirrels gathered and ate the acorns, so I figured I might be able to kill a squirrel with my slingshot. I walked into our front yard with my slingshot loaded and began to look for squirrels. The squirrels around our house were not as wary as the squirrels I had hunted in the mountains with Dad. The village squirrels climbed around in the trees as if they had no enemies at all. The mountain and country squirrels always attempted to hide from their enemies, especially human beings.

In a short time, I spotted a squirrel sitting on a limb eating an acorn. I pulled the pocket of my slingshot back as far as I could, because I knew squirrels were tough and hard to kill. When I let go of the pocket, the marble traveled so fast all I could see was a blur. The marble struck the squirrel on its side. The squirrel did not fall, but it ran to the trunk of the tree and got out of my sight. As I walked around the tree in an attempt to get another shot at the squirrel, it was climbing around the tree trunk just out of my sight. It had become a wary squirrel much sooner than I expected. I decided to do what Dad had taught me to do when confronted with a wary squirrel: just sit down and wait. Dad taught me that a squirrel would eventually check to see whether or not its enemy had left, and the curiosity of the squirrel would put it back into a position for a hunter to take another shot.

After about thirty minutes, the squirrel inched its way back around the trunk of the tree. I could hear the squirrel's claws digging in before I saw the squirrel. I had already pulled the pocket of my slingshot back as far as I could before it appeared. I had inserted a steel ball bearing into the slingshot. When the squirrel reached a place where I could actually see it, its body was flattened against the tree but its head stuck out as if it were looking for me. I had a window of about two square inches in which to shoot. As soon as I let go of the slingshot pocket, I knew I had a direct hit. The marble struck the squirrel right in its eye, and the squirrel tumbled to the ground. I picked it up by its hind legs and slammed its head against the tree to make sure it was dead, and then I carried it to the rear of our house, skinned and gutted it, and washed it. I took the squirrel inside the house and put it into our refrigerator and then went back outside to hunt more squirrels. I killed two more squirrels that day, and we had a very tasty fried squirrel meal. As a result of my success, I knew I would continue to hunt squirrels, other animals, and birds as long as we lived at that location. In fact, I hunted at least two or three times per week until we moved away. David and James would sometimes hunt with me, but I don't recall that William did a lot of hunting with us. However, William did occasionally participate when we played a game of makeshift golf in the yard around our house.

We had a couple of old wooden-shafted golf clubs that someone at the Paris Mountain Country Club had given to David when we caddied there. We also had a few golf balls. We saved some tin cans Mother had taken food from. We dug holes in our yard and placed the cans in the holes. We had the cans about twenty-five to thirty feet apart and scattered all the way around our house. Our golf course was similar to a putt-putt course without carpet. The terrain was bumpy and rough, but it suited our purpose. For weeks, when we were not in school, we were hunting or playing golf.

Unfortunately, playing golf in our yard ended abruptly. The thing that brought yard-golf to a screeching halt for me was a whipping I got from Dad. In fact, I don't remember anyone playing golf in the yard again.

One day I was playing golf in our yard with a friend named Don Hill, who lived just down the street. Don had never played golf before, so he was not very good at it. When he struck his golf ball with a club, we never knew in what direction it was going to travel; and, because I knew a little bit about the game, I was easily winning. Also contributing to my being able to win was the fact that I was eleven years old and he was only eight or nine. Don got very frustrated, then angry, because I was winning. To add to his frustration, I was laughing at his terrible golf game. Suddenly, Don slammed the golf club against the ball he was using, and the golf ball crashed right through my parents' bedroom window. Dad was sleeping at the time, and the noise awakened him. We heard Dad jump out of bed, and Don dropped the golf club and ran home. By the time Dad got dressed and reached the front door of our house, Don was already inside his house. When Dad opened the door, I was standing in the yard with the golf club in my hand.

Dad didn't even ask how it happened or who did it; he just ordered me to come to him. Dad went back into the bedroom and then returned. He handed his pocketknife to me and ordered me to go down next to the creek and cut some hickories for him. Then he made the statement, "Boy, I'm going to wear you out!" I had heard a statement similar to that before, just before one of us boys got a whipping. I started to try to tell Dad I didn't break the window, but he told me, "If you don't shut up, I'm going to whip you twice: once for breaking the window and again for lying." By that time, I was already crying, but then he said, "I'm going to whip your rear-end till it won't hold shucks." I had also heard that statement before, and I knew it meant a whipping was coming. I couldn't remember receiving a whipping from Dad since I was four years old, and I was petrified with fear. I knew it was useless to try to convince Dad I had not broken the window because he would never allow me the opportunity to contradict anything he already believed to be true. Just as he never believed my brothers when they were innocent of eating all of the bananas when I was three years old and he didn't believe William when he was innocent of stealing pears, he wasn't going to believe me about the window. His final words before I went to cut hickories were, "Boy, I told you to get yourself down to the creek and cut me some hickories!"

When I reached the creek, I found some hedge limbs that were young, slim, and tender. I figured they wouldn't hurt as much as the bigger, tough ones, so I cut three of them and carried them to Dad. Dad took one look at the hickories I had brought to him and made a remark about me trying to be a "smart-aleck." Then he started to braid the three limbs together. I was crying even more, so much that I could hardly breathe. When Dad finished braiding the limbs together, what he held in his hand appeared to be a large, twisted limb. I was frightened by the appearance of the limbs, but I was more frightened by the appearance of Dad; his face showed nothing but anger. He grabbed me by one arm and began to whip me with the limbs. I couldn't get away from him, so every time he swung, he hit me somewhere.

I was feeling the sting of the limbs all over my body, especially around my back, shoulders, and arms, but occasionally he hit me on my buttocks and legs. The limbs began to break and fall apart, but he continued whipping me until all he had left were some short pieces of the limbs. He threw them onto the floor, handed his knife to me again, and said, "Boy, I told you to get me some hickories. Now, you get yourself back down there and get me some real hickories." I was too scared to even attempt to do otherwise.

Although I was crying and snubbing uncontrollably, I went back to the creek to get more hickories. I was in a lot of pain, but I knew the worst was yet to come. I walked slower than I normally would have, but I didn't want to be so slow that I created more anger, so I began to search for hickories. That time, out of extreme fear, I cut some of the bigger, tougher limbs and carried them back to our house. As soon as Dad got them in his hands, he began to whip me with them. He was whipping me on the legs and buttocks, and I could feel the ends of the limbs snapping around onto the front of my legs and cutting through my clothing. I was wearing blue jeans, but they were so old they were worn thin, almost threadbare in places. I was screaming at the top of my lungs, and tears were streaming down my face and over my body. I was gasping for air because I was sobbing so heavily, and I felt as if I was going to die right there.

When Dad finally finished whipping me, he went back into his bedroom, and I went into our bathroom. When I looked at myself in the mirror, I saw welts all over my arms and back. I even had a couple of stripes on my neck. Some of the welts looked as if they might start bleeding just any second. I pulled my pants down to look at my legs, and to my horror, I was bleeding. I had numerous cuts about two to four inches long on the front of both legs. The cuts were superficial, but they were bleeding just the same, and I was in excruciating pain. I was too scared to call for Dad, so I just stayed in the bathroom and took my pants completely off. I stood next to the bathtub and turned on the cold water, which I caught with my hands and rubbed onto my wounds. I was able to wash all the blood away and the cold water seemed to stop the bleeding. Mother was working in the cotton mill, and all of my brothers were gone so I couldn't do anything but cry and wait for someone else to come home.

Dad must have been getting dressed for work because I heard him leave the house. After I was positive he was gone, I came out of the bathroom. When I looked at our clock, I knew for sure Dad had gone to work. I also knew Mother would be home within the next forty-five minutes.

When Mother arrived home, I was still whimpering and in a lot of pain. When I showed her what Dad had done, she reacted very angrily toward him. She helped me get cleaned up and applied some soothing medication to my wounds, and then she took me next door to our neighbors' house. To my embarrassment, she made me take off my pants so the neighbors could see my wounds. Mother remarked that she "ought to call the law." I explained to Mother and the neighbors how Don had broken the window and Dad wouldn't listen to me, and the neighbors were infuriated by Dad's actions. They encouraged Mother to call law enforcement authorities, and Mother told them she intended to. Mother and I went back to our house; however, she never called anyone. I guess she figured law enforcement authorities had never helped her in a situation like that before, so why should she think they would help her that time. I didn't press the issue because I feared another whipping. I just tended to my wounds, stayed out of Dad's sight, and slowly healed. I still have a very vivid memory of that whipping. Sometimes, when I dwell on it too long, tears still come into my eyes.

A few days after I was whipped, my little friend who had actually broken our window came to our house and admitted to Mother that he had done it.

He apologized and offered to pay for the damage, and Mother accepted his apology but not the pay. He was my friend, so I also accepted his apology and we remained friends. However, I never received an apology from Dad. In fact, although I know Mother told Dad about my friend's confession and apology, he never even acknowledged he had learned the truth about the window-breaking incident. That hurt me almost as much as the whipping, but I just tried to put it out of my mind by playing with my brothers and friends.

Playing with my brothers and friends kept my mind busy, and it was always a learning experience. It wasn't long after the whipping that I learned to ride a bicycle. Somehow, William had gotten an old, used bicycle. I guess he bought it with money he had earned at the grocery store where he was working. I had never ridden a bicycle before, and I'm not sure David and James had either. One day we were all out in the street playing, and William, David, and James were taking turns riding the bicycle. All of them were riding just fine. My little friend who had broken our window had a small bicycle of his own, and he was riding with my brothers. I wanted to learn how to ride, so I asked my brothers to teach me.

They got me onto the bicycle and gave me a push. They told me to pedal, but they didn't say anything about brakes. I didn't even know I had to reverse the pedals to stop the bicycle. I was pedaling away, traveling down the street, and Don Hill was riding alongside on his bicycle. He asked if I wanted to race with him, and I started pedaling as hard as I could. We were still side-by-side as we were approaching the small creek just below our house. I was not used to riding a bicycle so I was wobbling all over the road. Just as we got to the creek, I wobbled toward Don. I didn't hit him, but I must have frightened him because he ran off the roadway and splashed right into the creek. He must have fallen at least four or five feet straight down. I didn't know how to stop so I just kept going, but I was yelling for my brothers to stop me. They all ran into the road and grabbed the bicycle and me. When I got off the bicycle, I ran to see what happened to Don. He was soaking wet but not seriously hurt. However, I think I probably hurt him more by telling him I won the race. He accused me of cheating, but when I offered to race him again, he wisely declined the invitation. After a few days I learned to get on and off the bicycle, and I could ride as well as Don. We rode together many times, but we also did many other things together and with my brothers.

One of the things my brothers and I played together with our friends was football. We also played with some black boys who lived nearby. The street we lived on bordered a neighborhood that consisted of all black families. Some of their houses were as close as two hundred feet from our house. There was a vacant field separating the all-black neighborhood from our all-white neighborhood behind the row of houses across the street from us. Within days of our moving to that location, we saw numerous black children playing in the vacant field. We enjoyed playing, so we became interested in the area where we could see play taking place. Segregation was a way of life in our region of the country, so we had never even been close to a black person. We had only seen a few from a distance so we had no idea what they were like or whether or not they would be friendly, but we walked over to the field anyway.

When we got to the field, there was a game of football in progress, so we just sat on the ground and watched. The black boys seemed to be having a wonderful time, playing hard but laughing and joking with each other, and several black girls were sitting on the ground near their houses watching the game. The activity was very amusing. It was as if each of the black boys wanted to make a greater impression on the girls. They were playing football well, but that didn't seem to be their main objective. The objective seemed to be to impress and win the girl of their choice. I guess some of them must have figured if they could play against a bunch of scrawny white boys and beat them, it would make a bigger impression. They asked us to join them, which we did.

At first, the black boys wanted to play an all-black team against an all-white team. However, there were not enough white boys to have equal racial team numbers. Eventually, it was decided that we would just choose captains to choose their players alternately. What we wound up with was two racially mixed teams, each with big and small boys. When we began playing, it seemed as if everyone forgot there were different races in the game, just teams. Each team member was treated just as well as the next, also equally as bad. We played for hours without a cross word from anyone. Occasionally, from that day until we moved away, we played both football and baseball with the black boys, and I can remember only one time when a fight broke out. The fight involved only two boys, one black and one white. However, when the fight was over, we continued playing as if nothing had happened.

The thing that amazes me most is how the names we called each other back then have become so racially explosive in our world today. When we were playing with those black boys, they called us every name in the book. They even called us names that are, for the most part, slang words that black people today claim are reserved for their race only. We used the same slang words toward them, but we were friends. We all just laughed at each other, and we laughed together. Calling each other names did not create racism and hatred among us. We played together and visited each other's houses. We would not have been opposed to going to school with them, but the laws in our state prohibited that. We went to our school, and they went to theirs. They had to walk across the street from their homes to Sullivan Street Elementary School, and we had to walk almost a mile to Mills Mill Elementary School.

Mills Mill Community Building. Photo Courtesy of Greenville County Historical Society. Greenville, South Carolina.

We walked to downtown Greenville to attend movies whenever we could, and we occasionally saw some of the black children we played football with at the movies. Segregation laws prevented them from sitting on the main floor of the theatre and we could not sit in the balcony. I remember being upset because I thought they were being given the best seats in the theatre.

We continued playing with the black boys only occasionally after we discovered we had a baseball park and a community building with a gymnasium in our mill village.

We never had either available to us in the past, so we were excited about it. Both places had organized sports, but only residents of the mill village were allowed to participate. The black families did not live in the mill village, but because of segregation policies they would not have been allowed into the gymnasium or into the baseball park anyway.

As soon as we discovered a gymnasium was available to us, we began going to it almost every day. There were no weights or exercise equipment like a person expects to see in a modern gymnasium, just a full basketball court and some showers. We didn't have the appropriate shoes for a basketball court floor so we either played barefooted or with socks on. William was too busy to play basketball regularly, but the rest of us played every chance we got. David and James got really good at it, but I got too nervous and frustrated when someone began guarding me. I didn't like the invasion of my space by opposing players. As long as I was allowed to shoot without interference, I was quite good; but when anyone else got within two feet of me, I was lousy. Needless to say, I never learned to play as a team member, but David and James were both good team members. Both of them bought basketball shoes and joined the team that was sponsored by the cotton mill. I could win at games such as horse and around the world, but I never played on an organized team. I just hung around in the gym and watched David and James play basketball with their teammates. When a game was not in progress, I played basketball, but when the season was over, we all began going to the baseball park.

David, James, and I went to the baseball park regularly, and William went when he could. In the spring, the cotton mill administrators announced that the mill would be sponsoring baseball teams for some specified age groups. David and James were old enough to play in what was then called the Pony League. I was too young for that, so I signed up to play in the Little League.

We went to practice every day, and as time went by, each of us became more proficient. David and James quickly became good all-around ballplayers. I was good at running, throwing, and catching, but I couldn't have hit a baseball with a foot-wide board, especially not with a three-inch wide baseball bat. I loved the game, but I was really frustrated by the hitting problem. All of my teammates seemed to be able to hit a baseball, and I just couldn't understand why I couldn't hit one as well as they did. I played the entire first season of my life in absolute frustration. I was the team strikeout king, and some of my teammates reminded me of it daily. However, I hoped I was going to improve. Unfortunately, when baseball season ended, I was still not a very good hitter; I needed a lot of practice. I wanted to impress the girls in our neighborhood with my ability to play baseball; however, none of the girls would ever pay any attention to me. I thought it was because I couldn't hit a baseball, but I was probably wrong about that.

I had been attending school at Mills Mill Elementary for only a short time, but I had already made a number of friends. I was in the top reading and spelling groups in my class, so that helped a little. I really enjoyed going to school, but I wanted to have a girlfriend. Unfortunately, I was not nearly as bold as I had been in earlier years, and I just couldn't get up the nerve to approach any of the girls. I knew we were still dirt poor, and I didn't wear new and stylish clothing. I didn't think I was handsome enough for the girls I had seen and wanted to talk to, so I just kept to myself.

One day a group of girls approached and wanted to talk to me. I was elated that they would even look at me, and I was happy to talk with them. One of the first questions they asked was whether or not I had a girlfriend. I was embarrassed by the question, and I didn't want to admit I didn't have one. I thought they would be more impressed if they thought I had a girlfriend, so I told them I had a beautiful girlfriend who lived at Poe Mill. When they asked for a name, I gave them the first name that came to my mind. That turned out to be a big mistake, because the girl whose name I gave was never my girlfriend. She probably would never have thought about the possibility of being my girlfriend; however, neither would I have ever wanted to be her boyfriend. She was a highly intelligent girl, and at the time, I thought she was much too intelligent for me. When we all went to high school years later I was embarrassed again because the girls from both schools were in my class. Yes, they compared notes and told stories, and I was the big loser! However, I discovered that I was right about one thing. The girl whom I had falsely claimed as a girlfriend was indeed too intelligent for me. I think all of my other classmates and I felt intimidated by her intelligence. The girls from Mills Mill ridiculed me for claiming the girl from Poe Mill had been my girlfriend, but at least, if she had been, I would have chosen an intelligent one. I was interested in girls and I wanted a girlfriend; so even after I was embarrassed, I was hoping that one of the girls would like me. It never happened. I guess I was just not "cute" enough for them.

However, when summer came, I visited some relatives for two weeks in Liberty, South Carolina. Their names are Cliff and Margie Thomas, and their children are Wayne and Nancy. While visiting my relatives, I found a girl in Liberty who was much prettier than most of the girls in my class at school, and she became my girlfriend, at least for that one summer. We only saw each other briefly each day for a period of two weeks and we exchanged letters for the remainder of the summer. However, she was the first girl I ever claimed to be in love with, and although I never claimed her as a girlfriend after that summer and she may not ever have claimed me as a boyfriend, even for those two weeks, I had some wonderful times with her for a short while. I had never really kissed a girl with enthusiasm until I met her, but I will never forget when she and I hid behind my uncle's garage and kissed on a couple of occasions. We never even thought about going beyond kissing, but she was the delight of my life and I hope she remembers me as fondly as I remember her. During those two weeks of summer, my self-appraisal was very high. However insignificant my relationship was to the girl, I was proud that she would even talk to me. She was a very special person to all who knew her.

The end result of my two-week visit was that I gained a lot of confidence in myself, and I don't think I ever failed to at least make an attempt to talk to other girls I became interested in after that summer.

When school started back in the fall, I just ignored all of the girls in my class and dreamed about the one in the other town. Life for me was much easier that way. I enjoyed school, so I concentrated on schoolwork.

Although I enjoyed school very much and I had not missed a day since we moved to Mills Mill, I did play hooky on one occasion. As a matter of fact, it was the only day in our lives that David or I ever played hooky. One morning, David and I got dressed for school and left the house as if we were going to school. Somewhere along the way, we decided we did not want to attend school that day. We wanted to go up to Paris Mountain Country Club and caddy. We had no money, so we wanted to earn some. David was about thirteen, and I was about eleven. We walked to Green Avenue and began hitchhiking. Someone picked us up and took us through the city of Greenville to the intersection of Main Street and Buncombe Road. We walked on Buncombe to Poinsett Highway and then began hitchhiking until someone else picked us up and took us all the way to the golf course. Fortunately, some golfers there needed caddies. David and I each caddied for golfers who played eighteen holes, and then we received our pay from the club manager plus tips from the golfers. I don't recall how much money we earned, but to us it was a substantial amount. We then hitched a ride with some golfers back across town. By the time school was over, we were back in our mill village. We walked home as if we had just come from school. We never told anyone, and we never got caught. However, we also never tried our luck with playing hooky again. We just spent our money conservatively until it ran out and then found another way to earn money.

Although David and I were very close, we were not always agreeable. I recall one time when we had a disagreement that caused both of us a little pain. He got his from me, and I got mine from Mother.

Mother sent David and me to the Moon's grocery store about a block from our house. David decided we should ride the old, piece-of-junk bicycle he had gotten from somewhere; it could have been William's old bicycle—I just don't recall. Anyway, after we bought the items we were sent to purchase, David bought some candy. I don't recall whether or not he used his own money; I just recall that I wanted some of the candy. David refused to give any candy to me, and to make matters worse, he jumped onto the bicycle and took off without me. I yelled for him to stop, but he just kept going, so I quickly picked up a rock and threw it at him. To my surprise, the rock struck David on the back of his head. I saw David grab the back of his head, but he managed to continue riding the bicycle toward our house. I had to walk home, which took all of about four or five minutes. When I got home, David had already told Mother about my rock throwing. However, I don't think he bothered to mention the candy or that he had ridden off and left me behind. As soon as I walked into the house, Mother was all over me. She slapped me across the face, on the back of the head, on the shoulders and arms, and anywhere else she could hit me. I was ducking and dodging and trying to escape. I finally saw an opening and ran through the doorway. The assault was over, but the pain lasted a while. Of course, David felt the pain from the rock for a while, too. By the time our pain was gone, we were playing together again. We also visited the store together many times, but we never had another disagreeable incident that involved rock throwing. The store was one of our favorite places to visit, for the whole family, because we always found exactly what we were looking for. Of course, occasionally one of us would mistakenly pick up a wrong item. I remember an error David and I made at the store one day.

Mother asked David and me to go to the store to pick up a can of treat for our lunch. Treat is some kind of pressed meat; I think it is ham and other pork products pressed into a small block and canned. David and I bought what we thought was a can of treat, but when we got home we realized, after we had already opened the can, we had bought tripe. Tripe is the rubbery lining of the stomachs of cattle. When Mother realized she had tripe instead of treat, and it was too late to exchange it because the can had been opened, she decided to cook it anyway. We could not afford to go buy another can of anything. When she had cooked the tripe, we sat down to eat. I had already heard what tripe was so I opted not to eat any, and no one else wanted to eat tripe either. I think someone tried to chew a small piece but was unsuccessful because it was similar to trying to chew rubber. We were all just eating whatever else Mother had prepared. Then Dad said he would pay a quarter to any of us who would eat a slice of tripe. I immediately chose not to try it. David must have needed some money really badly because he said he would eat a slice of tripe. He put a small piece into his mouth and began to chew. After what seemed to be five minutes, he was still attempting to chew that small piece, and finally he swallowed it. Dad let him stop with the one piece and paid him. David earned a quarter, but it would have taken much more to get me to try tripe. When we had the tripe incident, the whole family seemed to see humor in it. We were laughing at David as he was chewing, and we laughed after he had received his quarter. Enjoying a humorous moment with the whole family involved had been a rarity during the first few years of my life, and I was impressed by the fact that it really was happening more often as I was getting older. We savored every second that the entire family was involved in a humorous moment. Happiness that involved the total family was like a wayward wind; it came and left quickly. On the other hand, sadness was like a dense fog; it sometimes surrounded all of us and lingered for a while.

There was an accident in 1953 involving William that almost cost him his life and caused our family great sadness for a few weeks. He was out late one night riding in a car with some of his friends from Poe Mill, and they were involved in a major traffic accident. William was thrown partially through the windshield of the car and was seriously injured. I remember when Mother and Dad received information that William was in the emergency room and how they scrambled out of the house to get to the hospital. I can't recall whether or not William was hospitalized, but I think he was. As I recall, I didn't see William until several days after the accident. He had been cut across his nose and numerous other places on his head, and his wounds had initially been life-threatening. I think I remember hearing someone say that one of the cuts on William had missed a main artery by a small fraction of an inch and that he was lucky to be alive. I loved all of my brothers, and I was happy William survived the accident.

It wasn't long after William's traffic accident wounds were completely healed that we moved away from Ridge Street. We had lived on Ridge Street about a year before Mills Mill administrators announced the mill was selling all of the village houses. Mother and Dad went to the opposite side of the mill village and picked out a four-and-a-half-room house at 278 Moore Street to buy. The house also had a full indoor bathroom. They were allowed to purchase the house they chose, so we moved in as soon as they had closed the deal. We still teetered on the brink of low income, but it appeared that we would be able to finally hold onto something of great importance: decent shelter that no one could force us out of as long as we could make mortgage payments.

We moved into the house on Moore Street in March 1953. The house was not the largest or most beautiful house in the mill village, but even though it lacked beauty and some conveniences, it was the nicest house we had ever lived in. The half-room had been a back porch at one time, but the previous owners had closed it in and made it into a small room about half the size of one of the other rooms. William was the oldest boy, so he was granted the opportunity to claim the half-room as his bedroom. It was a little cramped, but it worked for him. David, James, and I shared one bedroom. With William's bed out of the room, we had plenty of space for our three single beds.

Dad and Mother were earning more in wages than ever before. We had accumulated a few modern conveniences, and we were able to purchase a more varied food supply. We had also managed to discard most of our patched and hand-me-down clothing, but we could not yet afford to buy the most stylish clothing. Our clothing was always clean, but I remember some disparaging remarks made by some of my classmates. Sometimes I was humiliated, but I learned a lot about humility by being humiliated. I recall that I was wearing cheap, lace-up, leather shoes and tennis shoes made from cloth and rubber while many of my classmates were wearing all-leather penny loafers. I wanted to wear penny loafers also, but we had no money for them. I also had no money for a raincoat. I had to walk about a half-mile to school, and getting wet when it rained was just a fact of life. We just never seemed to have enough money for all of our needs. I think all of us children realized if we were ever going to have things we wanted, we would have to work for them. However, every time our parents bought something new, I believed it was a sign that they were slowly climbing the ladder to success.

Dad had the house insulated and siding put onto the exterior not long after we moved to Moore Street. The house was already underpinned, so the siding and insulation made the house much easier to heat in the winter, and although we had no air conditioner, the house was much cooler in the summer. We had an oil-burning heater that could burn continuously, and it heated almost the entire house in winters. Chopping wood, gathering kindling, and buying coal were no longer necessary. At last, we were comfortable in our own house.

Mother was very disappointed that the house had no kitchen cabinets, but it wasn't long before she hired a cabinetmaker to install wall-to-wall cabinets on two walls. That was the first time in my life we had built-in cabinets in our kitchen. The cabinetmaker also installed a new kitchen sink and a new floor covering. Mother already had a nice refrigerator and electric stove. To us, the kitchen was magnificent. I think Mother loved her kitchen more than anything she ever owned. She was so proud to invite others to see it and to sit down for a bite to eat. Even I was eager to invite my friends into our house. We were all proud. However, it would take a long time to pay for all that had been done to improve the house, and that meant all of us boys would have to find a way to earn money to assist with our personal needs.

William was already working in a grocery store, but he had switched stores several different times in attempts to earn higher wages. Although James was attempting to find work, no one would hire him because he was small and looked so much younger than he was. David always seemed to find a way to earn a little money, but he had no regular job either. I just followed David around and attempted to get him to let me have some of his money or let me help him earn some. I was willing to do whatever I could.

David and I used an old run-down nonmotorized lawn mower and a sling blade to earn about ten dollars per week for cutting the grass of some of the more affluent people who lived at the fringe of the mill village. We could cut all the grass we could handle within two miles of our house. The pay was not so great, but we could at least buy things for ourselves that our parents could not. We cut grass almost every day during the remainder of the spring and summer, so we were able to buy some things, such as tennis shoes, that we would not have gotten otherwise.

David also came up with another way to earn money, but he wouldn't let me share that with him. He used two bicycle wheels and some lumber to build a large cart he could roll to the baseball park and to other places in the mill village. He bought an ice scraper, different flavors of juices, ice, and cups, and then he went into the snow cone business. I don't recall how much he charged for a snow cone, but I do recall that he sold hundreds of them. He always had a little money in his pockets. He pushed that cart onto almost every street in the mill village, and I don't think he ever missed having the cart at a baseball game. I had great admiration for him. He was a hard worker during the day when I was playing baseball, but he still had plenty of time to play with our friends and me in the evenings when baseball was over.

The cotton mill was continuing to sponsor an adult baseball team, a Pony League team, and a Little League team. James was good enough to play on the adult team, David played on the Pony League Team, and I was playing on the Little League team. Playing baseball was the most important thing in my life, and I had high hopes of becoming a professional ballplayer. In fact, I had gotten quite good at it. I could run, catch, and throw as well as anyone else on my team. I hadn't been able to hit a baseball during the past season, but at the beginning of the new season I learned how to hit as well as anyone else on the team, even better than some.

A young man named Jim McAlister, who played on the adult team, offered to teach me how to hit a baseball just after we entered our second season. I had seen him hit many home runs. Sometimes, he hit the ball so hard that it would travel out of the ballpark and over a house across the street before landing in its backyard. He was a very good baseball player, and I admired him a lot because of his abilities. I was eager to learn from him.

The first thing I learned was how to hold a baseball bat in a cocked position off my shoulder. I could begin my swing without having to use extra fractions of a second to raise the bat. The next thing I learned was to watch the baseball from the time the pitcher released it until it struck my bat. He also told me I should start my swing just as the pitcher released the ball so the bat would already be in a forward motion as the ball traveled toward me. If the pitch were bad, I could stop the forward motion of the bat, and if the pitch were good, I could hit the ball. I paid very close attention to everything Jim said.

The first time I went to bat after receiving instructions from Jim, I hit my first home run. I was so excited I could hardly feel the ground or the bases as I ran around and tagged each base. I saw all of my teammates waiting for me when I started toward home plate. What a joyous time I had. They had never before seemed to care a lot for me as a teammate, but they were hugging me and congratulating me with such enthusiasm that I fell to the ground with all of them falling on top of me. I had finally become a complete baseball player because I learned to hit. I finally felt as if I was really a part of the team.

I was having a very good year. I had gained the respect and friendship of all of my teammates, and my batting average was good. I was a contributor on the field. I was selected as one of the regional all-stars when the season was almost over, and I was scheduled to travel to West Palm Beach, Florida, to play in the regional all-star game. I knew that several players on my team were probably better ballplayers than I, and I didn't understand why they were not chosen before me. I never learned how or why I had been selected to play as an all-star, but I was excited and ready to go. However, disaster struck, and my baseball season ended abruptly, as well as any hopes and dreams I had of someday becoming a professional baseball player. I received a devastating injury, but it was not related to baseball. I think I might not have been injured, at least not so severely, had I not been playing barefooted.

I was playing with my brothers and some of our friends behind a row of houses. We had one golf club and about ten golf balls, and we were hitting the golf balls into a pasture about a hundred yards away. The first time the golf balls were hit into the pasture, the owner of the balls hit them. However, once he had hit all of them, the person who could find one got an opportunity to hit it. As soon as the last ball was hit, we all ran as fast as we could to search for the golf balls. We had been through that routine several times before I received my injury.

We lined up to hit all of the golf balls after we retrieved them. I was first, so after I hit mine I watched the others. I was watching closely to see where the balls landed because I wanted to be sure to get some to hit again. As soon as the last ball was hit, I ran as fast as I could to a location where I believed a ball had stopped. I saw a golf ball lying on the ground across a gully from me. I thought someone was racing me to get the ball, so I jumped over the gully to get to it first. I felt a sharp pain in the bottom of my left foot when I landed. I started to jump up to run for another golf ball, but I fell to the ground again. I didn't realize I was seriously hurt until then. I couldn't get up. I sat up and turned my foot so I could see the bottom of it. I almost went into shock when I looked at my foot. There was a hole in the bottom of my foot as large in diameter as a silver dollar, and I could see the bone. There was no blood at all, just the hole. I looked around to see what I had landed on and discovered that I had landed on a small tree stump. I began to yell for my brothers, but I felt no pain so I didn't cry. David looked at my foot and immediately picked me up and started toward our house. My foot had started to bleed by that time, but it never bled a lot. The blood just kind of seeped out.

After David carried me out of the pasture and across the paved road, a man who was a neighbor took me from David and carried me home, and then someone took me to a doctor's office. The doctor examined me, cleaned the wound, and then sewed my foot up and released me.

I was back at home a short time after the doctor released me. However, I could not walk, and I had no crutches. I had to hop everywhere I went, so I didn't go very far. Needless to say, my baseball season ended and I would not be going to Florida. I was terribly disappointed about not going to Florida, because I had never been outside upstate South Carolina.

I figured I would just lie around and heal and then play baseball again the next season. Of course, I had to go to school, but when school was over each day, there was not much else I could do. Surely, I would heal quickly. After all, young people usually did.

Some of my friends would come by our house and carry me to school because I couldn't walk. Mother did not know how to drive an automobile, and Dad left for work much earlier than I needed to leave for school. David was already attending junior high school, so he couldn't help me. I had one classmate named Gerald McGarity who was much larger than I, and he could carry me to school on his back. He carried me the whole half-mile without stopping to rest more than twice. He also carried me to the lunchroom and onto the playground each day. I was very grateful to him, and he and I became close friends.

My wound still was not healing after several weeks, so I had to return to the doctor's office. The doctor performed surgery and probed around in the hole in my foot and found a piece of bark. He removed it and sewed my foot up again.

We had no television set and I had nothing to play with. Mother bought a kit for making potholders and gave it to me. She and Dad were both working the first shift in the cotton mill, and Mother wanted me to be busy so I wouldn't be bored. I sat on our front porch and made potholders every afternoon after school. Some of my friends sometimes came by to talk with me, and I would sit and make potholders and talk with them for hours.

One day a lady who lived across the street came over to see me. When she saw I was making potholders, she wanted to buy some of them. I sold several to her, and then I got into the business of making and selling potholders. I must have sold potholders to every neighbor within a three-block radius. I could send my friends to the store to buy candy and drinks for us because I was earning a little money. I never had a shortage of friends on our front porch.

Some of my friends had card and board games they began bringing to our house. My brothers and I played games with our friends for many hours each day. I recall that our favorite games were Monopoly and Rook.

After several months had gone by, I had to return to the doctor's office because my foot still was not healing. The doctor determined I needed surgery again. However, he said I needed to go to a hospital instead of having the surgery in his office, and I was taken to the hospital that same afternoon.

The next morning when I was taken into the operating room I was very frightened, but some nurses talked to me and helped to keep me calm. I was given a shot of some kind and then someone placed a mask over my face. I tried to fight against the mask, but I discovered that my arms and legs were strapped down. Suddenly I was hearing a buzzing sound, and the room was spinning and going dark. I found out later that I was put to sleep with ether. I woke up in another room with my mother standing at my bedside.

The doctor came into my room carrying a small glass container with something inside it. He held it up close to me so I could see it clearly and told me he had taken it from my foot. It was a piece of wood about half an inch long and a quarter of an inch in diameter. He said the wood had been lodged between a large tendon and a bone in my foot in such a position that X-rays had not detected it. He said without surgery my foot would not have healed. He said the foot should heal completely, but he doubted the hole would ever be completely closed. He said I should not even attempt to play baseball for a couple of years.

When I went home, I was more upset about not being able to play baseball than I was about being injured. I just continued going to school and hoping the doctor was wrong. However, I did not get to play in the Pony League the following season, and I was too old for Little League. I had lost a lot of my ability to be a good ballplayer, and I felt that it was imperative that I make a transition from one league to the next as a well-rounded, well-respected ballplayer. I wasn't able to do that, so I never played on another organized baseball team. The hole in my foot is still there after so many years.

My baseball career ended, but my brothers and I continued inventing and playing games with our friends. One of the creations we made was stilts, and we did a lot of stilt walking. I don't know where we got the idea, but we decided we were just not walking tall enough. We wanted to walk a little taller. We found some two-by-fours, nails, and some pieces of leather. We cut some short pieces from a two-by-four and nailed them to the longer two-by-fours, making places for our feet about four feet from the bottom of the long two-by-fours. Then, we attached pieces of leather to the ends of the foot pieces and to the long two-by-fours. When they were attached, we had created what looked similar to stirrups on a two-by-four. We then trimmed the tops of the two-by-fours to make handles for our hands. When we stood them on end, we had created stilts.

We had to get on top of something such as a porch or a trashcan to mount the stilts. We fell off many times before we finally learned how to maintain our balance on stilts, but once we learned how to maintain balance, we were walking tall. We really thought we were something.

We walked throughout the mill village on our stilts. Eventually, we learned to walk up and down steps and to step over short objects. Although I was not one of them, some learned how to walk on stilts without the use of their hands. I could only follow them around and admire their skill. We walked on our stilts almost every day after school, and the only thing that eventually stopped us from walking on stilts was a desire to go to new heights: we decided we could go even higher if we pole-vaulted.

Pole Vaulters L to R: Melvin Prather, Herman Patterson, David Porter, David Grant, Charles Sanders, Dan Rodgers, Doyle Porter, James Porter, Gary Underwood.

I don't know the name of the slender trees we used for pole-vaulting, but we found them near a creek about two blocks from our house. We looked for the tallest trees we could find that were small in diameter. We cut them down and trimmed all of the bark from them, and then we placed them in a location where they could dry out in the sun. It usually took several days for a tree to dry out completely. Although the trees were dry, they still maintained the flexibility necessary for pole-vaulting.

We began our pole-vaulting stunts at the creek. We ran toward the creek at full speed with our poles held high. Just as we reached the creek bank, we stuck the ends of our poles into the creek bed and jumped into the air. We were able to ride our poles over the creek and land on the opposite creek bank. We repeated the process to get back across the creek. We vaulted over the creek every day for a couple of weeks and occasionally afterwards. One day when I was attempting to vault over the creek, I thrust my pole into some soft mud in the bottom of the creek bed and the pole sank into the mud. My ride ended over the middle of the creek. I was hanging on to the pole but there was nowhere to go. I had to just let go and drop into the water. I tried to choose better places to cross the creek after that.

We got bored after we mastered jumping over the creek. We wanted to jump over something with height. We walked around our house and all the houses nearby, but we could see only a few garbage cans. We jumped over the garbage cans but that was too easy. We wanted to jump over something more difficult, and someone came up with the idea of jumping over a clothesline. The first person to attempt jumping over a clothesline straddled it. When he came down, the clothesline struck him in an area where no male wants to be struck. He fell to the ground screaming and crying. The clothesline did not break, but it was sagging a lot. After a short time, the injured person recovered enough to continue playing with us. However, he would not attempt to jump over the clothesline again. The rest of us jumped over the clothesline one at a time, and all of us made it over without touching it. We continued jumping over the clothesline until we decided it was no longer high enough and then we raised it. We jumped over it a couple of times but quickly got bored. We raised the line until there was no space left at the top of the post and we could not raise it any higher. We were soon bored with jumping over the clothesline, so we went looking for something higher.

We could not find anything else in the immediate area higher than our clothesline, so we decided to vault onto the roof of our house. We did a few practice vaults near the side of our house just to see if we could vault high enough to actually reach the roof. When we were confident we could reach the roof, we began attempting to do so. The first few vaults were failures. Our vaults came up short, so we placed our feet against the side of the house and returned to the ground. However, it was evident that we could vault high enough to achieve our objective of vaulting onto the roof. We just needed to get up enough nerve to do so. Our parents were working, so we didn't have to worry about getting caught by them. Otherwise, we would never have placed our feet against the side of our house.

We continued to vault to gain confidence, and the time came either to make the vault or forget it. One of my brothers went first, and he made it. He got about half of his body onto the roof and then, using his pole, pushed himself the rest of the way onto the roof. He stood up and gave a victory yell and then rode his pole back down to the ground. He said it was easy. Each of the rest of us took a turn, and we all made it onto the roof. We were having more fun than the law should allow. Then we realized it was about time for our parents to come home from work. We quickly put our poles under our house and went to a friend's house to play some other type of game. When our parents got home, they had no idea what we had been doing all day. We carried out the same routine for weeks until we finally figured out we could vault even higher by using a string and two tall poles. That was also much less dangerous. We continued pole-vaulting for several months, and we were good at it. However, none of us ever entered any competitive pole-vaulting events at school or otherwise. We were just a bunch of good old boys having fun.

Brushy Creek was only a couple of blocks from our house. It was the creek that provided water for the millpond. My brothers and I, along with numerous friends, often went to the creek in summers to play together. There were many large oak and other species of trees that lined the creek banks. We found a large oak tree that had huge limbs stretching over the creek. We decided to build a rope-swing that we could use to swing over the water and then let go and fall into the water.

Someone found a very large rope that was approximately one hundred feet in length. A couple of the older boys climbed the tree and tied the rope to a large limb that was quite high off the ground. We tied a knot in the loose end of the rope to create a makeshift handle. One of the older boys took the rope in hand and ran as far away from the tree as the rope would allow and then jumped from the creek bank at full speed. The rope carried him in a wide circle across the creek and then back toward the side from which he had jumped. As he was returning, he let go of the rope over the middle of the creek and splashed into the water below. The boy was not injured, but we discovered then that the creek was not deep enough for that activity.

Several boys ran home to get shovels and other tools for digging. We dug a large trench to divert the creek water to only one side of the creek bed, and then we began to dig a very large hole in the other side of the creek bed. By the time we finished digging, our hole was the size of a small swimming pool, and the depth of the water when we allowed it to enter the hole was approximately five feet. We then dug out the other side of the creek bed. The result was that we had a hole that was the size of a mid-size swimming pool about five feet deep. We took turns swinging over the creek and splashing into the water every time we got an opportunity. There were eventually as many as twenty-five boys and girls playing in the creek at one time.

Someone decided he wanted to have another way of falling into the water. Fortunately, he had possession of a one-inch-diameter cable and some plumbing pipes. He and several other boys climbed the oak tree and, using cable clamps, secured the cable to the tree trunk about fifteen feet off the ground. They then fashioned a _T_ with the plumbing pipes and slid the bottom section of the _T_ onto the cable. The result was that the pipes appeared to be an upside-down _T_, with the crossbar at the bottom serving as handles. The boys then attached the loose end of the cable at a height of about two feet to an oak tree on the opposite side of the creek. The cable stretched over the center of the swimming hole. We had to tie a string onto the handles so we could pull the handles to the tree from which we intended to slide. Each time someone slid across, we had to retrieve the handles with the use of the string.

One of the older boys took the handles in hand and jumped from the tree. He glided very fast directly over the swimming hole and then dropped to the water. The cable worked just fine, but the boy said the ride was really fast and a little scary. We took turns, and everyone seemed to be enjoying it. Then we had one younger boy who slid across and was so frightened that he didn't turn loose of the handles until he was just about to crash into the tree on the opposite side of the creek. He actually did crash into the creek bank. Fortunately, he was not injured. Everyone learned quickly that it was imperative to let go of the handles in time to splash into the water. After that incident, we spent many hours of many days gliding on the cable and swinging on the rope to splash into our swimming hole in the creek. We always seemed to find inexpensive or cost-free ways to enjoy life.

The village gymnasium was several blocks from our house after we moved to Moore Street, but we no longer had to make that trip. David either bought or found a basketball rim with net. He spent hours building a basketball goal for our backyard, and then he got a set of posthole diggers from somewhere and spent another hour digging a deep hole for the goal post. Once the basketball goal was in place, we had a wonderful time playing basketball with numerous friends. There were times when as many as twenty of us were playing at the same time. We played until dinner was ready and then went inside to eat. Sometimes, some of our friends were invited to eat with us. After eating dinner, we went back outside and played basketball until supper time. When supper was over, we played until it was so dark we could no longer see the goal from any distance at all. After dark, we played whatever game came to our minds until it was bedtime. We then went inside and stayed until the next morning. We kept that schedule as long as possible.

We were having a lot of fun but I never seemed to have any money, so I was eager to get back to work and earn some spending money. I was too young to get a real job, but I could help other people with their work and share the earnings. David had started helping one of our neighbors, Rob Bishop, deliver newspapers every morning, so I asked Rob if I could also help, and he said I could. Another neighbor, Dan Rodgers, had an afternoon paper route, so I asked him if I could assist him, and he hired me. For several months, I got up at five-thirty and helped David deliver newspapers, and then we came home and got dressed for school. I helped deliver newspapers with Dan after school, and then I came home to do homework. I had a little spending money most of the time, but my brothers and I also did some work for which we received no pay.

After I finished my homework each day, I had to help James and David wash clothes and hang them outside to dry. We washed clothes every day. I also helped James and David clean and dry our dishes. I hated washing dishes more than any other household chore. We usually were finished with our household chores by the time Mother and Dad got home from work. Mother cooked supper, and then we had to clean the kitchen again. Sometimes it seemed that our work was never done, but our work was not always the same either.

David became a close friend of Harry Green, who lived on the next street behind our house. One day when they were talking, Harry was explaining to David that he wanted a basement dug under his house. He asked David if he thought he could dig the basement for him. When David said he believed he could, the man hired him. The only tools David had were a pick, a mattock, a shovel, and a wheelbarrow, but he began working on the basement immediately, and I was there to watch. David was working very hard, but the ground under the house was just so hard that David's pick would hardly penetrate it. He was always sweating profusely, and I helped keep him supplied with ice water. I kept hoping David would share some of his earnings with me.

David was hardly making a dent in the ground under the house after several days of digging. He loosened some dirt and shoveled it out to the wheelbarrow, and then he had to come from under the house to haul the dirt away before he could dig anymore. The job was more than one person could handle, but David was determined to do it anyway. He made an arrangement to haul the dirt from the basement to another neighbor's yard where the dirt would be used as fill dirt. The neighbor promised to pay David for each load of dirt.

I guess David was overworked or he was tired of watching me watching him, so he asked me to help him. I was happy and eager to help until I started attempting to dig. I was astonished at how hard the ground under that house was, but I knew I had no other way to earn money. David wouldn't share his earnings with me unless I pulled my load, and I knew that. I dug until I couldn't swing the pick anymore, and then I rested while David dug. That meant David did about 90 percent of the work, but I thought I was earning 50 percent of the money. When we loosened enough dirt to fill the wheelbarrow, we shoveled it from under the house. While David hauled the dirt away, I would be digging, or pretending to dig, until he returned.

We worked that way for weeks, but we still had not dug what I would consider to be a basement. We dug a large hole in the ground, about twelve feet by twelve feet and about four or five feet deep. However, the man who hired David seemed to be satisfied, and he paid David. In turn, David paid me. That's when I learned I had not been earning 50 percent of the money, only what David thought my work had been worth. When David went to collect his money for the dirt he had hauled to the other neighbor's yard, the neighbor refused to pay David. Of course, David was upset, and he told Dad. When Dad confronted the neighbor, the neighbor told some story about how he was just giving David a place to dump the dirt, and he denied he had promised to pay for the dirt. To this day, David has never collected any money for all the dirt he hauled to that neighbor's yard. David and I learned a lot about being honest, because a person whom we had respected cheated David.

After the basement work, David went to work at a gas and auto service station. I couldn't help him there, so I had to start cutting grass and raking leaves again. It was hard work, but I had no other way to earn money.

Dad became close friends with Harry Green when he lived behind us and David worked on the basement. Harry moved a couple of blocks away to a place where he owned several acres of land at the fringe of the mill village. Harry offered to let Dad plant a garden on his land. Harry even agreed to buy some of the vegetables Dad would grow. Harry owned a café in the village named Peg's Place, and he could use the vegetables there. Dad worked hard to get the large garden spot ready, and then he planted vegetables. However, Dad didn't have time to hoe and rake the big garden all alone; he needed help, so Mother and all of us boys had to assist Dad with the garden chores. We didn't look forward to working in the garden, but we knew it meant we would have some very good meals. Of course, the gardening did not take up a lot of our time. We had plenty of time to participate in sports activities, go to the swimming hole, hunt and fish, and otherwise enjoy the spring and summer. We were not slaves to the garden; we just dreaded the work.

I was thrilled that our family was eating so well at last. We had gone through times when we had little or no food at all, and suddenly we had enough food to eat well every day and still have vegetables to can for use in the winter. We didn't have a lot of money, but we had plenty of food for the remainder of my growing-up years. We had a new garden every year, beginning in the spring that I turned thirteen.

I looked forward to eating all of the different types of vegetables we had in our garden each year, but I enjoyed the cantaloupes more than any other thing we planted. All of us loved cantaloupe at any time of the day, but I preferred to have it for breakfast. Mother sliced it and put it into a shallow bowl, and then made some of the best biscuits anyone ever tasted. While the biscuits were baking, she cooked some bacon or fatback meat. Some people know fatback meat as "salt pork." When the meat had cooked, she used the grease to make gravy, much like the gravy served in some fast-food restaurants today, but Mother's was better. To top that off, we had fresh whole milk, straight from a cow, with about two inches of cream at the surface. Milk was delivered to our house daily from a local farmer. Even now, I can't think of any meal I would prefer over cantaloupe, biscuits, gravy, fatback meat, and fresh milk.

Mother had an old cabinet that had a large flour bin built into it at the top. There was a built-in sifter at the bottom of the flour bin. Mother kept a large, oval-shaped, wooden bowl underneath the cabinet work-space. She took out the wooden bowl, sifted flour into it, and prepared some of the best biscuits anyone has ever tasted. She mixed all of her ingredients by hand. When she had the dough at just the right consistency, she pinched off a piece and rolled it in her hands until she was pleased with it. Then she placed it into her baking pan and flattened it with the back of her hand, leaving her knuckle prints in it. When the biscuits rose while baking, the knuckle prints disappeared. When the biscuits were baked, they were irresistible.

We usually had a few biscuits left over from breakfast, and Mother put them on the stovetop. I usually went into the kitchen later in the day, got a couple of biscuits, and headed to the garden. I pulled up green spring onions or picked a tomato or cucumber. I ate whatever I happened to have chosen from the garden, along with the biscuits, as I walked through the woods. The snacks were delicious to me. I preferred Mother's biscuits instead of a candy bar, and I loved vegetables almost as much as the biscuits. The vegetables were delicious straight from the plants, but Mother found many other ways to serve them to us.

Using our tomatoes and other vegetables, Mother made some of the best vegetable soup I have ever eaten. She picked the tomatoes when they were just ripe enough and then she got a pot of water boiling. She dipped each tomato into the boiling water for just a couple of seconds and then dipped it into cold water. The process caused the tomato skins to just slide off the tomatoes and none of the delicious juices were lost. She cooked the tomatoes with the other vegetables she had added to the pot, and we had vegetable soup. I can almost taste it now.

A few years ago, a movie titled *Fried Green Tomatoes* came out. Just reading the title made me hungry, but when I watched the movie and saw there really were fried green tomatoes in it, I was salivating. I had not had any fried green tomatoes in years. Mother fried green tomatoes when I was growing up, but she didn't cook them in the same fashion as they were cooked in the movie. She cut the green tomatoes into small pieces and rolled them in a batter of flour or cornmeal and spices, and then she sliced okra into small round pieces and rolled it in the same batter she had just rolled the tomatoes in. When she finished rolling the tomatoes and okra in the batter, she placed both vegetables into a large frying pan and fried them together. That dish was another favorite of mine.

Another way I enjoyed tomatoes was in a tomato sandwich. I just put a little mayonnaise on a couple of slices of bread and added sliced tomatoes, pepper, and salt. My tomato sandwiches were delicious. I also loved tomatoes on hamburgers, in garden salads, and in different types of sauces. I learned to use tomatoes to make spaghetti sauce, lasagna sauce, and a variety of other sauces. I have always loved the taste of fresh tomato juice, and even though I have to buy it, I love tomato ketchup.

Although I loved okra fried with green tomatoes, I also loved okra fried alone. When Mother fried okra, none was ever left when we walked away from the table. However, she also served boiled okra occasionally, and I loved boiled okra just as much as fried okra. When Mother boiled okra, she washed it good and put it into a pot of boiling water to cook until it was tender. When we ate the boiled okra, we held it in our hands, by the stem end, and bit the whole okra pod from the stem end. Boiled okra was so slimy we couldn't bite off just half a pod; we had to bite off the whole pod. Otherwise, slimy okra would drip all over us. The taste of boiled okra was different from that of fried okra, but it was just as good.

Yellow squash grew well in our garden, and it grew really fast. The plants got about two feet tall and produced so much squash that we had to pick it almost every day. Mother canned a lot of squash and served the rest to the family. I learned how to make squash casseroles that would make my taste buds go wild, using a mixture of squash, onions, carrots, cream of celery soup, and bread crumbs. I still make them. Mother also fried squash, much the same as she did the okra and green tomatoes, and it was very good.

Potatoes were also planted in our garden. A person who has never dug potatoes from the ground should try it at least one time. The work is hard, but the reward of uncovering a large, beautiful potato makes it worth the effort. Having the freshest potatoes possible is fantastic. No matter how one cooks them, they are usually better than any potatoes anyone can buy in a grocery store.

It always amazed me that we could buy potatoes, cut them into small pieces, bury the pieces in the ground, and wake up one morning to see potato plants in the garden. Of course, I eventually learned what a seed potato was, with its little sprouts all over it. I'm still awed by the very acts of nature that allow human beings to plant seeds and then harvest such wonderful foods.

The potato is probably one of the most versatile foods in existence, right up there with soybeans. Boiled potatoes, baked potatoes, French fries, potato chips, stewed potatoes, potato pancakes, potato bread, potato casseroles, and potato soup are only some of the ways I enjoy potatoes.

We also had sweet potatoes. Long before I started school, I was introduced to baked sweet potatoes. I thought they were the best-tasting food I had ever eaten, and I just begged for one every day. Mother also made candied sweet potatoes. I learned how to make a sweet potato soufflé that is very good. Anyone who likes coconut, pecans, raisins, and marshmallows would enjoy one of my soufflés. However, the one way I preferred sweet potatoes was in a cobbler. Mother could make the best cobbler in the entire county. I remember when she baked them in the oven of her old woodstove. There was something about that old woodstove that just put a tremendous amount of added flavor into a cobbler. We sat around drooling and waiting for the pie to come out of the oven. Most of the time, the cobbler was served as dessert, but once in awhile one was cooked for eating whenever we were hungry for it. I always tried to be first, and last, to the pie pan. While fighting with three older brothers and a sister, I ate as much of the cobbler as I could, and then I wanted to lick the pan. That's how good Mother's cobblers were. We also had peach, apple, strawberry, and blackberry cobblers. Mother could make a great cobbler with just about any type of fruit.

Green beans from our garden were on our table every Sunday at dinnertime when the plants were bearing. Dinner was the midday meal that people today call "lunch." Where did "lunch" come from? We had breakfast, dinner, and supper. Now, it's breakfast, lunch, and dinner. Where did supper go? We have a late breakfast and skip lunch, but we call the meal "brunch." If some people still call their evening meal "supper," when they have a late dinner and skip supper, maybe they should call the meal "dinper." Maybe we have so much obesity in our country because a meal was added and now people are eating breakfast, lunch, dinner, and supper. Who knows?

In our garden, we usually had two types of green beans. One was half-runners, and the other was pole beans. Both were good. Mother had a large, black, iron pot with three tiny legs on it. I guess the pot held about ten quarts, and when Mother cooked green beans, she always cooked them in the iron pot. She placed the beans into the pot with a thick slice of fatback meat and let the beans cook for hours. The grease from the meat gave the beans a good flavor, and the long cooking time made them especially tender. I know doctors tell people that cooking with pork is bad for their health, but that's all Mother ever used, and she is over ninety years old and still going strong. Maybe cooking with pork is bad for people, but we had some of the best green beans, as well as other foods, that could be found anywhere in the southeastern United States.

We would never have had a garden without corn, but I didn't like pulling, shucking, or silking it. However, I certainly enjoyed eating it. We had creamed corn, boiled corn on the cob, and corn in vegetable soup.

We also always had several rows of colored butterbeans. It seems as if they were the most difficult of all of the vegetables we had. Picking green beans was bad enough, but we had to feel each butterbean to be sure it was filled out before we picked it. "Filled out" means the little butterbeans inside the outer shells are fully grown. If they were not, we were not to pick them. There might be a cluster of ten to twelve beans, but if a couple of them were not filled out, we couldn't just jerk the whole cluster from the plant. To make matters worse— much worse—the butterbean plants grew very close to the ground. We couldn't walk on our knees or crawl, so the task of picking butterbeans required a lot of stooping. It was back-bending, back-aching, feeling-like-back-breaking work! I hated the sight of a row of butterbeans, but when Dad told us to pick, we picked. When I picked some that were not filled out, I suffered consequences. I tried to be careful because I knew mistakes were not tolerated.

After we finished picking butterbeans, we had to sit and shell them until the last one was shelled. I hated that, too. Butterbeans had the toughest shells of any bean I have ever encountered, and opening a butterbean required the use of my fingernails. My fingernails were always broken, and the ends of my fingers were always sore. I never understood how Dad expected me to play a decent game of anything with such sore fingers. However, when the butterbeans were cooked, I was usually the first one to dip into the pot to fill my plate with them. There was nothing better than a plate full of butterbeans, Mother's homemade chow-chow, cornbread, and buttermilk. I ate until I could eat no more.

Another vegetable we always had was cabbage. Cabbage was much easier to pick than other vegetables: we just cut it off near the bottom of the plant. We had steamed cabbage, fried cabbage, and cabbage in Mother's homemade chow-chow and sauerkraut. I didn't like the smell of cabbage when it was cooking, but I loved the taste of it when it was served. I also loved cabbage in cole slaw.

We had cucumber vines running all over the garden, and we loved to eat cucumbers straight from the vine. However, Mother made some very good bread-and-butter pickles in her churn, and I loved to eat the pickles. We also had bell peppers and hot peppers, which we ate straight from the plants or in Mother's chow-chow. Of course, peppers were used to flavor many foods that we ate.

When the strawberries and peaches were ripe, it was time to drag out the ice cream churn. There was nothing better than sitting around under a large oak tree on a hot summer day with a bowl of freshly churned homemade ice cream. We had an old ice cream churn with a metal container inside a wooden bucket with a hand crank on top of it. We filled the metal container with the ice cream mixture and sealed it, and then we filled the outer wooden bucket with ice and rock salt and began turning the crank. It took a long time for the ice cream to harden, so one person would begin turning the churn crank and another would take over when the first person grew tired. By the time the ice cream was ready, we would be perspiring. It seemed as if the ice cream was always better because we had to work so hard to make it. It always tasted good, but even if it hadn't, we would have enjoyed the refreshing coolness of it anyway.

One other thing I remember getting from our garden is watermelons. We would put one into the refrigerator and leave it overnight, and then we would cut it at about midday. I loved cold watermelon, especially on a hot summer day. Even though I sometimes felt as if I were going to burst, I would eat watermelon until the last bite was gone. I even scraped the rind until all of the red color was gone. I just couldn't seem to get enough.

I guess I remember our garden so well because of the years we had gone through when we sometimes had no food at all on our table. It was wonderful to see that Mother was able to cook and enjoy a delicious meal rather than skipping meals because she worried so much about her children's hunger and nutrition. I looked at the planting and harvesting of our garden as a major turning point in our lives. It didn't cost us a lot of money to buy and plant seeds, and Dad and Mother had more money to take care of household needs and pay down debts because they didn't have to spend everything they earned on food. Because we had ample food, all of us boys could enjoy our work, play, and adventures much more than we could have otherwise. We continued to have a garden each summer, and the work and enjoyment was always similar each year.

The gardens always enabled Mother to serve many delicious meals to our friends and relatives when they visited our house. We also were able to carry ample food supplies to the Thomas family reunion each summer. When we arrived at our relatives' home, the large twenty-five-foot-long table usually already had a variety of foods sitting on it. Every family brought food, and the table was full when we finished placing all of our food on it. The Thomas family always had a feast at the reunions.

The reunions were also good times for all of us boys and Grace to visit with all of our relatives. We had an opportunity to see some of our cousins we sometimes didn't see any other time but reunions, and we spent as much time with them as possible. It was nice to see how each one changed in appearance and maturity as the years passed. It was always obvious that they were growing older. Meanwhile, all of us were getting older as well.

When David entered the tenth grade at Parker High School, I entered the eighth grade at L. P. Hollis Junior High School. William and James were seniors at Parker.

William Porter, James Porter.

I don't recall whether or not my brothers rode a public bus or rode with friends in private vehicles, but public school buses did not come into our neighborhood. I recall I had to walk to school each day, and the distance was about two miles by road. However, I walked with a group of friends, and we chose to walk through the woods and alongside the railroad tracks, a route that made our trek about one mile shorter. Our walks to school were pleasant most of the time because we chatted and played along the way. I had unpleasant walks only when it rained because I still did not have a raincoat. However, I do remember a couple of occasions when I was frightened as I was walking to school, and I don't think I will ever forget them.

The first incident occurred one morning when a friend and I were walking to school by way of the railroad tracks. We discovered the body of a dead man lying adjacent to the tracks. When we took a close look at the man, it looked as if someone had struck him on the head with an axe. He had several deep gashes on his head. We thought the man must have been murdered, and our first thought was that the murderer could still be in the area. The thought of being killed by blows from an axe was frightening, so we ran as fast as we could to a café in the area. We reported finding the dead man to the café owner, and he called law enforcement authorities. We were considerably late for school that day because we had to wait for law enforcement authorities to arrive and lead them to the body. After answering numerous questions from the authorities, we got a ride to school in their vehicle. A sheriff's deputy explained to our school principal why we were late, so our tardiness was excused. After school, we walked home by way of the road because we had not yet been told that a train had killed the man. We learned a train had killed the man later that evening. We resumed walking to school by way of the railroad tracks the next day.

The second incident also occurred one morning when I was walking to school with friends. We knew a bootlegger lived near the railroad tracks, and he buried glass jars full of moonshine whiskey along the railroad embankment. We dug up jars of moonshine and passed them around among our classmates and ourselves on several occasions. Each of us would drink a small amount, but we always passed the jar around until it was empty. We disposed of the jar and then walked into the school as though we were innocent of any wrongdoing. Fortunately, school authorities and our parents never caught us. Anyway, as we were walking along the tracks that morning, we decided to dig up another jar of moonshine. We went down the railroad embankment and dug up a quart jar, and when we were back on the tracks, we began passing it around. Suddenly, we heard a very loud *boom*! We turned to look in the direction the noise came from, and there was the bootlegger, pointing a shotgun as us. We ran and escaped from the bootlegger, but I will never forget the sounds emitted from his shotgun. He fired four shots as we ran away. Somehow, we managed to maintain possession of the moonshine, and we passed it around until the jar was empty. As we passed the jar around to our classmates, we described our frightening, hair-raising experience to them.

A couple of weeks later, a mysterious fire occurred along the railroad embankment where the bootlegger stored his moonshine. As the fire raced across the embankment, small explosions of jars of moonshine occurred. The moonshine was additional fuel for the fire and made it more difficult for the firefighters. It wasn't long before sheriff's deputies began to arrive. The bootlegger was arrested, and I never saw him again. I also never looked for his moonshine again. Of course, the memory of the shotgun was deterrent enough to keep me away from the bootlegger's territory, but that memory wasn't enough to stop my friends and me from being mischievous, even downright malicious at times. I remember a few incidents very clearly. One of the most hilarious events I was ever involved in was playing a devious prank on one of our neighbors.

No one had a fence around his yard in our mill village, and everyone knew all of his neighbors. My brothers and I knew everyone in the entire village. We could go to anyone in the village for assistance or just yell for help if we needed it. Almost every adult in the village looked after the children in the village as though everyone in the village were family members. We never had to worry about someone coming to our aid. We knew someone would. We even left the doors to our home open day and night because we never had fear that burglars would come. We had screen doors only to keep insects out. To me, one of the great things about living in the village was the absence of fences. We could take shortcuts through almost any yard in the village without being scolded. However, one man who lived alone in our neighborhood was not very kind when we walked or ran across his yard. He acted as though he disliked children even when we attempted to be nice to him. He was the person we decided to aggravate with our little prank.

We began by knocking on his door at night and then running to hide in the bushes across the street before he could get the door opened. When he opened the door, no one would be there. He would stand on his porch and look around for a couple of minutes and then go back inside and close the door. We repeated that prank many times.

When Halloween arrived, we decided the man needed some special attention. We found a ball of kite string more than a hundred yards in length, and then we crept onto the man's porch and tied one end of the string to his screened door handle. As we walked across the street, we unrolled the string and allowed it to lie loosely on the ground, and we held onto the loose end. When we were safely hidden in the bushes, we pulled the man's screen door open with the string and then let the door slam shut. He must have had a strong spring on the door because it made a loud sound when it slammed shut. The man came to the door, turned on his porch light and looked around, and then he went back inside, closed the door and turned off the light. We waited a couple of minutes and then opened and shut the door again. The man went through the same process of opening the door, turning on the light, and looking around. We repeated our prank at least ten times before the man decided to attempt to catch us. The last time we pulled the door open and let it slam, he must have been just inside, standing ready to open the door quickly. We opened the door and let it slam, and the man was instantly on the porch with a shotgun in his hands. We remained hidden, and the man fired the shotgun into the air. He stood on his porch for at least five minutes, but he never discovered the string. When he finally went back inside, we jumped from the bushes and ran away.

A couple of days later, I went to the barbershop for a haircut. The man was sitting in the barber's chair telling the barber about our prank. He had discovered a piece of our string we left tied to his door. I acted innocent, but I laughed. The man never discovered who we were, and we pulled another prank on him the following Halloween.

By the time the next Halloween arrived, the man had a chain-link fence installed around his yard, the only fence in the village for several years. However, the fence did not stop us from pulling our prank. Prior to darkness, several of us boys had gathered in the mill village pasture, and we had taken a large, paper grocery bag with us. As many of us that could, defecated, and then, using sticks, placed the defecation into the grocery bag. We waited until about ten o'clock and then visited the man's house. We crept onto the man's porch, placed the bag in front of his door, and set the bag on fire. We knocked loudly on the man's door and then ran away to hide. We were hiding in the bushes by the time the man opened the door and saw the fire. He immediately began the stomp on the bag of defecation to extinguish the fire. It wasn't until he had the fire out that he realized he had defecation all over his feet. He yelled out that he was going to get us, whoever we were, and we ran away as fast as we could. Fortunately, we never got caught. We went to

218

the pasture, ate our trick-or-treat candy and fruit we had collected earlier, and laughed until our sides were hurting. I guess we thought everything we did was humorous, but humor did not always come our way from others.

It was about that time of my life when I experienced one case of harsh reaction to a remark I made to Mother and the only apology that any family member ever got from Dad. One day I was attempting to get Mother to buy something for me and she kept refusing. After about thirty minutes of begging and getting refusals, I got the wise idea to ask Mother if I was adopted. She asked me why I would ask such a stupid question. That should have been my warning not to say anything else, but I failed to heed it. I told Mother that I wanted to know whether or not I was adopted because I didn't think she treated me like the rest of the family. I didn't get the words out of my mouth good before I felt the stinging pain of her hand across my face. She slapped me everywhere she could land a blow. I was ducking and dodging all over the room. She was in a rage, and I got out of there as quickly as I could. I never asked her another question that I thought she might consider to be stupid. However, I guess she had just shown me that she would treat me just like she did the rest of the family, with a quick reaction and harsh discipline. I left the house and went to walk in the woods.

The apology from Dad was given just a couple of weeks after the incident with Mother. David was working that week, but it was Thursday and he would not receive his pay until Friday or Saturday. He went to the neighborhood grocery store and borrowed twenty dollars from the owner, Gordon Blair, promising to pay it back when he got paid. David was not aware Gordon put the twenty dollars on Dad's charge account. Later the same day, Dad went to the grocery store to pick up a couple of items and pay any money he owed on his charge account. Gordon placed all of Dad's bills on the counter and began to ring them up. Dad noticed the bill for twenty dollars and asked about it. Gordon told Dad I had borrowed the money. Obviously, Gordon had mistakenly identified the wrong son, but Dad had no way of knowing that. He paid the account in full and then came home full of anger.

Dad grabbed me by the arm and proceeded to take off his belt. I could see the anger in his face, and I knew I was about to be whipped with the belt. I asked Dad what I had done and he replied that I knew good and well what I had done. He told me I had borrowed money at the grocery store and put it on his account. When I denied it, he said he was going to whip me for lying. I started to cry because I was being accused of something I had not done, and just like the punishment after the golf ball incident, I knew I was about to receive a terrible whipping. I kept saying I was innocent, and he kept saying I was guilty. I was somehow able to convince him I was innocent, or he was remembering the golf ball incident, because he didn't whip me. Instead, he told me to go to the store with him and he would prove I had borrowed the money. I told him I was willing and ready to go, and we began walking toward the store. About a block from the grocery store, Dad suddenly stopped and turned around. He told me to go back to the house. I told him I wanted to continue to the store to prove my innocence, but he insisted that I go home, so I did. I went into my bedroom and lay across my bed and cried. Dad went into our living room and sat in his chair.

When David came home, the first thing Dad asked him was whether or not he had borrowed any money from the grocery store. David told Dad he had borrowed twenty dollars but the money was not supposed to be placed on Dad's charge account; it was supposed to be charged to David. The only explanation for writing a bill in Dad's name was that perhaps Gordon just wanted to be sure he got his money back. Fortunately for me, Dad learned the truth that time before he whipped me with the belt.

When all of the other family members were home, Dad called me into the living room. He told them the full story, and then he apologized to me in front of the family. I went to bed that night relieved that I had not been whipped but still hurting from being accused of doing something I was innocent of. Dad had already gone to work when I got up the next morning. I headed to the woods, where I stayed all day, thinking about running away from home but fearing the consequences if I should get caught. I spent a lot of time in the woods after that incident.

I loved being in the woods almost as much as I ever loved playing baseball. I guess it was the fact that I could be at peace in the woods that I was so drawn to the woods and streams. My self-appraisal was very high when I was alone in the woods. It didn't matter whether I was hunting, fishing, frog gigging, catching snakes, or just sitting on the ground leaning back against a large oak tree. In that environment, I was always more than just contented: I was happy.

I began spending a lot of time in and around the woods and streams that were within walking distance of our house. I also visited several of my uncles who owned farms with woods and streams on them. I got my slingshot out and practiced until I was as good as I had ever been, probably better. I carried the slingshot around my neck, and I always had marbles in my pants pocket. Every time I went into the woods and fields, I was prepared to hunt and shoot small animals and birds. For the next few years, I experienced some of the most exciting adventures I could have ever imagined. I also made some mistakes I regret still today, but even when I was making mistakes, I was having fun.

I once visited my uncle King Nix, his wife Iola, and their two daughters Mildred and Margaret in Pickens County for a week.

I wasn't allowed to take my shotgun, but I was allowed to take my slingshot and a few dozen marbles. One day I was walking along the edge of the woods at the rear of their house when a large chicken walked into sight. I knew the chicken belonged to King because I had seen it earlier, closer to the house.

I thought the chicken was too far away for me to kill it with my slingshot, but I wanted to try to scare it anyway. I placed a marble into the pocket of my slingshot and fired. *Bam!* I hit the chicken squarely on the head. The chicken began to flap its wings and was bouncing all over the ground. I was scared to death that King would either see the chicken or hear all the commotion. I ran about a quarter of a mile and hid in an apple orchard. After about an hour, I walked back to the area

Uncle King and Aunt Iola.

221

Bertha Thomas (Clyde's first wife), Gladys Thomas,
King Nix, Margie Thomas, Cannie Thomas.

where I shot the chicken and discovered the chicken was dead. The first thing I thought of was cooking the chicken, but then I thought King would kill me if he found out I had killed his chicken. I picked the chicken up and carried it about a half mile through the woods and then covered it with limbs and brush. I never told King about killing his chicken, and he never asked me about it. I regretted that mistake because I loved Uncle King dearly. However, I also feared him, and I was afraid he would either whip me or tell Dad. I knew Dad would give me a beating that I would never forget, so I kept my mouth shut. I enjoyed the rest of my visit with my relatives, and I visited them again many times, without my slingshot.

I visited another uncle, Clyde Thomas, his wife Bertha, and their boys Lester and Larry, who lived in Pickens County. I was allowed to take my shotgun. Clyde allowed me to hunt with his beagles while he worked at his barbershop in town. I loved to hunt rabbits, so I was just as happy as I could be. On the third day I was at my uncle's house, I went rabbit hunting early in the morning. Clyde and Lester had already left for town, but Bertha and

Larry were inside the house. I had all of the beagles with me as I crossed a field of deep grass and weeds adjacent to the house, or so I thought. When I was no more than fifty yards away from the house, I thought I saw a rabbit running through the tall grass and weeds. It appeared to be running from the dogs. I shouldered and fired my shotgun quickly. The next sound I heard was the terrifying yelp of a beagle that I had just shot! The poor dog cried for what seemed to be a full minute, and then there was complete silence. I knew immediately I had killed one of Clyde's dogs. I also knew Bertha and Larry had to have heard the noises of both my shotgun and the dog. I was extremely frightened.

I started acting as if I was calling the dogs, but in reality I was dragging the dead dog and yelling for the other dogs to follow me. Of course, the other dogs did not follow me, and how could I blame them? They probably thought I was planning to shoot all of them. I pulled the dead dog at least a mile through the woods and fields before I finally stopped because I was just totally exhausted. I covered the dog with heavy brush, and then I pretended I was hunting again.

I was trying all day to figure out what I would say when asked what happened to Clyde's dog. To my surprise, not one word was mentioned that evening about dogs or hunting. I went to sleep that night, but I slept very little. I was so worried that Clyde was going to burst into the bedroom any minute and give me a beating.

The next morning, I was called to the dining room for breakfast. When I got into the dining room, Clyde, Bertha, Lester, and Larry were already sitting around the table. We began to eat, but then Clyde asked about his dog. He asked me when I had last seen his dog, Queenie. I was absolutely petrified with fright, but I managed to answer his question. I said the last time I had seen the dog was when we were about a mile to a mile and a half from

Clyde and Ida Thomas.

his house. Clyde never asked me another question. He just remarked that the rest of his dogs were in the yard, but Queenie wasn't there. We finished eating, and Clyde left for work. To this day, I don't know whether or not Clyde knew I had killed his dog. However, I visited him many times before his death, and he never once mentioned Queenie.

I have to believe Bertha and Larry knew I had killed Clyde's dog. Either they didn't realize what I had done, or they were just as afraid to tell Clyde as I was. The only other reason I could think of was that they just wanted to protect me from a whipping by Clyde and another whipping by Dad. If they knew I had killed the dog and protected me, I am grateful for that. However, I am still very sorry I killed Clyde's dog. I would never have intentionally harmed a hunting dog, especially one belonging to my uncle. Since Clyde's death, I have thought about him many times, and I always remember him as a gruff-talking but softhearted uncle who always treated me with much care and concern. I am happy I was able spend time with him. Thankfully, I have never made a mistake of killing a hunting dog again. However, I did continue with my outdoor adventures, including hunting.

There was a place on Grove Road about a mile from our house called Earle's Pasture. It must have contained two or three hundred acres of some of the most beautiful woodlands and pastures I have ever seen, and it had a large creek running through it. Greenville Memorial Hospital and many hospital-related buildings now occupy that land.

From the Earle family home, Faris Road was about a half mile to the left. The forest between the Earle home and Faris Road contained many large and tall oak, poplar, and hickory trees that reminded me of the trees that were on Paris Mountain where Dad first taught me to hunt squirrels.

Although the property was privately owned and we were probably not supposed to enter it, David and I, along with several of our friends, went there often. We walked across Grove Road, but we always made sure the Earle family could not see us. We didn't want to anger anyone; we just wanted to have some fun. Our version of fun was swimming in the creek and hunting anything that moved on the land.

The first time we entered Earle's Pasture, it seemed as if we walked two miles through the woods before we discovered the creek. It was in the summertime, and the temperature was high. That's probably why the walk seemed so long. The creek just seemed to tell us to jump in, so we did. Of course, we took off all of our clothes first. There is nothing more refreshing than the feel of cool, rushing water on a person's body after a long, sweaty walk through a forest. We must have played around in the water for a good three hours. If anyone knew we were there, they never bothered us. That was the first of many skinny-dipping trips we enjoyed in the creek. Over time, a number of people joined us, but no one ever stopped us. I have seen as many as twenty teenagers, boys and girls, some naked, swimming and playing in the creek.

One day three of my friends and I decided to go rabbit hunting in Earle's Pasture. I had my slingshot, one friend had a BB gun, one had a large knife, and the other had no weapon at all. However, the friend with no weapon had a large Chinese Chow dog that he allowed to go along. I had never seen a dog like that, especially on a rabbit-hunting trip. With the pitiful arsenal of weapons we had, I don't think anyone really expected us to come even close to getting a rabbit.

We entered a field that had a lot of briar patches. I'm not sure if the patches were blackberry vines or just scrub briars. We were walking by one patch of briars when a rabbit jumped up at the edge and ran into the thickest part of the patch. We surrounded the briar patch to prevent the rabbit from escaping. The friend with the dog was directly across the patch from me. I had a marble in the pocket of my slingshot, and I was prepared to shoot. The dog kept going into the briar patch, but it kept returning to its owner. It never barked once. After about five minutes, I got down on my knees to see if I could look under the vines. It was then that I saw the rabbit just sitting in the middle of the briar patch. It appeared to be a little nonchalant about the commotion we were making. I pulled back the pocket of my slingshot as far as I could and then let it go. The marble struck the rabbit right between its eyes and it fell to the ground dead. I told my friend to hold onto his dog and then I crawled on my belly under the briars to retrieve the rabbit. We might have had a pitiful arsenal of weapons, but we had a rabbit! I placed the rabbit into a pocket of my jacket and continued hunting.

We walked about another forty yards before another rabbit jumped up. The dog saw the rabbit jump up and gave chase. The rabbit ran no more than forty to fifty feet before the dog caught it. The dog chomped on the rabbit's neck and shook it one time and the rabbit was instantly dead. I couldn't believe what I had just seen. I had always hunted with beagles, but none of them had ever come close to catching a rabbit. In fact, we used beagles because we didn't want them to catch a rabbit. We just wanted them to chase a rabbit until we could get a shot at it. Regardless, my friends and I were proving that we were good hunters. Luck or no luck, we had two rabbits! I've seen a lot of hunters come home from a rabbit-hunting trip with less.

While we were walking across the field to get to another briar patch, a bird flew just in front of us. I threw up my slingshot and fired, and the bird fell dead to the ground. My friends were congratulating me and acting as if they believed I must have been the most accurate slingshot user alive. I knew luck had been on my side again.

We continued to hunt for a while and then we sat down in the woods to rest, talking about whatever came to mind. I asked my friend if I could see his knife. I was flabbergasted when he pulled it from its sheath. He had a knife called a Bowie knife. The knife was named Bowie, because Jim Bowie, the frontiersman who died in the Battle of the Alamo in San Antonio, Texas, carried a knife of that style and size. My friend's knife was beautiful. It was about fifteen inches long and had a bone handle. While I was admiring the knife, one of my other friends remarked that the knife owner could throw the knife as well as I could shoot my slingshot. When I expressed doubt, the knife owner took the knife and threw it at a tree about ten paces away. The knife stuck about an inch into the tree. Next, my friend announced that he was going to attempt to throw the knife into a small knot on the tree. The knot was about three inches in diameter. I didn't think he would even come close; however, he stuck the knife almost in the center of the knot. I expressed no more doubts, and I didn't attempt to shoot at the knot with my slingshot either. After I had just knocked a flying bird from the air, I didn't want to chance being embarrassed by missing a knot that was perfectly still on the side of a tree.

Also, I never bothered to challenge my friend with the BB gun. I had seen one friend's expertise with a knife, and I had seen another friend's dog catch a running rabbit. I just assumed my other friend was equally as good with his BB gun as I was with my slingshot.

Although I hunted with my friends regularly, I also spent a lot of time in the woods and fields alone. I also went alone to the creeks and ponds in the area regularly. In fact, when I was not hunting or playing with my brothers and friends, I was usually involved in some other activity in the woods, at the creek, or at the millpond. I especially enjoyed visiting the millpond because I loved to gig frogs and eat their legs.

I got started gigging frogs because I accidentally saw some frog gigs for sale at the small grocery store near our house. I had just been paid for a grass-cutting job, so I had a little money with me. Just the thought of hunting and gigging frogs intrigued me, so although I had gone to the store to buy candy and a drink, I didn't hesitate to buy a frog gig first. I had heard some frogs down at the millpond that sounded as if they were big. Most of the time, the frogs began to croak at first darkness of night and they would croak all night. Sometimes, it seemed as if there must have been five hundred frogs croaking at the same time. I had never eaten frog legs but I had heard they were delicious, so I decided to try my luck at gigging frogs and eating their legs.

A frog gig did not come already mounted on a pole, at least not any that I had ever seen. The gigger had to find some type of pole on which to mount the gig, and gig poles were not sold in our neighborhood store. I went down to the creek to find a small sapling I could cut down to use as a gig pole. After a long search, I found the ideal tree, about fifteen feet tall. It was also quite straight and had very few limbs. Initially, I cut off both ends of the pole to make it close to ten feet in length, and then I trimmed all of the bark from it. I whittled the larger end of the pole to a point that would fit into the funnel-shaped top end of the gig. After being satisfied with the fit of the pole into the gig, I placed the pole in a spot where I knew the sun would shine on it for many hours each day.

The pole needed to be dried out so it would lose most of its flexibility. After several days of drying out, the pole was ready for me to mount my gig on it. I mounted the gig with a large nail, and I was ready to go frog gigging.

The sky was still light when I arrived at the millpond, but the sun had already gone below the horizon. I discovered I could not walk around the perimeter of the pond as I had expected to, because the weeds and plants surrounding the pond had thorny bushes among them. I had never noticed them before because I had always just walked into the pond by way of the creek that fed the pond. I just returned home, planning to do some scouting around the pond the next day. I also discovered I needed some fresh flashlight batteries.

The next day I arrived at the millpond at about ten o'clock in the morning. I had plenty of time to figure out how I was going to maneuver around the pond to gig frogs. I attempted to find a pathway around the perimeter of the pond, but there was none. Finally, I decided to see whether or not I could get into the pond by way of the creek and just walk in the water around the inside perimeter of the pond. I took off my shoes and placed them on the creek bank and entered the water. The creek had a mostly sandy bottom, but it was also rocky in places. However, when I entered the millpond, I was walking in slimy, soft mud. It was a good thing I had taken off my shoes because the mud would have sucked them right from my feet. I guess the good thing about my scouting was I was learning what to expect when I returned to gig frogs. The water around the edge of the pond was just above my knees. Of course, at the dam and in the middle of the pond, it was much deeper. I had to walk down one side of the pond, return to the creek, cross to the other side, and then walk down the other side of the pond. More time was consumed, but I could see no other way to gig on both sides of the pond.

I returned to the millpond that night just as it was getting dark. The frogs were already croaking. In fact, the frogs were croaking so loud that I could hear nothing else. The low bass sounds of the frogs let me know that they were large bullfrogs, not just some little toads. They were everywhere.

I entered the creek about twenty yards from the pond and walked toward the pond, staying close to the bank. I had a large sack that we called a "croaker sack," but other people called it "gunnysack." I tied the sack to my belt to keep it from floating away or sinking, and I tied a piece of strong twine we called "mill band" onto one end of my flashlight and attached the other end to my belt to prevent the loss of my flashlight if I dropped it into the water.

My flashlight held three batteries that made the light shine very brightly. I was barefooted and wearing blue jeans to protect my legs if I walked into a snag. I had on a warm shirt because the water was cold.

I was shining my flashlight as I walked toward the shoreline just ahead of me. When I had almost reached the pond, I saw the eyes of a frog on the bank of the creek. I shined the light into the eyes of the frog and crept slowly toward it. I stopped when I had reached a point where I was sure I could gig the frog. I slowly raised the gig, and then I thrust the gig into the back of the frog. The frog was attempting to get away but I was holding it against the ground with the gig. I ran my hand down the pole until I could feel the frog, and then I got a good grip on the frog and lifted it out of the water. I discovered there was no way the frog could have gotten off the gig. The gig had penetrated the body of the frog, and the spurs on the gig would not have allowed the frog to escape. It took a minute or so for me to get the frog off the gig, and then I put the frog into my croaker sack. I had successfully gigged my first frog. I went looking for more, staying at the pond about four hours that night. I successfully gigged about forty frogs, some of them so big they had legs about the size of a large chicken leg. The frogs were very heavy, and because most of them were still alive and moving, they were difficult to carry. I had gotten a lot of frogs, but more than I had gigged had hopped into the pond to escape being caught. I knew if frog legs were as good to eat as I had been told, I had several good meals in my bag. I also knew I had found an excellent place to hunt for frogs, and I would return often.

It was very late at night when I finally arrived home but I still had to cut off the legs of the frogs, skin them, wash them, and put them into the refrigerator. I also had to get rid of the remains. It must have been close to three o'clock in the morning by the time I finished. When I went to bed, I was so tired I slept until noon.

I decided I wanted to eat frog legs for lunch, so I got about a dozen out to prepare for cooking. I had cooked chicken legs many times, so I just prepared the frog legs the same way I had prepared the chicken legs. To my surprise, when I put the frog legs into a pan of hot grease, they began to quiver so hard I thought they were going to jump right out of the pan. I called Mother into the kitchen so she could see the frog legs quiver. She had never cooked frog legs, so she was amused. I was ready to eat when the frog legs were fully cooked. The meat was white and looked very much like the meat of a fried chicken breast, and the legs cooked very much like chicken. It even had a pleasant aroma like chicken. I knew I would be going back to the millpond when I took the first bite. The frog legs were absolutely delicious. I offered some to Mother, but she wouldn't even taste them. What a loss for her. I ate all I had cooked, and I could have eaten more. However, I knew I had several more meals waiting in the refrigerator, and I would be gigging again soon.

One night when I went gigging at the millpond, I got an unexpected surprise. I was walking in the water around the inside perimeter of the pond, shining my light, when I saw the body of a large frog, but I could not see the eyes of the frog. I walked closer to get a better look. Suddenly, I realized I could not see the eyes of the frog because a huge snake had the entire head of the frog in its mouth. For just a few seconds, I was frightened silly. However, I realized I was in no danger from the snake because the snake was attempting to swallow the frog and it couldn't crawl, swim, or attack me. It had so much of the frog in its mouth it could not have turned it loose even if it wanted to. I watched the snake swallowing the frog for a few minutes, and then I decided to gig the snake. I thrust the gig into the snake just behind its head and the snake began to coil around my gig and pole. I just walked back up to the creek to a place where I could get out of the water and carried the snake and frog onto the top of the creek bank. I used my hunting knife to cut the snake's head off. I knew I would never encounter that snake at the millpond again. I also knew I had just eliminated a major competitor for the frogs.

Many species of creatures lived in and around the creek that fed into the millpond. One day when I was looking for minnows, I saw a crawfish slither under a rock at the bottom of the stream. Some people called them "crayfish," but in our area we called them "crawfish." I decided to try catching the crawfish.

I was already barefooted, so I just stepped into the water and gently picked up the rock I had seen the crawfish go under. The crawfish was still there, and it appeared as if it were trying to hide. I placed the rock on the creek bank and put my hands into the water to catch the crawfish. I knew crawfish could swim backwards very fast but moved forward very slowly. I put one hand behind the crawfish and placed my other hand in front of it. The crawfish swam backwards right into my hand, and then it swam quickly out again. I had not reacted quickly enough to catch it. I watched it until it stopped swimming and cupped my hands and moved slowly toward it. The crawfish backed up against the creek bank at the bottom of the creek. I could see that it had very large claws—I called them "pinchers." I had to be careful, or I would get pinched. The pinch of a crawfish claw is sometimes painful. I decided I would attempt to catch the crawfish by grabbing its body behind its claws. I moved one hand down very slowly behind the crawfish until I was almost touching it. I grabbed the crawfish quickly. When I pulled the crawfish from the water it was trying to pinch me, but my fingers were behind its claws, so it couldn't. I saw two more crawfish dart through the water and hide under rocks as I stepped out of the water. I knew I had found a crawfish hole. I decided I would catch as many crawfish as I could; however, I had nothing to put captured crawfish into. Even though I was originally looking for minnows, I had brought nothing to put them into. I guess I was a poor planner that day.

I decided I would just kill the crawfish I had caught and leave. I could always come back another day. I held the crawfish in one hand and carefully pulled its claws off with the other hand. The crawfish was defenseless without its claws. I took the end of its head between my fingers and pinched it off. I was surprised to see two little white pieces of bone-like material inside the crawfish's head. When I took them out, I noticed that each piece of material resembled one side of a pearl. It appeared that I was holding a whole pearl in my hand when I put the two pieces together. I was fascinated by the appearance, so I decided to catch another crawfish to see if it had the same material in its head. I placed the two pieces I had already gotten into my pocket and reentered the water. I had soon caught another crawfish, and sure enough, there were two pieces of the same bonelike material, gleaming white in color. I continued to catch crawfish until I had about eighty pieces of the bonelike material in my pocket. I was excited because I thought I had discovered a source of pearls no one else knew about.

I ran most of the way home and walked fast the rest of the way. I couldn't wait to show my pearls to Mother. I was terribly disappointed because when I showed them to Mother, she was not in the least impressed. I just put the material in my bedroom and went outside to play.

The next morning I took the pearllike material to school and showed them to my teacher. She acted as if she were very excited to see them. Her reaction was just the opposite of the reaction I had gotten from Mother. The teacher asked a lot of questions about what the material was and where I had gotten all the pieces. After I explained everything I knew about the material to the teacher, she asked me if I would sell them to her. I guess I must have been speechless because I had not expected to have an offer to buy the material. I didn't say anything, but then the teacher told me she would pay me a nickel for each piece of the material. I was ecstatic. I couldn't believe I was going to earn a fortune from a bunch of crawfish parts, and I didn't hesitate to sell them to my teacher. She told me she would buy all of that material I could bring to her. I was in business.

After I had been hard at work catching crawfish for about three weeks, my teacher called me to the front of the class to show something to me. When she showed it to me, I knew immediately why she had bought the crawfish parts. She had made one of the most beautiful pearllike necklaces I have ever seen in my life. She said she glued the pieces in place and then polished them. They were glued to tiny pieces of silver and gold colored material in such a way that they looked as if they were whole pearls imbedded into the metal. I still don't know how she did it, but the metal pieces were attached to each other to make it into a solid necklace. My teacher was very proud of her necklace, and she wore it to school quite often after that day.

My teacher must have been a jewelry hobbyist or a real jeweler. She made bracelets, earrings, finger rings, and a variety of other necklaces, using crawfish parts she bought from me. Everything she made was pretty, but I thought the first necklace was the most beautiful piece. It was my favorite as well as hers. I have always been proud that I was able to contribute to such a piece of art, even if I did make a small fortune from my treasure hunts.

In the summertime, I went to the creek often. I was looking for minnows to fish with most of the time, and I had found a lot of minnows and caught a lot of fish. However, one day I found something to fish with that I had not expected. I was walking around in the creek turning over rocks to find minnows when I noticed a salamander. I wasn't really interested in it, but I put it into my minnow bucket anyway. I caught several minnows and another salamander. When I caught all the minnows I wanted, I was ready to go fishing. I just took the salamanders along for the ride.

I began to fish with minnows when I got to the fishing lake. I caught three or four small fish, but I lost several minnows in the process. I was almost out of minnows so I decided to fish with a minnow on one line and a salamander on the other. I had never fished with a salamander, so I had no idea whether or not they were good fish bait. I threw the line with the salamander on it into the lake and let it sink to the bottom and then did the same with a minnow. About twenty minutes later, one of my rods was jerked so hard it almost fell into the lake. I grabbed it and jerked it back hard, setting a hook into the mouth of a fish. I had the drag on my reel set fairly tight, but the fish was taking line as if I had no drag at all. I was holding on to the rod and attempting to reel, but I wasn't having much success. I decided to just tighten the drag some more and let the fish take line. The only hope I had of catching the fish was for the fish to get tired enough to stop fighting. After a few minutes, I was able to reel the fish in a little, but then the fish pulled more line out. As the fish tired, I was able to reel it in closer and closer. The fish finally came to the surface of the water and just rolled over and gave up. I reeled it ashore, and I was jubilant. I had caught the biggest fish of my life. I looked to see what species the fish was, and I saw that it was a bass. Then I noticed I had caught it with the salamander.

I hooked my stringer through the gills of the fish before I even thought about taking the hook from the fish's mouth. I picked the fish up with the stringer and carried it away from the water and took the hook from its mouth. I did not want to take a chance that the fish might get away. I tied my stringer to a tree and then reeled in the line with a minnow on it. I reeled in both lines, packed up, and went home; however, I stopped at the grocery store to weigh the fish before I went home.

I was barely able to carry the big bass the distance to the grocery store. I asked the meat market manager to weigh the fish, and he acted as if he were delighted to do so. He told me the fish weighed seven pounds and three ounces. I was so excited I could hardly talk. The meat market manager asked me if I would like for him to filet the fish, and I almost screamed out the word, "*yes*." He didn't even scale the fish; he just cut right through the scales and skin. He cut both sides from the fish, turned them skin-down on his table, and cut the filet from the skin. I had never seen anyone cut filets from a fish before, and I was fascinated that he could do it so fast. The filets were so large that he cut them into smaller pieces. He wrapped them for me, and I just gave the other fish I had caught to the meat market manager. He seemed to be happy, and I was certainly happy as I walked home with enough fish filets to feed the whole family. We had a very tasteful meal the next day. As soon as I got a chance, I was back at the creek looking for salamanders.

I walked down to the creek after a heavy rain to see how high the water level was. I did not realize it had rained so much, but the water was just about to overflow the creek banks. The water was extremely muddy and ugly, but I stood near the creek and watched it flow by anyway.

I had been standing there for about fifteen minutes when I suddenly started noticing some small black objects floating on top of the water. I took a closer look and saw that the small objects seemed to be trying to swim. I got as close to the rushing water as I dared and looked even closer. To my amazement, I saw that the small objects were hundreds of tiny catfish, no longer than two inches. I wanted to catch some of them but I had nothing to put them into, so I ran home as fast as I could and got a bucket and then ran back to the creek.

Little catfish were still floating and swimming by when I got back to the creek. I lay on my stomach and reached out into the water as far as I could, and I was able to scoop up some of the fish as they floated by. I kept scooping until I could no longer see fish floating by, and then I ran downstream as fast as I could run. I stopped and looked into the creek when I reached a place where I knew I could possibly catch more fish. Fish were floating by, so I quickly lay down and began to scoop them up. I scooped up all the fish I could see and then went home.

I saw several of my friends as I was walking home. I called them over and showed the catfish to them. When they asked me what I was going to do with the catfish, I told them I was going to raise them until they got big enough to eat, and then I was going to eat them. All of my friends followed me home. I got a large tin tub and filled it with water from our faucet, and then I scooped the fish from the bucket and put them into the tub. I then put the bucket away and left to play with my friends. I bragged to everyone I saw about my catfish and told them about my plan to raise and eat them. I must have told half the people in the mill village, and I think my friends must have told the other half. It seemed as if everyone knew the story within an hour. I returned home after playing with my friends and bragging about my catfish for about three hours.

I didn't know what I was going to feed to the catfish, but I decided they might like a crumbled-up biscuit. I went into the house, got a biscuit, and went out to feed the catfish. I crumbled the bread and dropped it into the tub and went inside for the night.

I got up the next morning and immediately went outside to check on my catfish. I was horrified when I looked into the tub. All of the tiny catfish were floating on top of the water, dead. I was just devastated. They had been so lively the night before. How could such a thing happen?

I saw some of my friends and told them what had happened. They just laughed and started telling everyone they came in contact with. Everyone in the mill village knew of my catastrophe within two hours.

I went to a small café in the mill village later in the evening, and as soon as I walked through the front door, I was greeted by about twelve people shouting,

"Hey, Catfish!" The laughter was more than I wanted to hear, but I just laughed with them and hoped they would soon shut up. They didn't, and I got stuck with the nickname "Catfish" for the remainder of my life. However, I seldom see any of the people now who hung the nickname on me, so I rarely hear it. I read about a baseball player many years later who was nicknamed "Catfish." He was Catfish Hunter, one of the premier pitchers in baseball. He seemed to be pleased with his nickname so I figured I probably should be pleased with mine also. If I run into one of my old friends, I'll just smile and answer to "Catfish."

I usually carried my slingshot draped around my neck almost everywhere I went. Anytime I was carrying the slingshot, I was also carrying a pocket full of marbles. One day when I was walking to the baseball park to play with some of my friends, a cat walked into the road a few yards in front of me. I could see that the cat had something in its mouth, but I couldn't tell what it was. I stopped walking, took my slingshot from around my neck, and loaded it with a marble. I shot the cat in the side, making it drop whatever was in its mouth. The cat quickly ran away, and I went over to see what dropped from its mouth. I was sad to see that the cat had dropped a small chipmunk that appeared to be dead. The chipmunk appeared to be just a baby, and I picked it up just to look at it. As I was holding the little chipmunk, it began to quiver and was trying to move its legs. I turned around and carried the chipmunk home as fast as I could run. I just forgot all about baseball. If I could keep the chipmunk alive, I would possibly have a new pet. I was very excited about that possibility.

The chipmunk was moving a lot more by the time I reached our house. I grabbed the first thing I could find to put the chipmunk into to keep it from escaping. I took a wide-mouth gallon jar from our kitchen and punched holes in the lid so the chipmunk could get air, and then I put the chipmunk gently into the jar. The jar was to be only a temporary cage.

I found some screen wire and a few boards and built a large cage for the chipmunk. I ran to the woods and collected some acorns and put some water and the acorns into the cage. The chipmunk was very much alive by that time, and it was attempting to find a way out of the jar.

I kept a couple of acorns in my hand to attempt to feed them to the chipmunk. I picked up the jar, opened it, and reached into the jar to take the chipmunk out. I was a little scared because I thought the chipmunk might bite me, but I was hoping it would not. When I gently wrapped my hand around the body of the chipmunk, it did not resist or attempt to bite me at all. Instead of acting frightened, it acted as if it was pleased to be in my hand. I wondered whether or not it realized I had saved it from being eaten by a cat. I just sat on the ground and petted the little chipmunk for a long while and then offered an acorn to it. To my surprise and delight, the chipmunk took the acorn and, sitting in my hand, began to nibble the outer shell away from the acorn. I was astonished. I just couldn't believe a wild animal would act so tame so quickly. I watched in amazement as the chipmunk devoured the entire acorn while sitting in my hand. I put the chipmunk into my shirt pocket rather than the cage. I also dropped a couple of small acorns into the pocket.

I walked throughout the neighborhood with the chipmunk in my shirt pocket, and I took the chipmunk to the baseball park to show it to my friends. As soon as my friends saw the chipmunk, they acted as if they understood why I had not arrived to play with them earlier. I think all of them were envious, but they were very careful not to scare the little chipmunk. We all watched as the chipmunk devoured another acorn. I then left for home, where I placed the chipmunk in its cage and headed for the woods. I carried a large bucket with me and gathered acorns until the bucket was completely full. I took the acorns home and stored them in my bedroom. I intended to feed a few acorns to the chipmunk each day.

I got the chipmunk out and petted and played with it for hours each day. I gave acorns to the chipmunk, and it sat in my pocket and ate them. Occasionally I would clean out the acorn shells, and the chipmunk would curl up and go to sleep in the pocket. Then, one day the chipmunk ran from my pocket to my shoulder. I thought it was attempting to escape, but I was afraid I would hurt it if I grabbed it too quickly. However, the chipmunk stopped on top of my shoulder and began to eat an acorn. I couldn't stop myself from laughing. I thought the chipmunk was the most amazing animal I had ever seen. When the chipmunk finished eating the acorn, I dropped another one into my shirt pocket. The chipmunk scurried into the pocket, got the acorn, and returned to my shoulder and began to eat. I was even more amazed. In fact, I think I loved the chipmunk a little more each minute, and it seemed to love me. Undoubtedly, the chipmunk was the most fascinating pet I had ever had.

After about two months, I decided to take the chipmunk to school. When I announced to my classmates that I had a chipmunk in my pocket, they all wanted to see it. I dropped an acorn into my pocket, and the chipmunk scurried up to my shoulder to eat the acorn. All of the girls thought the chipmunk was just so cute, but the boys just thought it was a neat pet. I had the full attention of the whole class.

One of the boys in my class wanted to hold the chipmunk, but I told him no. I told him it might bite him, but he responded by asking whether or not it had ever bitten me. When I told him it had not bitten me, he insisted that I let him hold it. He was much larger than I was and he was considered a tough guy, so I decided to let him hold the chipmunk rather than get into a fight. I placed the chipmunk in his hands. I have no idea what happened next, but my classmate was suddenly jumping around wildly, screaming, and shaking his hand violently. When I looked toward his hand, I saw the little chipmunk clinging to the end of his fingers. Suddenly I saw the chipmunk flying across the classroom, and I ran across the room to get it. It was lying on the floor and appeared to be stunned, but it was not dead. I picked it up and began to gently stroke its head and back. I put the chipmunk into my shirt pocket as I walked back across the room. When I reached my classmate, he was holding his bleeding hand up so the teacher could get a better look at it. There was a hole through the fingernail on the top of his finger and another hole in the bottom side of the same finger. The chipmunk had bitten all the way through my classmate's finger, and the teacher sent my classmate to the office to receive first aid. No one else asked to hold the chipmunk, and I never took it to school again.

One day I was playing with my chipmunk in the clover in our backyard. The clover was about four to six inches tall. I put the chipmunk down in the clover and walked about five steps away. The chipmunk found its way to me, scrambled up my clothing, and got into my shirt pocket. It had been doing that trick for weeks. I put it down again and, to my surprise, it didn't come to me. The clover was so deep I could not see where the chipmunk was, and I couldn't see its movements. I just thought the best thing for me to do was to be still. I was hoping the chipmunk would come to me or I would see some clover move so I could tell where it was and pick it up. After about thirty minutes of watching and waiting, I decided I had better look for the chipmunk, so I started toward where I had put it down. With the very first step I took, I stepped right on the little chipmunk's head and crushed it. The chipmunk died instantly, and I cried like a baby. I loved that little chipmunk more than any other pet I ever had.

Hours later, when I had gotten myself halfway under control, I put the dead chipmunk into a small box and buried it near the house. I missed the little chipmunk terribly, and I had a difficult time thinking about anything else for a long time. However, life must go on, and I eventually got interested in other things. When I remember the little chipmunk, except for the death, the memories are all pleasant.

Someone apparently cut all the large trees down and hauled most of them away in an area near the creek. There were many small trees, scrub brush, and vines left behind. Remains of fallen trees were also scattered about, and there were many large tree stumps. I had never hunted there because I didn't think I would find anything interesting. However, somehow the place intrigued me. Every time I passed the area, my curiosity was aroused and my interest in the area continued to grow. There was one very large, hollow oak tree still standing at the edge of the area, and it was located within eight feet of the creek bank. The last time I was passing by the area, I stopped at the large oak tree to smoke a cigarette. I stuffed the remainder of my package of cigarettes into the bottom of the hollow tree to keep them dry, as well as hidden from my family.

I decided to go down to the creek a few days later to smoke a cigarette. I got down on my knees and reached into the hollow tree to get my cigarettes, but I didn't feel them. I thought I had put them close to the entrance of the hole where I could easily retrieve them, so my first thought was that someone else had discovered my hiding place. However, I thought there was no way anyone else could have discovered the hiding place. I thought I just had not reached far enough into the hole. I got down low enough to look into the hole, which was within three inches of ground level, and stuck my head right up next to the hole so I could see into it. I saw the cigarettes lying inside the hole but they were a little further back than I remembered putting them. Just as I was straining to reach for the cigarettes, with my face touching the tree at the entrance of the hole, a large king snake crawled out of the hole. The snake actually touched my face as it came out of the hole. I jumped to my feet so fast I didn't even realize I had done so, and I probably screamed. I was so shaken by the snake; I could do nothing but watch as it crawled away. It crawled into the area where all of the fallen trees and stumps were, and I didn't bother following it. I just smoked a couple of cigarettes and calmed down. However, I was also thinking I had just discovered something else to hunt; I could hunt snakes. I had never thought of having a pet snake before, but I was thinking about it then.

I began to prepare for a snake hunt a couple of days later. I knew having a long, forked stick was required for hunting snakes. I also knew there were several different species of snakes in the area, some of them poisonous. I just hoped I would know the difference. I certainly didn't want to be bitten by a poisonous snake.

I took my hunting knife into the area where I had gotten my frog gig pole and found a small, straight sapling and cut it down. Near the top of the tree, the branches formed a perfect *Y*. That was unusual for a treetop, but perfect for snake hunting. I cut the prongs of the tree very short and shortened the length of the tree by cutting off the opposite end. The total length of my snake hunting stick was about six feet. I trimmed all of the bark from the tree and placed it in a sunny place to dry out. I wanted a stick that was not flexible and one that would be strong. I knew I would have to hold a snake to the ground while I took hold of it behind the head. Otherwise, I would not be able to pick a snake up without being bitten.

A few days later, I entered the area where I had last seen the king snake. I was armed with the forked stick, a hunting knife, and a wide-mouth gallon jar.

I walked around for about an hour and saw nothing. I finally found a snake while overturning some of the fallen trees. As soon as I uncovered the snake, it coiled into a defensive position and was ready to strike. I stepped back and, using my stick, pushed the snake to one side. The snake attempted to strike the stick and then recoiled. I pushed the snake again, and the snake struck the stick. *Click!* The sound of the snake's fangs striking the stick was frightening, but I was determined I was going to capture it. I had no idea what species of snake it was, but I really didn't care at that point. I pushed the snake again and it attempted to strike. Before the snake could recoil, I had the forks of the stick over its body, but when I looked closely I could see that the stick was too far back from the snake's head. I had to try again. After two more unsuccessful attempts, I was able to get the forks of the stick in just the right place over the snake's body. I held the snake down with the stick and slowly got a firm grip around the snake's body, just behind its head. When I was sure I had a firm enough grip, I lifted the stick. The snake immediately wrapped itself around my arm and was trying to pull its head from my hand. I was scared at that point, but I knew I couldn't loosen my grip or I would be bitten for sure. I estimated the length of the snake to be about three and a half feet. It was a brownish color, with some very beautiful designs on its body. Its head was shiny and about the shade of a dirty penny, and it was rather large in diameter.

When I walked over to put the snake into my jar, I realized I had not yet opened the jar. How was I going to open the jar and maintain a grip on the snake at the same time? How stupid could I be? After a couple of minutes of thought, I put the jar between my legs and squeezed my legs tightly around the jar. With my free hand, I unscrewed the lid and removed it from the jar. I set the jar on the ground and, using my free hand, began to uncoil the snake from my arm. As I uncoiled the snake, I was placing the snake into the jar, tail first. When I had the entire snake into the jar, I held the jar lid in one hand and quickly released the snake's head, jerked my hand away, and slammed the lid onto the jar at the same time. Success! I had captured my first snake! I screwed the lid tightly onto the jar and punched a few holes in the lid with my hunting knife, and then I headed for home.

I was intending to show my snake to my family and then go show it to my friends. However, I didn't get any further than Dad, who was the first person I showed the snake to. When I showed the snake to Dad, he jumped back and told me I had a copperhead snake in the jar. He said if that snake had bitten me it was so poisonous I probably wouldn't have even made it home. I probably would have died before I could have gotten to the paved road. Dad's tone of voice and obvious fright scared me, but I still wanted to keep the snake. Dad told me to get the snake out of the house and take it to the pasture and kill it with a long stick. I left the house and headed back to the creek; however, I hid the snake, still in the jar, in some bushes near the creek. I went back home empty-handed, and Dad must have assumed I had killed the snake because he didn't ask about it.

The next day when I left for school I went by and picked up the snake and carried it to school. When my teacher saw the snake, she took it from me immediately and said she was going to display it on our science table, but then she took the snake from our classroom. When the teacher returned, she didn't have the snake. I asked where the snake was, and the teacher told me I would see it the next day on the science table.

When I arrived at school the next day, I went immediately to the science table. I found my snake, but it appeared to be dead, floating around in some sort of liquid. A new lid, with no holes, was on the jar. I asked my teacher what happened to the snake, and she said she had pickled it in a formaldehyde solution. She said the formaldehyde was a preservative, and students would be able to enjoy the snake for several years. I was a little upset that the snake was dead, but I knew it would have been too dangerous to keep in the classroom while it was alive. I just accepted the fact that the snake was dead and there was nothing I could do about it. I wasn't about to go home and complain to Dad and let him discover I had disobeyed him by not killing the snake myself. However, I had already decided that I would capture more snakes for our science table. I did, and my teacher pickled every one of them and displayed them on our science table. I was proud to be the only student in the class with snakes on exhibit.

One day when I was snake hunting, I found a black racer about two and a half feet long. I knew black racers weren't poisonous, so I just picked it up by its mid-section. It didn't try to bite me, so I let it crawl over my arms, from one arm to the other. I left my snake pole at the creek and went home. I knew I couldn't let anyone at home know I had a snake so I put the snake into my pocket and kept my hand in my pocket. I went through the house as quickly as I could without arousing anyone's curiosity. When I reached my bedroom, I was trying to figure out what I was going to do with the snake. I didn't have anything to put the snake into, so I just pulled back the quilt on my bed and put the snake down and covered it with the quilt. I closed my bedroom door as I left the room, and then I went outside to play with my friends.

When I came back home for the night, I went into my bedroom and found the snake exactly where I had left it. I left the snake there and went back into our living room where I stayed until bedtime. When I went to bed for the night, I made sure the bedroom doors were all closed, and then I put the snake on the floor so it could crawl around in the room while I slept.

The next morning I got dressed, put the snake in my pocket, and left for school. I saw a group of girls standing together talking, and I approached the girls and asked them if they would like a surprise. When they said they would like a surprise, I pulled the snake from my pocket and dangled it in front of them. All of the girls screamed, and one of them ran to report me to our teacher. I would have been in trouble, but I told the teacher I had just brought another snake to exhibit on our science table and I didn't really mean to frighten anyone. What a lie, but I got away with it. The teacher pickled my snake. That was the last time I ever thought of having a snake for a pet. They just caused too much trouble. Even if a snake I had captured wouldn't hurt anyone, it would cause someone to hurt himself. Occasionally I carried another snake in my pocket, but eventually I got bored with snakes and moved on to something else.

One morning I was walking along the edge of the woods at Mills Mill Elementary School with my slingshot around my neck and my pocket about half full of marbles. I was hunting for squirrels or birds, whichever I could find. I thought I saw something move in a tree about forty yards in front of me so I crept in that direction. I looked into the lower branches of the tree and saw some type of bird sitting on a limb. I moved around the tree to get a better look, but when I moved too close, the bird flew from the tree. I immediately saw that the bird was a very young sparrow hawk. The proper name for "sparrow hawk" is "American kestrel," but in our area we have always called them "sparrow hawks." The hawk had not yet learned to fly well and could go only a few yards before landing again. I gave chase, and within four to five minutes I caught the young hawk. I looked around to see whether or not I might see more young hawks, and I saw two more sitting in a tree together. I shook the limbs of the tree, and one hawk fell to the ground and the other one flew a few yards away. I caught the one on the ground and then chased the other one. I caught it within five minutes. I had three hawks in my hands, but I was still looking for more when I spotted a fourth young hawk sitting in another tree. When I approached it, it flew away. It was immediately obvious that it was larger, stronger, and could fly better than the three I had already caught. I gave chase, but every time I got close, it flew another fifty to a hundred feet away. I decided I would have to shoot the hawk with my slingshot to catch it, but I couldn't shoot it with three hawks in my hands. I left for home, running as fast as I could.

I found a large cardboard box and put the three hawks into it, and then ran back to the area where I had last seen the fourth hawk. Two full-grown hawks were sitting in the tree with the young hawk, but they flew away immediately as I approached the tree. When I shook some lower limbs, the young hawk flew to another tree about forty yards away. I was convinced I would never be able to catch that hawk without first shooting it with my slingshot. I took my slingshot from around my neck and loaded a marble into the pocket. When I let go, the marble struck the hawk on a wing and it tumbled to the ground. I caught it quickly and then headed for home. I didn't bother to look for more young hawks because I didn't think there would be any more.

I put the injured hawk into the box with the others, and then I went looking for materials to build a cage. I found enough chicken wire and lumber to build a cage large enough to allow the birds space to fly back and forth across it. I built the cage and put the hawks inside it. I found some small boards and built a shelter for the hawks to sleep in or to get inside when the weather was bad. I put some soft hay into the box for making a nest. Then I went hunting for birds to feed them. I killed three or four birds and put them inside the cage. The hawks acted as if they wanted no part of the birds, and I was getting a little worried that they might starve themselves to death. I went inside for the night.

The next morning, I rushed outside to check on the hawks. All four of them were eating the birds I had left the day before. At least I knew the hawks knew how to eat, and they wouldn't starve themselves to death. I got my slingshot and went looking for more birds. I fed birds to the hawks every day, and they ate heartily. Within a few weeks, the hawks were fully grown.

I was killing blue jays, robins, thrushes, sparrows, finches, and starlings. I thought blue jays and starlings were just pests, and the other species of birds I killed were plentiful, so I figured I wasn't eliminating a species. I would not kill a cardinal, bluebird, or oriole because I thought they were just too beautiful to kill. I would not kill a mockingbird because I loved to hear them sing, and I would not kill a Carolina wren because that was our state bird. I didn't just kill birds indiscriminately as I had a few years earlier.

To learn more about the eating habits of sparrow hawks, I went to the library and read a couple of articles. I found some information that surprised me. I discovered that the adult male sparrow hawk was normally the provider for its young, not the female. Until then, I would have believed that the mother would have taken that role. I learned that sparrow hawks eat a lot of insects, especially grasshoppers. I continued killing birds, but I also caught a lot of grasshoppers. The hawks seemed content.

I would take one hawk at a time from the cage and play with it. They were just slightly larger than a robin, about the size of a mourning dove. They were the most beautiful birds I have ever seen in all of my life. They were multicolored, with a mixture of black, blue, white, yellow, and a rust-brown. The designs on the birds are absolutely magnificent. More people need to see American kestrels up close.

I cared for my hawks as if they were small children. I guess I became their surrogate father. I loved them equally as much as I had loved the chipmunk I had when I was slightly younger.

When I received an invitation to visit one of my uncles in Pickens County, I knew I could not leave the hawks for a full week without having someone feed them for me. I asked a good friend if he would take care of them while I was gone, and he promised me that he would. He had a BB gun, so I knew he could shoot some birds. I was comforted by the fact that my friend would take care of my hawks, so I left for a week.

When I got back home, I was eager to go check on my hawks. However, when I got to the cage, I found a sight that I did *not* want to see. I found three beautiful, healthy-looking hawks and the remains of a fourth hawk. My trusted friend had not fed my hawks, and the three healthy ones had killed and eaten one of their own. All that was left of the dead hawk were the feet, feathers, and beak. I was devastated, and I was sick! However, I was lucky that three hawks had survived. I ran inside, got my slingshot and some marbles, and went bird hunting. I killed several birds and put them into the cage. The remaining hawks jumped on the birds immediately and began to eat them. I just stood and watched the hawks for at least two hours, and in that time I decided it was time to free the hawks back into the wild. I really had mixed emotions about that. I wanted to keep the hawks as pets, but I realized they were grown and they needed to be free to soar in the sky and hunt for themselves.

I carried all three hawks to Dunean Baseball Park and walked into the outfield grass. I released all three hawks, one at a time, and they all flew around the inside of the park fence. I watched as they flew higher and higher, and I was still watching when they landed and perched on the crossbar of a ballpark light pole. I had been fascinated by their flight. I held up a dead bird I had pulled from a pocket and called to the hawks. To my surprise and absolute amazement, the hawks came to me. Seeing three hawks swooping down from that height with the speed they were flying was a little unnerving, but all of them landed safely on my arm and shoulder. I gave each of them a dead bird and made them fly off. They returned to the light pole. After about thirty minutes, I left the ballpark and the hawks behind.

I carried dead birds to the ballpark and fed the hawks regularly, but one day, when I called for the hawks, they didn't come to me. Although I could see them clearly, no matter how much I called, they wouldn't come to me. I knew they no longer needed to depend on me for food, but I was crushed that my close relationship with them had ended. I was sad, but I knew nature intended things to be that way. I lay on the grass and watched the hawks for about an hour, but they never left their perch. I left the ballpark and returned home. I never attempted to call the hawks to me again, although I could see them regularly flying over the ballpark and the surrounding fields and woods. I missed being able to hold and pet them, but I was happy to see them enjoying their freedom. I continued to hunt, fish, and ramble around in the woods and fields, but after I released the hawks, I never captured more than one other wild animal with the intention of keeping it as a pet. I caught a baby white-tailed deer and raised it in my backyard. It died of natural causes, and that ended my wild pet days.

When I got a little older, I began to hunt for white-tailed deer, black bears, and wild boar. I have never killed a bear, but I have been with a hunting party on several occasions when a member of the party killed one. The last bear I recall being killed when I was along was quite large: it weighed in at 451 pounds. Each party member took some of the meat, but the person who actually shot a bear always kept the bear skin and head as a trophy.

I found that killing white-tailed deer was not nearly as difficult as I had been led to believe. I always thought they were so wary that no one could get anywhere close to them. However, the first white-tailed deer I killed, I walked to within twenty yards of it. It was standing in the edge of the woods and looking into an open field. I was walking slowly and quietly in the woods, going to a deer stand in a tree close by. When I saw the deer, I couldn't believe my eyes. It was huge and had a large rack of antlers. I slowly raised my rifle and aimed at the deer, and the deer never turned its head toward me or acted as if it might have seen or heard me. I moved my rifle around for about thirty seconds before I fired. I wanted to shoot the deer in a place that would cause instant death but, at the same time, preserve as much of the meat as possible. When I fired, the deer fell straight to the ground and kicked a few times before remaining still. I shot it through the heart. It turned out to be an eight pointer that weighed 181 pounds.

Over the years, I have killed numerous deer. I once killed four in one day. I have gotten to the point that hunting deer doesn't excite me as it did when I was young. I guess I will just have to let other people hunt them, and I will share their meat. Although I have killed some large deer—the largest had ten points—I have never hung a deer head as a trophy. I know I am a good hunter and that's enough to satisfy me. I don't need to hang trophies to prove myself to anyone else.

Boar hunting, however, is a very rigorous and dangerous sport. A hunter can never tell when a wild boar might charge at him or when a dangerous snake might confront him. Although there is no season for hunting wild boar in South Carolina, the best time to hunt them in the swamps is when the weather is warm because the hunters usually have to walk in water that is sometimes waist deep. The hunter must always be vigilant because of the danger of cottonmouth water moccasins and other poisonous snakes. In the mountains, it is best to hunt wild boar when the weather is cold and the rattlesnakes are hibernating.

I always hunted wild boar simply for the meat. Wild boar meat contains little fat and is quite tasty when barbequed. When a small amount of domestic hog fat is added, it is also delicious as sausage.

I started hunting wild boar when a friend of mine who had some plot hound dogs asked me to join him on a hunt. He and I, along with one other person, took three dogs into the swamps of the Savannah River at the South Carolina and Georgia border. I was a little wary of walking in the black water, because I couldn't see two inches below the surface. I was constantly thinking I might step into a deep hole and all of my clothing and equipment would get wet. However, when the dogs jumped some wild hogs, I forgot all about danger. When the dogs caught a hog and were holding it by its jowls with their teeth, I ran up and shot the hog between its shoulders. When we pulled the dogs away, we discovered I had just killed a small female that had a litter of small piglets in the brush nearby. We tried to catch some of the small pigs, but they were too fast for us. We began to tie a stick in the mouth of the hog so we could drag it from the swamp. I leaned over to tie a knot, and my friend smeared blood from the hog all over my face. I knew the blood was part of a ritual for hunters when they get their first kill of a big game species, so I just laughed with my friends and left the blood on my face. One of my friends killed another hog about thirty minutes later, and we headed for home.

There was one boar-hunting trip I will never forget. I was walking through black swamp water about forty yards from the nearest land when I saw a log floating on top of the water about thirty yards in front of me. As I walked toward the log, I saw that there was a huge cottonmouth water moccasin lying on top of the log. I pulled my .44-magnum pistol and loaded it with snake shot. My intention was to walk closer and shoot the snake. When I was about fifteen yards from the snake, I raised my pistol to aim at the snake, not wanting to miss such a large, poisonous snake. But just as I was about to shoot the snake, it suddenly slid from the log into the black water. I couldn't see it at all. I backed away from the log, but I was watching for the snake to surface. The snake surfaced about ten yards from me, and then went under the water again before I could shoot. I turned and ran toward dry land as fast as I could, and I must have been running on top of the water because I was on shore quickly.

Over the years, I have killed numerous wild hogs and many domestic ones as well. One thing I know for certain is that I am no longer as physically fit as I used to be, and I probably have given up hunting wild boar forever. Some things need to be passed on to younger generations, and hunting wild boar is one of them.

I had a lot of fun in the fields, woods, and streams. I also had a lot of fun playing with my brothers and friends. However, there was also work to be done. I had to continue working in our garden with other family members in the evenings and on Saturday mornings during summer months, but time was moving on.

William and James graduated from high school in June 1955, and James immediately joined the U.S. Air Force. James was seeking freedom and independence to find his own way. I was proud of James, and I think the rest of the family was also proud of him. He had left our village behind and would never return to work in a cotton mill. Neither of us knew it at the time, but James was blazing a trail I would one day follow.

Dwight D. Eisenhower was president of the United States when James joined the air force in 1955. I believed James was safe in the military because the Korean War had ended in July 1953 and the United States was not involved in any wars, with the exception of the Cold War with the United Soviet Socialist Republic.

George Bell Timmerman was in his first term as governor of South Carolina in 1955, and J. Kenneth Cass was the mayor of the City of Greenville.

The population of Greenville County had grown from approximately 168,000 in 1950 to approximately 185,000 in 1955, and the population of the City of Greenville had grown from approximately 58,000 in 1950 to approximately 61,000 in 1955. Efforts of recruitment by state and county officials were paying off, and manufacturing was rapidly growing in Greenville County. Much of the new industry coming into Greenville County was nontextile. The diversity began to offer children of cotton mill workers new paths to success.

William continued to live at home and worked at a business about five or six miles from our house. Because he had no car and public buses did not travel a route that would take him close to his place of employment, he walked to work most of the time, occasionally getting a ride with someone else. He was paying room and board money to Dad, so he was having a difficult time saving any money for himself. On numerous occasions, William attempted to join different branches of the military, but physical problems caused him to be denied entry. I knew William wanted freedom and independence to find his own way, and I felt badly for him because he just couldn't seem to get the one break he needed. He was unable to find employment where he could earn enough money to move away from home and begin a life of his own. He was working long, hard hours at a difficult job, but he still couldn't get enough money together to even buy himself a car. His situation made me even more determined that I would someday leave our neighborhood behind to seek a different way of life.

David was working at a gas station about one mile from home. I don't know whether or not he had to give a portion of his earnings to Dad at that time, but he seemed always to have some money in his wallet. He had begun to date, so I was unable to get money from him because he was saving it for his girlfriend. I never could understand why he preferred to spend money on a girl instead of on his younger brother. Of course, I believed I knew why. I thought the female of the human species was never satisfied with whatever the male she was interested in had the ability to give. She always wanted a little more or something different. It wasn't her fault; it was just the nature of females. When Adam and Eve were the only two humans on earth, Eve set the precedent for female behavior. I believed Eve took the forbidden fruit from the serpent because Adam did not have the ability by way of authority to give it to her. Once she had it, she taunted Adam with it until he, in an attempt to please her, accepted a portion of it; the world has been in chaos ever since. Of course, just because I believed that little self-concocted story, it's not necessarily true. I just wanted some of David's money!

I was still cutting grass, running errands, and doing odd jobs to earn a little spending money, and I was living in my own little world. I recall many trips to the woods, fields, ponds, and creeks, but hardly anything relating to school or my family life. I do recall that I began to get interested in music, and I joined the mixed chorus at school. I enjoyed being a part of a group that achieved and performed, and I also enjoyed listening to professional musical performers. I think it was about 1955 or 1956 that rock and roll music began to become popular, and I was an enthusiastic listener. There were two restaurants in the mill village only one block from our house, and a third restaurant four blocks away. The restaurants were regular hangouts for the teenagers and young unmarried adults from our village and at least two other mill villages. The names of the restaurants were Peg's Place, Shamrock, and the Coffee Pot. Rock and roll music was played at those restaurants almost constantly, and each restaurant had a dance floor.

There would be as many as thirty to forty young people gathered at a restaurant almost every evening. Like many of my classmates and friends I wanted to learn to dance, but I could not overcome my lack of confidence and fear of looking like an idiot if I couldn't dance well. I felt as if all eyes would be watching me if I got onto a dance floor, and I was sometimes just too embarrassed to try it. I just sat, watched, and admired all of my friends, classmates, and others who were brave enough to take the risk regardless of what someone else might think. I sometimes attempted to dance anyway, but I spent most of my time at the restaurants eating and chatting with friends.

I was also very interested in baseball, and I listened to a lot of baseball games on the radio. I was a fan of the New York Yankees and the Brooklyn Dodgers, and I was thrilled that those two teams seemed to have a major rivalry, because the rivalry seemed to make baseball all the more exciting. I spent a lot of time watching our local baseball teams, and I felt fortunate to be living so close to Dunean Baseball Park, which I could see a portion of from my bedroom window. In some ways, my life was very exciting, but in other ways, it was just sort of ho-hum.

David had his job to go to, and I had household chores to do. I spent most of my time at home, at the ballpark, at the village café, or in the woods and fields. However, I was also very interested in the opposite sex, and I was dating occasionally. A date at that time of my life was walking a girl to church and home afterwards, visiting a girl at her home, or walking a girl to a baseball game where I enjoyed the game and conversation. The girls probably didn't even consider our times together to be dates, but I did.

Dad and Mother were working hard in the cotton mill, and they were managing to pay down their debts. I was still helping to deliver newspapers, but I wasn't earning enough money to be a real contributor to our household income. I think William and David were paying some money from their paychecks to Dad, but I don't know whether or not it was still being called room-and-board money.

I don't know how much the absence of James had to do with anything, but I noticed that the family seemed to be somewhat subdued. I believe his leaving so abruptly had a lasting effect on Dad and Mother, and I think they both missed James very much. Mother seemed to worry about James a lot, and Dad didn't say much about him. William, David, and I had matured considerably, and there seemed to be a lot of harmony among all of us. The family, as a whole, had become closer. We saw Grace often, but we missed James. I hoped James would do well in the military, but I also hoped he would come back to live in our area when he was discharged. However, James made it very clear that he intended to stay in the military and make it his career. He didn't seem to be interested in coming back to live in our area. The year I spent in the ninth grade went by like a blur. I do not recall anything of significance occurring during the entire year.

In September 1956, when I entered the tenth grade at Parker High School, David began his senior year at Parker High School.

William was still living at home with us, James was in the military, and Grace and Carl were happily married. Life seemed to be much better for all of us, especially Dad and Mother. William and David had jobs and contributed to the family income, thereby enabling Dad and Mother to pay down debts and provide better for the family. Dad and Mother seemed to be much more relaxed than they had been a few years earlier. Because World War II and the Korean conflict were behind us and the economy was much better, wages had been increased and physical and mental strains relating to survival and raising children had been greatly reduced for Dad and Mother. William and James were both adults, and David was almost an adult. I was fifteen, so David and I were still vulnerable to parental discipline. However, our home seemed to be more harmonious than ever before. As difficult as it was for me to believe, I received some new clothing. For the first time, I received a brand-new coat instead of a hand-me-down. Dad and Mother provided me with money for transportation, lunch, and school supplies, and I did not have to

David Porter

work anywhere during my sophomore year of high school. I did some odd jobs to earn a little extra spending money, but I did not have to worry about providing money to add to the family income. I spent my time either in school, studying at home, at the ballpark, in the woods and fields, at church, at the village café, or with some of my male friends. I also spent a lot of time roaming around town and visiting other mill villages looking for girls to begin a relationship with. I did not have an automobile available to me, and I had little or no money. My relationships with girls were like my socks; they were changed daily. I still spent a lot of time visiting girls and attempting to have relationships with them.

David and I spent as much time together as possible, but I didn't see him until late every evening. Then, he was working, so we didn't spend a lot of time together. We played baseball, football, and basketball together on weekends whenever we could. I remember that David was playing baseball with me and some of our friends when I hit my first baseball out of the park and onto the porch of a house across the street. I even thought it was a fluke, but then I repeated the feat several more times within the next few minutes. I was really proud because I have never seen any of my brothers hit a baseball out of the park and across the street like I did. That's not to say they never

Parker High School. Photo Courtesy of Greenville County Historical Society. Greenville, South Carolina.

did, I just never witnessed it. I was happy that David was there to witness my success. I also remember that I became good enough at golf to defeat all of my brothers. I was proud of my achievements, and I think they were proud of me also. If they were a little envious, that was good for me.

Parker High School offered a variety of technical and vocational training for boys and girls. I had the opportunity to choose mechanical drawing, woodworking, electrical training, textiles, auto mechanics, or shop. However, I had decided several years earlier that I wanted to be a business owner some day, so I chose to study bookkeeping, accounting, and typing. I was also enrolled in general math, English, history, and choral music. I knew I could not afford to go to college, so I chose not to take college preparatory courses. If college scholarships were available at the time, I was not aware of it.

Although I chose not to take classes in textiles, I visited the area where textiles were being taught many times. I lived in cotton mill villages practically all of my life, but I knew almost nothing about the operation of the mills. I knew Dad and Mother went to work every day clean and vibrant and came home from work dirty, sweaty, and tired. Also, they usually had cotton dust and lint all over them, especially in their hair. The cotton mill workers and their children often were called "lint-heads," a very derogatory and much-resented term. It seemed to me that anyone who did not work in a cotton mill had no respect for those who did. I knew life inside a cotton mill was not easy, but neither was the life of a child of cotton mill workers away from a cotton mill. By the time I had begun high school, I had already been in numerous fights over being called a lint-head.

When I visited the textiles classes, I talked to the teachers and students about cotton mill operations; by listening to them, I learned about the process for turning raw cotton into cloth. I also had an opportunity to visit an area cotton mill, and mill workers explained the entire process as I was touring the mill.

I saw a huge room, called the opening room, where cotton bales were brought to be opened. After the cotton was opened, it was torn apart and cleaned by a large machine. Workers sent the clean cotton into a room called the picker room where it was cleaned again and then smoothed into sheets.

Next, the cotton went to a carding machine that cleaned it again and then twisted it into roping. The roping was sent into a drawing frame, where it was combined and thinned. At that point, I think the cotton was called yarn, and the yarn was then twisted and spun into thread. Next, the thread was placed on a spooling frame to be combined from a number of bobbins to make it bigger and stronger. When that process was finished, the thread was sent to the weave room, where it was woven into cloth. Finally, the cloth was sent to a cloth room, where it was inspected and prepared for shipment.

In addition to learning about processing cotton into cloth, I also learned a little about the history of the textile industry in Greenville. I was told that the first cotton mill to locate in Greenville County was Pelham Mill, and it was built in 1820. A short time later, Fork Shoals Mill was erected, and it wasn't long before a host of other mills were located in Greenville and surrounding counties. Eventually, Greenville County, South Carolina, was proclaimed to be the Textile Center of the World. I have personally visited the following textile mills or villages: Poe Mill, Mills Mill, Southern Bleachery, Fork Shoals, Camperdown, Conestee, Southern Worsted, Union Bleachery, American Spinning, Woodside, Monaghan, Dunean, Pelzer, Piedmont, Pelham, Greer, Brandon, Judson, Poinsett, Slater-Marietta, Lydia, Saco-Lowell, Woodside in Liberty, and Norris in Cateechee.

After talking to textiles teachers and students, I had no doubt that I had been wise to choose other subjects, but that doesn't mean I was the smartest student on campus; I still had my problems. I was satisfied with my choices of study, but I was the only boy in most of my classes. Sometimes I was thrilled to be the only boy in class because I sometimes sat at a table with cheerleaders and band majorettes. I was ecstatic to be surrounded by so much beauty, and I did a lot of fantasizing about desired relationships. I enjoyed being in the company of females, but sometimes I wished a few boys would join me because I missed the male companionship. Many times, I sought out my male friends at lunchtime and sat with them. We talked about the girls for an hour, and then I returned to class to talk with the girls I had just been talking about. My days at school were always interesting.

Greenville High School. Photo Courtesy of Greenville County
Historical Society. Greenville, South Carolina.

I had relationships with many of the girls at my school, but I also developed relationships with girls from Greenville High School.

In addition, I was interested in girls from nearby small towns and other mill villages. Occasionally, I would meet one when I was roaming. I never wanted the girls I met to know Dad worked in a cotton mill because, at that time in my life, I was ashamed and embarrassed to be a child of cotton mill workers. I told many of them Dad was a preacher. Sometimes it helped; sometimes it didn't.

While I was a sophomore in high school, I learned Dad had received training to become a preacher when I was about six years old. I knew he had stopped drinking and had begun attending church regularly when I was young, but I was unaware of his calling to become a preacher. By the time I learned about his seminary studies, he was an ordained church deacon, a Sunday school teacher, and the worship service song leader. I don't recall ever seeing the word "Reverend" or the abbreviation "Rev." in front of his name, but he rarely missed any church service or activity. He studied his Bible regularly, and he had read the Bible from cover to cover several times. He was well liked by church members and community neighbors. I have been told by Mother and other family members that Dad was actually ordained as a minister but just never became an active preacher. Dad probably could have become an active preacher if he had stuck with the training and applied himself, but I think he was forced to choose between an uncertain survival as a preacher and a certain job in a cotton mill. With five small children to raise, Dad chose to work at a job he knew for certain would provide at least some means of survival during World War II and the Korean War. After those tragedies were over, survival was still a problem so he felt that he needed to remain in a job he knew well and serve his church in a variety of other ways.

When I learned Dad had studied for the ministry, I used that information to justify lying to people about his means of earning a living because I thought being a preacher was somehow more honorable and prestigious than being a cotton mill employee. I wanted to impress people, and lying and denying were my way of dealing with my low self-appraisal. If I convinced other people that my dad was important to the community, I felt more important. Because most preachers were looked on in high esteem and were thought to be financially secure, I thought people would think I was well above the poverty level and an honorable person. In reality, I was just digging myself a hole so deep I could not escape from it. Eventually I was caught, and my lying had to come to a screeching halt. I am very thankful I began to realize that working in a cotton mill was hard and dirty but very honorable. I gained a new and genuine perspective on the struggles and work of Dad and Mother. I became very proud of my heritage rather than being ashamed of it, and I have told many people, with pride, about my years of growing up.

Maturity enhanced my perspective of what is honorable and important. I learned it is not how a person earns a living that counts; it's whether or not the work is honest. I learned being truthful is more important than building false friendships. I learned equal justice for all does not mean that everyone should receive identical treatment, earn equal amounts of money, or own the same things. It just means everyone should receive fair treatment and be given opportunities for personal growth, and what they do with it is their choice, not society's fault. I learned numerous other helpful ideas and ideals, but that still didn't totally prevent me from making mistakes or doing things I knew were wrong at the time. However, the positive messages were stored within the depths of my mind, and I eventually disposed of the negative messages to become an honest and productive person. My first year of high school was an important experience that has probably influenced my life more than any other single year. I think personal growth was my biggest and most important achievement even though my grades in school didn't show a lot of promise for a bright future.

I was elected by my classmates to represent my class as a senator in our school government, and I also served as a traffic monitor on the school grounds and in the school hallways. I was honored to hold those positions, regardless of their insignificance.

David did well in school, and a few weeks before he graduated in June 1957, he got a job as a bookkeeper for a textile company. He bought a 1953 Chevrolet that he drove to work and other places. Because David was working and dating regularly, I did not spend a lot of time with him anymore; however, when he was around, we spent as much time together as we could. Our lives remained that way for the next year.

I spent some of my time during the summer at the ballpark or roaming in the woods and fields. However, I went with friends to a couple of swimming lakes on the east side of Greenville whenever I could. The lakes were Woods Lake and Pine Grove Lake. Almost every teenager in Greenville County went to those two swimming lakes. There would be hundreds at each lake every day during the summer.

After swimming, we usually went to one of the Clock drive-in restaurants to eat and chat with friends that showed up. The Clock drive-ins were regular hang-outs for teenagers. They were good places to meet the opposite sex. We also cruised Main Street in Greenville in attempts to meet the opposite sex. On Friday and Saturday nights, the roadway would be so jammed with carloads of teenagers, traffic was practically at a complete standstill.

There were also many times that we went to drive-in theatres. The names of the theatres were Skyland, Augusta Road, White Horse, and Belmont. Sometimes, the drive-in theatres charged only one dollar for each automobile regardless of the number of people in the automobile. We took full advantage of that. We packed as many teenagers as possible into the passenger seats and several of us got into the trunk. Once we were inside and parked, the persons in the trunk got out and sat on the ground to watch the movie. We also pulled that trick when the theatre was charging full admission for each individual. The automobile trunks in the fifties were large, and that was to our advantage. Two people paid, and four more got in free. I spent a lot of time with my friends. Our summers and weekends were very busy when I had opportunities to travel with them.

When school started back in September 1957, I began my junior year in much the same fashion I had ended my sophomore year. I was in classes with all girls again and loving every minute of it. Although I was not dating any girl in my class, I was at least mature enough to talk to some of them with a little more confidence than I had been in the previous year. Instead of always seeking out boys to have lunch with, I had lunch more often with girls. I might not have been the brightest or the most handsome student in my class, but I was the luckiest. I was dating girls who were younger than I was, and I was getting valuable information about female expectations from my classmates. I didn't have a car, so I needed all the advantages I could get. Unfortunately, I was not as popular as I wished.

One of my classmates was a girl named Fran Bishop. I had attended school with her since I was in the fifth grade, and she lived in the same mill village that I did. She talked to me every day, but her conversation was not about the two of us: her conversation was about her relationship with my oldest brother, William. The two of them had been dating for a long time, and she was talking about their getting married. I just shrugged my shoulders and laughed because I knew William was not going to marry her. Wrong! In October, Fran quit school, and she and William were married. Once they were married, I quickly saw that William had made a good choice. Fran became a beloved member of our family immediately. They moved into a house in our mill village. William was no longer living with us, so the house was even quieter and lonelier.

Even though life was not easy for William and Fran, William had chosen not to work in a cotton mill. I knew he wanted to have a career he could eventually retire from, and I was proud of him and his efforts to move in that direction. Of course, I would have been proud of him regardless of the type of work he chose.

Nothing else of significance occurred for the next few months, and my grades were nothing to brag about. I spent my evenings and Saturdays at the ballpark or in the woods and fields, and I attended church regularly. David was still living at home, but he was busy most of the time. Life continued that way for me until about February 1958, and then new experiences came my way.

I got a job as a dishwasher (the one household chore I hated most) in the General Grill, a restaurant across the street from the Greenville General Hospital. The grill was about three miles from our house, and I worked from 3:30 p.m. until 11 p.m. Monday through Friday each week. The work was very difficult because I had to scrub all of the pots and pans while the dishwasher cleaned the glassware and stainless steel utensils. The water was very hot, so I was constantly perspiring as I worked over a deep metal sink. When I finished cleaning the pots and pans, I had to unload the glassware and stainless steel from the dishwasher and put them away. I placed the clean pots and pans into the dishwasher and ran very hot water over them for sterilization and then put them away. The cook was continuously busy, which meant I was rarely able to take a break. It didn't take long for me to learn work in a cotton mill was not the only work that was hard and dirty. I also learned a cotton mill was not the only place to get a low-paying job. My respect for Dad and Mother and the hard work they had performed for the benefit of our family grew. However, the matter that placed thorns on my rosebush was the fact that Dad informed me I was going to have to begin paying room and board to him and Mother. I was shocked, but I knew Dad was serious and I had no choice. It was either pay room and board to live in the house with my parents or move out and survive the best way I could. I knew I could not survive alone and I was very frightened, so I began paying Dad each week. I immediately knew many of my dreams would never be realized as long as I continued living with my parents. I had a little extra spending money after paying Dad each week, but I barely had enough to go to a couple of movies and enjoy a few hamburgers

261

and milkshakes at the village café. I wanted to buy a car so I could drive to school and take girls on dates, but that was out of the question. I wanted to buy a stereo so I could listen to the music I loved so much. I couldn't even afford that. I worked hard, but I had nothing to show for it. I have never believed a child who is still in high school should have to pay room and board to the parents. That was one of the most difficult situations I ever had to face, and it made me want to leave home as quickly as I could safely get away.

Several of my friends had cars, and I rode to school and back with one of them, but I had to walk to work or any other place I wanted to go. My circumstances were nothing like I had envisioned a year earlier. I had never thought Dad would control my life the way he did once I had begun to work and date girls. Because of his control, demand for money, and the restrictions he put on me, I was constantly thinking about ways to leave home and never be found by him. Fear of being caught was greater than I could cope with, so I never acted on my plans to leave home. I attempted to understand that, in Dad's own way, he truly believed everything he did for us, or to us, was for our own good. I believe his intentions were good, but intentions do not make all decisions correct. Because I did not believe all of Dad's decisions were correct or good for me, I sometimes disobeyed. In May 1958, I made a decision that cost me a whipping, but I was determined to become a person instead of Dad's whipping boy and a means of income for him. I was seventeen years old.

I had a date to attend church with a girl who lived in another nearby mill village, and the church we planned to attend was located about one block from her house. When I announced to Dad and Mother that I had a date to take the girl to church, Dad immediately told me I was not going to do any such thing. He told me I was going to church with him. Since both churches were the same denomination, I didn't understand why Dad had reacted the way he did, so I protested his decision. When Dad threatened me, I discontinued my argument and agreed to go with him.

When the time came to leave for church, Dad forced me to go with him. In our church, just like the girl's church, there were two evening services. The first service required different age groups to meet in separate classes, and the second service required all age groups to meet in the sanctuary. Dad went to his first class and I went to mine.

The whole time the first service was in progress, I don't think I heard one word the teacher spoke. I was concentrating on what was happening to me and thinking about what the girl would think of me when I failed to show up at her church. The girl was very beautiful and intelligent, and I believed I was madly in love with her. The last thing I wanted to happen was that I would lose the girl because of Dad's control. The more I thought about my circumstances, the angrier I got. I knew I was going to do something I would later regret, but I was determined not to let the girl think I didn't care for her.

As soon as the first service ended, I walked outside the church and looked around for Dad. When I didn't see him, I started running as fast as I could toward the other church. The girl's church was about a mile from our church, and I ran every step of the way to get there before her second service began. When I arrived at her church, she was just about to walk inside. I was breathing very heavily so she remained outside with me until I could breathe somewhat normally again, and then we went inside. I sat with the girl until the service was over and then I walked her home, where I stayed about thirty minutes before going to my home.

As soon as I walked through the door at home, Dad asked where I had been. When I replied I had been at church, he said he had not seen me there. I told him I had gone to church with the girl, and then I watched as he took his belt off and approached me with his face flushed with anger and his knuckles white from gripping the belt. I don't know how I kept from being frightened, but I did not feel fear. Maybe it was because I was a little older and tougher than in earlier years, but as he began to whip me with the belt, I just stood still and looked into his eyes. Although the pain from the belt was excruciating, I refused to shed tears, dance around as I had in the past, or scream for mercy. Dad was whipping me unmercifully and I was feeling every blow, but I just continued to look at his eyes and refused to cry. After I had been whipped for what seemed like ten minutes, the pain was getting so severe I felt I could not bear it much longer. I yelled that Dad could whip me for going to the girl's church, but God didn't care which church I attended. God was happy that I attended *any* church. Immediately, the whipping stopped.

I went to my bedroom and looked at myself in the dresser mirror. I was not bleeding, but I had a few welts scattered on my body. I lay across my bed and tears began to stream from my eyes, but I was as quiet as I could be. I didn't want Dad to hear anything that would give him the idea I was suffering, because I thought that would give him satisfaction. Dad had gone to our living room.

A short time later, I heard Dad go into the bathroom and begin to vomit. Apparently, he had worked himself up so much with anger while he was waiting for me to come home and while he was whipping me he had made himself sick. He vomited for a few minutes and then went into his bedroom. I didn't see him again that night.

I don't know whether or not Dad decided not to whip me again because I refused to cry, dance, and scream, or maybe he thought about what I said and realized I was right, but that was the last whipping I ever received from him. As a matter of fact, that was the last whipping I received from anyone. I thought about leaving home more than ever after that whipping, but I continued to live there and endure whatever came my way. I knew I was leaving as soon as I turned eighteen, and that was less than a year away.

I continued to go to school and work until school ended in June, and then I quit my job so I could play softball for the team the cotton mill sponsored. Dad and Mother voiced no objections to my playing softball, nor did they object to my not working during the summer. I cut grass and did odd jobs to earn a little spending money, but I spent a lot of time in the woods, fields, and streams. I also dated whenever I could get a date.

At seventeen, dating was not easy without a car because most girls expected to be taken somewhere; therefore, I had difficulty getting dates. I attempted to get Dad to let me learn how to drive his car, but he refused to discuss it. He had a straight shift car, and I wanted to just sit in it with the brakes on and learn how to change gears, but he refused to allow that also. I was disgusted with my situation, and I thought it was unfair that all of my friends were driving cars and I had to walk everywhere, including to the homes of girls I was interested in. There were many girls I was interested in that I never even bothered to ask for a date because I was just too embarrassed to tell them I couldn't take them anywhere. I wanted to ask David about double-dating with him, but I knew he was very serious about his girlfriend and was thinking about marriage. In fact, David announced he was getting married, so I just abandoned any ideas of dating with him and continued my life as usual.

David turned nineteen in June 1958, and he married Ann Eubanks shortly thereafter. Ann also quickly became a beloved member of our family. When David moved away, I was more alone than ever. Except for weekends, when at least one of my siblings would visit, our house was quiet. However, prior to the beginning of school in September, I was rarely at home during the day for the remainder of that summer. I was either rambling in the woods and fields or at the ballpark. I tried to spend as much time as possible in the woods and fields because that was the environment where I felt most comfortable.

When Halloween arrived in 1958, I knew it would be the last Halloween I lived in the mill village because I was not planning to stay there when I graduated from high school. I wanted that Halloween to be a memorable one. I visited another mill village and found a large group of my friends, along with some young men whom I did not know. We were much too old for trick-or-treat, so we were just sitting around talking and laughing. We were trying to think of something to do. One of my friends mentioned that he had heard his father talk about putting one of his neighbor's cows on his neighbor's porch as a Halloween prank. We knew there were a few cows in the village pasture, so we decided to do something with a cow. We talked about it for a while and decided we would put a cow on the flat roof of the neighborhood café. The roof was flat, but the walls of each side of the building extended about two feet above the roof. The walls made a perfect fence to prevent a cow from falling off.

We had no idea how we would get a cow to the roof, but we started collecting things such as a halter rope for a horse, a very large and strong rope that was about a hundred feet in length, some smaller lengths of rope, a large canvas tent, some nylon tie-down straps, and other miscellaneous items. Within two hours, we had enough equipment to make an attempt to lift a cow onto the café rooftop. We also recruited enough bigger and stronger older boys and young men to assist us.

We fashioned an animal-sized sling with the short ropes and tent, and then we went to the pasture to find the ideal cow. We found a small cow that we thought we might be able to hoist up to the rooftop, managed to catch it, and led it to the café, pushing and pulling along the way. It took about an hour just to get the cow to the building.

About twelve young men and older and stronger boys climbed to the rooftop while the rest of us put the cow into the crudely crafted sling. When everyone was ready, more of us climbed to the rooftop, and we hoisted the cow off the ground. The cow was frightened and began to bellow and kick. We put the cow back on the ground and modified the sling to make sure the cow could not fall out of it, and then we hoisted the cow to the top of the wall. We had not anticipated that getting the cow over the edge of the wall would be just as difficult as hoisting the cow to the top, so we were surprised by that. However, we eventually managed to pull the cow over the wall. When the cow was released from the sling, it ran toward the edge of the building. We thought it was going to jump off, but it stopped short. We climbed down from the rooftop and ran away as fast as we could.

The next morning, when the café owner came to work, the cow was bellowing from the rooftop. The café owner called the sheriff's department and the fire department, but neither could get the cow down. Finally, a small crane had to be brought in to lift the cow from the rooftop and place it back on the ground. No participant in the prank was ever caught, but the event is still occasionally the subject of conversation.

Although I was a senior in high school, I had no idea what my future would be. I was continuing with bookkeeping, accounting, and typing classes, as well as English, history, math, and choral music. I was still the only boy in most of my classes, but I was having a great time. School was fun, but when November came, my fun came to an abrupt halt. Dad told me I had to go back to work and pay room and board to him again. He said I had gotten by without paying during the summer, but summer was over. He expected me to pay him weekly. I knew I couldn't win an argument with Dad, so I agreed to get a job as soon as possible.

I did odd jobs to earn enough to pay Dad each week, but I didn't get a regular job immediately. I still wanted to buy a car, but I knew the more I earned, the more Dad would take. Buying a car was out of the question. I really wasn't trying to get a job at all because I knew I was leaving home as soon as I graduated from high school. I had the high school yearbook staff print under my picture that I planned to join the air force, and I tried to keep a low profile around Dad. I was still paying Dad with money I earned doing odd jobs, but just after Christmas Dad told me to get a job, and he didn't mean maybe. I began to seriously look for a job.

Southern Franklin Processing Company, located only two blocks from our house, hired me. It was not a cotton mill, but there were a lot of similarities. My job was to take full spools of yarn from a frame of some type, toss them into a cart, and take them to the dye room on another floor. When I compared my job to Dad's, I was doing practically the same thing he was doing in the cotton mill. I could have been called a doffer. The only noticeable difference between my job and Dad's was that I was removing cones of yarn from the frames and he was removing bobbins of thread. In my mind, there were some other obvious differences. I wasn't nearly as fast as Dad; I didn't make any attempt to be fast, and I wasn't looking for anything to brag about. I just wanted to get out of the plant as quickly as possible when shift-change time came.

From the time I began working in the dye plant until I graduated from high school, Monday through Friday of each week was nothing but school, work, and sleep. On Saturdays, I stayed as far away from home as I could. I dated when I could find a girl who didn't mind that I had to walk to her house and we couldn't go anywhere. On Sundays, I attended morning and evening church services. At least one of my siblings came to visit every Sunday, and I was always there to enjoy their company. I never told them at the time, but spending time with them was the most pleasure I had during those several months.

Doyle Porter

Airman Doyle Porter – Age 18.

In early summer of 1959, Dwight Eisenhower was serving his second term as president of the United States, and Ernest Hollings had recently been sworn in as governor of South Carolina. Also, J. Kenneth Cass was continuing his service as mayor of Greenville, and J. R. Martin was serving as the Greenville County sheriff.

Other than industrial growth and rapid population growth, I don't recall anything of real significance occurring in South Carolina during my last six months of high school. I recall that the addition of Alaska to the United States on January 3, 1959, made national and international news. I do not recall any other events or incidents that claimed national attention. That doesn't mean there weren't any; I just don't recall any.

I graduated from high school in June 1959, and in July I was a member of the U.S. Air Force. I didn't tell anyone I had actually joined the Air Force until the fourteenth of July, and I left for Columbia, South Carolina, the next morning at 7 a.m. I was inducted into the air force on the sixteenth of July, and I was in San Antonio, Texas, for basic training on the seventeenth of July.

As the plane left South Carolina for Texas, I was looking down, but I knew I was on my way up. Although I loved my family and my many mill village friends and I fully understood that working in cotton mills was honest, hard, and honorable work, I was off to seek a new and better way of life for myself. I knew my journey would not end with the military nor would it be short or easy. My only hopes were that I would not fail to achieve my dream of becoming the owner of a business someday and that my earnings would be sufficient to enable me to live a comfortable life.

Doyle Porter – Age 20 – in Germany.

Epilogue

*J*oining the military and leaving family and friends behind was not as easy as I had imagined, but I have never experienced regrets. I left behind the strong possibility that I would have continued as an employee of the processing plant or would have become a cotton mill employee. My destiny was totally unknown to me at the time, but I was to meet many thousands of new personalities, including President Richard Nixon, President Gerald Ford, and President Ronald Reagan. I also met presidential candidates Governor George Wallace and U.S. Senator Hubert Humphrey. I faced many difficult and some not-so-difficult challenges and have had many life-altering experiences over the course of my then-unknown future. I was so ignorant of the world outside of my little domain in upstate South Carolina that almost every new experience was also a new challenge for me, and my life was altered by experiences that would have been insignificant to many other people. I was eager to broaden my horizons, so I attempted to learn something from every new experience. As a result, my life has been exciting, sometimes difficult, many times pleasing, somewhat productive, and always progressive.

Many of my friends had traveled the three hundred miles to visit Myrtle Beach or some other beach in South Carolina when I was a teenager, but I had never even traveled as far south as Columbia, which is only one hundred miles from Greenville. Traveling to Myrtle Beach had been a recurrent dream for me, but I had never been given the opportunity. I had no knowledge of what the territory south of Clinton, South Carolina, looked like, and I had no idea what was waiting for me at Fort Jackson in Columbia.

When I arrived at Fort Jackson, primarily a U.S. Army base at the time, I immediately realized that I no longer had any support from family or friends, and the drill instructor made it very clear that he was not interested in rendering assistance to anyone who could not properly care for himself. I was thankful that I only had to stay at Fort Jackson long enough to be sworn into the U.S. Air Force. Immediately after being sworn in, I was transported to the airport and placed on an airplane destined for San Antonio, Texas.

When I arrived in San Antonio, Texas, I was met by military personnel and was transported by bus to Lackland Air Force Base, where I received basic training for three months. Upon arrival at Lackland, I immediately realized that the drill instructor at Fort Jackson had been a really nice guy. At first, I thought I had arrived in hell. The temperature at Lackland was in excess of one hundred degrees, and I thought the drill instructor at Lackland just had to be a relative of Satan. However, I got used to the heat, and the drill instructor got me through basic training. The only national news I heard while I was at Lackland was that Hawaii became the fiftieth state of the United States on August 21, 1959. My training was related to the military only. When I left Texas to go to Turner Air Force Base in Albany, Georgia, I was a little closer to being a man than a boy.

A significant transformation in family relations took place after I joined the military. The first time I noticed the change was when I came home on leave from Georgia. When I arrived at home, the first thing I noticed was that I actually received an affectionate hug from each of my parents. They talked to me as an adult, and they were actually asking what they could do for me. We communicated—I talked while they listened and vice versa, with no interruptions. That brand of family communication was new to me, but I thoroughly enjoyed every minute of it. I was getting the respect an adult should receive, and that was a gigantic step in the right direction.

Each time I came home on leave, the relationship between my parents and me seemed to be just a wee bit better. Several events brought about a causal effect. First, my parents owned a home for the first time in their lives; second, they were better off financially than they had ever been; third, they had been able to buy a nice automobile and had extra money to provide for themselves; and fourth, they no longer had the responsibilities of raising children. They were free to do whatever they wanted to do, within the constraints of their budget. Several events had also occurred that affected my life in a positive way. First, I had become a young adult; second, I had joined the military and escaped from the cotton mills; third, I no longer feared my parents or their discipline; fourth,

Mother and Dad's 50th wedding anniversary. Back Row L to R: Doyle, William. Front Row L to R: Grace, Mother, Dad, David (James was absent)

Mr. And Mrs. Doyle R. and Pamela A. Porter – 2000.

I had learned to drive and owned an automobile; and fifth, I was dating several girls. I could not have been happier in any other circumstances.

When my siblings began to have children, our parents amazed me with the love and affection they showered onto their grandchildren. They played with them and gave them more attention than I had ever dreamed of. They even babysat regularly. The children received, abundantly, the spoken and exhibited love and affection that my siblings and I did not receive when we were growing up. It was good to see our parents actually enjoying life. After I completed my military service of four years, I returned home, got married, and fathered three children.

Watching my parents with their grandchildren reminded me that, aside from what I considered harsh discipline when we were growing up, my parents demonstrated much love and comfort, and they raised my siblings and me in the best way they knew how and could afford to. Although my father is now deceased, I cherish many of the memories I have of him. Mother is getting older, not as strong in body as she used to be, still very strong willed and sometimes contrary, but I love her very much. Family love is probably the closest to being unconditional of all of the different relationships in the universe. We don't fall in love with family members; we just love them because they are family members. There might be some exceptions, but I believe, as a general rule, that is an accurate statement.

I have owned my own business for many years. I have traveled to many destinations within the United States, and I have also traveled to many foreign countries. I have reached a point in my life where I consider my self-worth to be at least equal to my net worth. On anyone's balance sheet, that equals more assets than liabilities. I have no supers, section men, boss men, or overseers. Except for my wife, Pamela, government regulating agencies, and the Internal Revenue Service, I don't have to answer to anyone other than God. I have escaped the dust of the South Carolina farms and cotton mills, and I have lived a full life. My siblings have also been successful in their lives.